ANCESTRAL IMAGES

IMAGES

The Iconography of Human Origins

STEPHANIE MOSER

Foreword by Clive Gamble

SUTTON PUBLISHING

First published in 1998 by
Sutton Publishing Limited · Phoenix Mill
Thrupp · Stroud · Gloucestershire · GL5 2BU

Published in the U.S. by Cornell University Press, Ithaca, New York.

British Library Cataloguing in Publication Data
A catalogue record for this book is available from the British Library

ISBN 0 7509 1178 6

To Alex

™ ALAN SUTTON™ and SUTTON™ are the
trade marks of Sutton Publishing Limited

Typeset in 10.5/13 pt Garamond
Typesetting and origination by
Sutton Publishing Limited
Printed in Great Britain by
Butler & Tanner, Frome, Somerset.

Contents

List of Illustrations

Colour Plates

Between pp. 88–9

Preface

This book constitutes an introduction to a vast topic. The question of how we, in our most ancient form, have been visually represented over the centuries has demanded forays into many areas of artistic, historical and scientific study. In undertaking an interdisciplinary project of this kind, I have experienced both great satisfaction and frustration. On the one hand, learning about the range and diversity of scholarly work that is being undertaken on historic images has been immensely enjoyable. On the other, the selection and highlighting of particular findings for the purposes of my own discussion has been a little daunting. While disciplinary boundaries and academic territoriality in the field of visual analysis are not as pronounced as they used to be, there is always a fear of taking things out of context. I can only hope that I have managed to fulfil my objective of providing a glimpse into the long tradition of depicting the past without doing an injustice to the many visual traditions to which I refer.

Many individuals from art galleries, libraries, museums and picture libraries gave assistance in locating works and providing biographical information on artists and illustrators. While all those who helped are too numerous to list here, I would like to make a special note of thanks to staff from the Department of Manuscripts at the British Library, the Department of History of Art Library at the University of Oxford, the Department of Prints and Drawings at the British Museum, the Illustrated London News Picture Library, the Library of Western Art in the Ashmolean Museum, the Mary Evans Picture Library, the Musée d'Orsay, the Musée des Beaux-Arts Reims, the Musée des Antiquités Nationale at St Germain-en-Laye, the Royal Society of Arts of London Library, the Royal Library in The Hague, the Rijks Museum in Amsterdam, the Society of Antiquaries Library and the Victoria and Albert Museum.

A number of people assisted with information on particular authors, illustrators and historical contexts, notably Pim Allison, Michael Campbell, John Creighton, Frances and Martin Flatman, Brian Golding, John House, Sandra Langereis, John Michell, Irina Meltzer, Hiram

Morgan and Tessa Webber. I am also grateful to the colleagues in my department who have answered queries on their research areas, and here a very special note of thanks must go to Brian Sparkes. Tim Champion, Thomas Dowson, Clive Gamble, JD Hill, David Hinton, Simon Keay, Yvonne Marshall and David Peacock have also provided assistance on their areas of expertise. A number of individuals read the manuscript in its first draft, all of whom provided useful comments and suggestions. Here I would like to thank Clive Gamble, Yvonne Marshall, Nick Merriman, Stephanie Pratt, Jonathan Sawday, Sam Smiles and Brian Sparkes. Finally, my commissioning editor Rupert Harding has been an endless source of support and assistance, and my editor Sue Thomas has greatly helped with copy-editing the text.

I am grateful to the School of Research and Graduate Studies at Southampton and the Department of Archaeology at Southampton for assisting with research funds for this project. I would also like to thank Robert Cannon, Tim Champion, Simon Keay, Eric Moser, Brian Sparkes and Mark van Vugt for help with translating various documents and texts. For photographic work I would like to thank Andy Vowles from the Cartographic Unit in the Department of Geography at the University of Southampton, and for the title of the book I would like to thank Russell Jones.

A large number of people have been very supportive and interested in this project and here I would like to thank my colleagues in the Department of Archaeology at Southampton, including Nick Bradford, my dissertation students who graduated in 1997 and Debra Lusty. I would also like to take this opportunity to express my indebtedness to a few scholars who have been so influential and helpful over the past years. To Alison Wylie, Clive Gamble, Tom Patterson and Meg Conkey, I owe an enormous thanks.

Finally, I want to thank Alex for all his help with complicated computer problems, but more importantly, for his ideas and for his unending support of my work over the past three years.

Foreword

Clive Gamble

The first history book I ever had was a picture book. It was also my introduction to the mysterious land of human prehistory. The book was R.J. Unstead's *Looking at History: Britain from cavemen to the present day*, first published in one volume in 1955.[1] It was richly illustrated with over one thousand drawings and some colour plates and photographs. It was light on text and the dates of kings and queens, so it was a winner for junior schoolchildren, especially as it showed you the inside of dungeons and the London mob in full cry. It dealt with everyday matters – clothing, houses of the rich and poor, travel, play and the changing work of the British people – rather than foreign policy and the many wars of succession that I have long since forgotten.

Neither, as I learnt much later, was I alone in following this tale of progress written and illustrated as a social history for children. Unstead died in 1988 and I happened to see his obituary in the national press. Although I still had his book I had to dig deep in the loft to find it. One reason for unearthing it stemmed from my surprise on reading in the obituary about his publishing sales. *Looking at History* sold an astonishing eight million copies and was followed by fifty sequels. Here, surely, was a major influence on the historical imagination of not just me but the children of postwar Britain. I sat down to look again, this time as an archaeologist rather than an eight-year-old.

Visual threads: where do cavemen come from?

The illustrations jumped out at me like old friends. Book one, *From Cavemen to Vikings*, had always been my favourite. I had even added to it by colouring in some of J.C.B. Knight's realistic sketches. But now I could spot the sources of some of the pictures: for example, the Battersea shield being carried by an Iron Age chief across a river. Here too were the Romans being very up-to-date by inventing central heating, while over the page the Anglo-Saxons were coping with the Danes and doing useful things such as building Westminster Abbey.

But what of course really caught my attention this time were the cavemen, my area of expertise as a Palaeolithic archaeologist. I remembered the pictures of hunting, life in the cave and the exotic wild animals with which they shared their world. What I could not remember was if any of these images had had much impact on me. I must have looked at them hundreds of times when I was a schoolchild, but I could not claim now they had shaped my future interests.

And yet, as you will no doubt also discover in Stephanie Moser's wonderful, scales-falling-from-the-eyes account of the visual language of our discovered origins, these images, and many more like them, had burrowed their way into my vision of that remote past. They had encouraged that vision, made it possible even, yet at the same time I could also now see they had put it in blinkers.

The drawings made it possible to present that long portion of our past that lacks dramatic monuments and which only has rather unpromising small pieces of stone and bone as its main evidence. Imagine trying to put the Old Stone Age into words for schoolchildren, or for that matter any audience, and you see the difficulty. Here is a case where one picture is worth not only five hundred words but also half a million years.

But such possibilities come with a price attached. These are powerful, arresting images that shoulder aside alternative visions. Their power is such that the scenes which are commonly reconstructed become the only ones we will see of human origins. So, our experience of the remote past is controlled neither by the evidence we can dig up nor by the scientific analyses we can perform on it, but instead by what we already expect to see of it. The importance of Moser's book is that, for the first time, the strands of such visual control are traced deep into our western past. We now understand that the power of these images stems not so much from the subject matter of human origins, but rather from the way they have been woven from the iconic vocabulary of a visual language. This common language has over the past three millennia portrayed different constructions of Europe and its world.

As we shall see in chapter 2, the images begin with the empires of Greece and Rome and their concerns with those peoples who lived beyond the frontier. This was the first glimpse of the 'Other' in European civilization. It remains a potent category to the present day. Over the intervening period the 'Other' has needed constant redefinition as empires waxed, waned and entered into new relationships with those same outsiders who, in opposition, provided a means to define what it was to be civilized. Accordingly, the classical authors provided the 'Other' with a place in time as well as space in their accounts of the progress of humankind towards their own privileged position as citizens of Athens and Rome.

From a human origins perspective the accounts of human progress by Vitruvius and Lucretius, which you can find in chapter 2, were borrowed by nineteenth- and twentieth-century archaeologists.[2] In a similar fashion the artists they commissioned to flesh out their finds of fossil skeletons and stone tools appropriated the icons closely associated with mythological figures, such as Herakles, depicted on the vases of antiquity – a case of classical artists illustrating an even more ancient age for humanity. By borrowing the familiar it was possible to construct a believable story about deep antiquity from strange and unfamiliar evidence such as stone tools.

Neither did the 'Other' have to live far away or in another time. Within classical society there were further social categories which could provide rich sources for determining the shape of human ancestors even before any archaeological evidence was forthcoming. In his theory of natural slavery Aristotle advanced the idea that,

> Nature would like to distinguish between the bodies of free men and slaves, making the one strong for servile labour, the other upright and although useless for service, useful for the political life in the arts of both peace and war.[3]

Consider for a moment the common depiction of Neanderthals who inhabited Europe before the appearance of people like ourselves, often known as the Crô-Magnons after an early find in a French cave of that name (Table 1). The former are portrayed as stooped, shambling but very strong, which they would need to be as they are invariably shown grappling with large beasts such as mammoths and woolly rhinos. As the historian Anthony Pagden has written of Aristotle's theory, the natural slave 'should always be a slouching beast of great physical strength'.[4] With such expectations about the differences between people backed by no less an authority than Aristotle, it is unsurprising to find in the classics-obsessed atmosphere of the nineteenth century that theories of human origins were not so much a case of 'if the cap fits, wear it' but rather 'let's cram those fossil heads into what we think is appropriate historical headgear'. By comparison, those later Crô-Magnons, ourselves, are drawn as upright, intelligent and far-sighted, with a 'finely chiselled head poised on a well balanced vertebral column', as the eminent archaeologist Sir Grahame Clark once put it.[5] We emerged, visually, as the natural masters of our own ancestors. Human progress became a palpable image, a theoretical certainty for our Victorian ancestors. As a result, our remote ancestors were not so much enslaved as domesticated within a tradition that judged individuals, races and nations by their position on the ladder of civilization.[6]

The classical period therefore set the template for a scientific branch of enquiry, human origins, the details of which it could not even conceive. Their vision of outsiders, which was to prove so useful at a later date in portraying the idea and evidence of remote human ancestry, was then woven with new strands into the medieval imagination. This weft was important because the nineteenth century, which gave us archaeology and cavemen, natural selection and human evolution, was also drawing, at a time of great social, political and economic change, on the medieval past. They drew on it to instil a sense of order and authority which was every bit as important as the classical bedrock from which the values of industrial Europe were hewn. So, railway stations were built to look like gothic cathedrals, poets intoned chivalric deeds, while thousands flocked to re-created tournaments where 'traditional' pageantry was invented.

The medieval period was highly varied and had many different imaginations. It does, however, provide another example of how the 'Other' has been redefined in European history. Compared to the classical empires of

Greece and Rome the medieval period generally saw smaller and shorter-lived empires but larger codes of the mind, most notably chivalry and Christianity. Interestingly, as Moser documents, they depicted the fabulous races of the classical period, the real 'Other' of travellers' tales, viewed from the luxury of distance. The images they chose were concerned with definitions of who, and where, was inside and outside civilized society. Many of these are comical and fantastic until we start spotting among them the icons which denote cavemen. These include that all-too familiar visual kit bag of nakedness, hairiness, fur wrap, club, physical deformities and living in wild places far beyond the city wall.

Just stop for a moment and ask some simple factual questions. Have we ever found a wooden club, especially a particularly gnarled one that any design-conscious Neanderthal simply must carry as an accessory? The answer is no, although one of the delights of the Piltdown hoax in 1912 was that one of the 'artefacts' planted with the fossil remains was described as similar to a cricket bat.[7] Then ask yourself, what archaeological evidence exists to indicate our ancestors were excessively hairy? Surely baldness cannot just be a recent evolutionary development? But how often is it shown in reconstructions? Hardly ever, as you will see in the following chapters. Furthermore, the honest answer to a common question is that we still do not know for sure that our earliest ancestors wore clothes. All we can say is that needles are a late development, but the absence of such an item for many hundreds of thousands of years is not by itself evidence for the lack of clothes. I would take my hat off to anyone, ancient or modern, who could live naked outdoors in northern Europe, however hairy they might be, during either a temperate or glacial climate, it doesn't matter which, in January. It just won't work and, as I have discussed on many occasions with students young and old, the reason we only reluctantly give them clothes is because we are conditioned not to do so by the images of life in the Old Stone Age. In turn these scientific images are borrowing from those medieval pictures of the naked, fabulous races. Naked, because they were the classic 'Other', club-wielding, because knights carried swords and outlaws either staffs, like Little John, or clubs like the wildmen.

Of all the fabulous races my favourite, because they are cavemen long before cavemen were even thought of, are the Blemmyae. They lived among other places in the deserts of Libya. Their faces were on their chests, reminiscent of the slumped posture of Neanderthals, and they are shown carrying clubs and roaming naked in wild craggy places where we might reasonably expect to find a cave.

A major twist in the visual threads which Moser has traced was applied after 1492 with the spectacular rise of the world empires and the slow ascendancy of science. These societies forged the nation-states of Europe. They also rediscovered the peoples of the world and then proceeded to describe, classify and assign them a place using a social ladder of progress and moral change. Their claims were legitimated by the past and they wove the images of the 'Other', that rich tapestry of human ethnic and cultural diversity, into their visual accounts. Many of these depictions made sense of the discoveries of continents of new peoples by reference to established ways of showing outsiders and other people. In this way Europe assimilated the world it now sought to administer.

So finally, in the story of the visual history of human origins, we come to the rise of science in the nineteenth century. Far from discarding the classical and national claims on our visual language of the past, scientists, in the shape of archaeologists and palaeontologists, embraced it. Science expanded our knowledge of ourselves through observation, classification and explanation. But for the new sciences, of which archaeology was a leading example, there was a real need to establish their subject matter in a concise, understandable form. The visual language which achieved this borrowed rather than introduced new images. What we learn from Moser's book is that familiarity breeds *content* when it comes to reconstructing our origins. Cavemen, as we see them now in the multitude of images that depict their lives and appearance, were spun from many different threads drawn together during the past two-and-a-half thousand years. They are as much a creation of a classical artist decorating a pot, or a monk illuminating a margin, as they are of an archaeologist meticulously digging a cave for their remains. Cavemen have met a recurrent need to voice and depict the alternative to civilization. And by being depicted in this manner, so the other life has been rejected and the appropriateness of the familiar affirmed.

Dinosaurs and cavemen

Should we be surprised? Without such images and reconstructions how do we come to believe in such a remote past and understand it? What can we grasp on to that is familiar unless we can see it on our own terms?

Consider how, from an even older prehistory, familiarity is achieved with dinosaurs. Here there are attention-grabbing big bones, even bigger teeth and mounted skeletons that create their own dramatic worlds for our imaginations to explore. Perhaps familiarity through association, however far-fetched, is one reason why dinosaurs, knobbly-kneed cavemen and ourselves are so often shown together. Sometimes the juxtaposition serves to make a joke, and none better than Gary Larsson's wonderful cartoons, made even funnier by the fact that he knows what he is doing:

> I've always felt that I've committed some heresy by doing cartoons . . . that mixed dinosaurs with primitive people. I think there should be cartoon confessionals where we could go and say things like, 'Father, I have sinned – I have drawn dinosaurs and hominids together in the same cartoon.'[8]

The special effects spectaculars of *Jurassic Park* and the *Lost World* would be diminished without a familiar, human element. Tyrannosaurus road rage in San Diego is so much more believable, because we understand how it feels, than a stroll through some tropical forest 50 million years before humans were even walking.

The way in which these cinema dinosaurs are recreated as flesh-and-blood possibilities by computer wizards is no different from my old school textbook with its pen-and-ink sketches of early humans shivering in a British cave. As Unstead wrote, these were 'imaginative reconstructions, made after careful research'. [9] That is the same claim now heard from Animatronics or any other living scientific illustrator. There is pride in these images and their representation of scientific accuracy. They provide visual insights into the business of doing science that those outside the process can readily understand. The images gain credibility from the detailed way in which they transfer specific knowledge about the unfamiliar into the generally familiar. Looking at prehistory is only possible because we have been taught how to look and learn. As Moser says in Chapter 1, these pictures contribute to the business of building scientific theories while at the same time exploring theoretical territory which is often difficult to convey in words. Crucially, they are persuasive because we know why the archaeologist/artist chose to show the reconstruction in that way.

Blinkered vision

But that is where the problem of putting blinkers on our vision comes into play. The problem lies in the translation from evidence to image. What can be shown about our origins? The answer, as Moser neatly documents, comes down to some five or six standard scenes. These deal with hunting, tool-making, eating, making fire, combat with wild beasts and the earliest art. She's absolutely right! All of these, and no more, were in my schoolboy textbook. Just to make sure, I looked up a more recent version, *Early Humans: A prehistoric world*, which came out thirty years after *Looking at History*.[10] This is a pop-up book for children. It has a Neanderthal burial scene, a common favourite ever since Ralph Solecki wrote his book *Shanidar – the first flower people* in 1971. This title caught the spirit of the times by describing, from a cave in Iraq, the excavation of a flower-strewn Neanderthal skeleton. *Early Humans* also has a pop-up construction gang of Crô-Magnon men building a house frame out of mammoth tusks. Both of these are based on evidence which came to light after the first decades of this century. Otherwise it is hunting big animals, making tools and eating, just as expected.

It is also very noticeable how the thirty years have preserved the gender bias. The pictures leave you in no doubt that it was a MAN'S world in the Palaeolithic. This is conveyed either by the position of the sexes in the scenes (foreground, background, standing, sitting), more of which below, but also by sheer numbers. Although sexing the pictures is not as easy as might be expected for unclothed subjects, I came up with the following head account:

	males	females	children
Looking at History (1955)	20	4	2
Early Humans (1987)	47	9	6

By my reckoning males continue to dominate our presentation of human origins to schoolchildren at an alarming 75 per cent! This simple statistic underlines the powerful grip of these images despite the shifts in social attitudes in the same period of time, not to mention the avalanche of archaeological discovery and scientific publications.

The point is whether these scenes are all that is possible. Why have these activities come to dominate our ability to reconstruct the past and so, as Wiktor Stoczkowski has commented, put chains on our imagination?

Not surprisingly, these questions raise a big issue for someone like me who is researching this period. I want to know to what extent will, or can, any discoveries or new theories about human origins be translated into fresh images for both scientific and popular consumption. Since our subject is known to most people through this visual language then, what can be done?

I will spend the rest of this foreword building on Moser's survey of images and how they communicate about ideas, by looking at some of those ideas which could only take flight if represented. In the roots of the tradition of depicting human origins lies an answer to my question, but first, if we are to treat them archaeologically, we need a timetable.

A timetable for human origins in Europe

It is 200 years exactly since a perspicacious Suffolk gentleman, John Frere, wrote a letter to the Society of Antiquaries of London, describing a number of flint implements that had come to light in a brick pit at Hoxne.[11] His observations were important for several reasons. First, he identified the stones – which we would now call Acheulean handaxes and date to some 350,000 years ago – as human implements. Secondly, in addition to some astute observations on the stratigraphy of the pit, he concluded that they were weapons of war and belonged 'to a very remote period, indeed, even beyond that of the present world'. Finally, he illustrated two of the pieces in a scientific specimen style. These engravings make it possible to identify precisely the surviving specimens in the Frere collection, which is loaned by the Society to the British Museum.

With hindsight Frere is a Palaeolithic hero, although his letter, published in the journal *Archaeologia* in 1800, was ignored for another half century. This puts him in a similar category to Gregor Mendel whose observation on the ratios by which parental characters were inherited in peas was well ahead of its 'genetic' time when published in 1855. Perhaps if Frere had illustrated his finds, not in the tradition of depicting fossils, but as an imaginative reconstruction of how such handaxes were used and who wielded them, he would have made a more immediate impact. Instead he had to wait for the cause of human antiquity to be established and proved. This was done through the association of human remains, either stone tools or more rarely skeletal evidence, with extinct animals and ice age geology.

Generally, 1859 is regarded as a watershed year in the history of human origins, when Sir Joseph Prestwich, a geologist, and Sir John Evans, the first great British expert on stone tools, visited the gravel pits at Abbeville and

Amiens.[12] These pits had been producing implements and the bones of extinct animals for many years and causing controversy over how they might be interpreted. The heavyweight presence of Prestwich and Evans, who personally dug artefacts at great depth out of the sides of the pits, was crucial. They presented their results to the Royal Society in London and the antiquity of human origins was sealed. Evans recalls that he only saw the Hoxne artefacts on his return from France, which led him back belatedly to Frere's original account.[13]

Of course, 1859 is better known scientifically as the year Darwin published the *Origin of Species*. While this book neither uses the word evolution nor examines human origins it unmistakably set the conceptual agenda which was fully realized in Darwin's *Descent of Man* in 1871. In the intervening years the archaeological contribution by those following his ideas was to stress the progressive tendency in human evolution, as shown by changes in technology. Sir John Lubbock, Darwin's neighbour in Kent, and General Pitt Rivers saw to that. Lubbock published his influential book *Pre-Historic Times* in 1865, in which he first coined the term 'Palaeolithic' to describe implements made of stone recovered from the drift deposits and cave sediments dating to the ice ages.[14] Lubbock's father-in-law, Pitt Rivers, whose collections went to found the museum of that name in Oxford, had very definite ideas about their presentation and display. Objects were organized to illustrate the law of progress, with items proceeding from crude to fine examples, coarse to sophisticated manufacture. Neither gentleman used reconstructions. Their pictures of flints, bronze and iron objects spoke for themselves once they were arranged into chapters or display cabinets. Lubbock did illustrate his argument for progress with descriptions and some engravings of the customs and technology of modern peoples, as had Daniel Wilson in his earlier work on *Prehistoric Man* of 1862. Thereafter it became commonplace to use ethnography as an example of living prehistory, based on the continued use of stone, bronze and iron.

But what of the human fossil remains which might have given a greater impetus to imaginative reconstruction? It is sometimes forgotten that the pace of discovery and verification of ancient human material was very slow. Lubbock and Wilson had hardly any fossil material to discuss and what existed was often contentious. The early finds, such as Paviland and Neander, were explained away as either recent or pathological.

This paucity of material is brought out in Table 1 where I have listed, up to the First World War, the more complete or significant finds. Many more finds of single bones were found during this period and some large collections are now lost. The discoveries I have listed were the data around which the account of human evolution was written. With one important exception from Java, they all come from Europe. The importance of this continent to human origins was only challenged in the 1930s with finds from Indonesia and China, and then surpassed from the late 1950s onwards by major discoveries of very early humans in eastern and southern Africa.

Table 1. A timetable of major fossil discoveries 1822–1914 and the major reconstructions of Palaeolithic life. Key images are shown in ***bold italics*** while major books and events are in CAPITALS.

FINDSPOT	ILLUSTRATOR/ SCIENTIST	DATE	FOSSIL FIND
Wales			
Paviland		1822	*Homo sapiens* 'the red lady'
Belgium			
Engis		1829–30	Neanderthal
		1830–3	LYELL, PRINCIPLES OF GEOLOGY
Gibraltar			
Forbes Quarry		1848	Neanderthal
Germany			
Neander Valley		1856	Neanderthal
		1859	HUMAN ANTIQUITY ESTABLISHED
	Boitard	1861	***Fossil Man*** fig. 5.24
		1863	HUXLEY, MAN'S PLACE IN NATURE
		1865	LUBBOCK, PRE-HISTORIC TIMES
Belgium			
Reuviau		1867	*Homo sapiens*
Trou Magrite		1867	*Homo sapiens*
France			
Crô-Magnon		1868	*Homo sapiens*
		1871	DARWIN, THE DESCENT OF MAN
	Harper's Weekly	1873	***Neanderthal man*** fig. 5.26
Belgium			
Spy Caves		1886	Neanderthal
	Cleuziou	1887	***Pithecanthropus*** fig. 5.27 the theory
Java			
Trinil		1891	*Homo erectus/Pithecanthropus*
	Max	1894	***Pithecanthropus*** fig. 5.28 the reality
	Hutchinson	1896	***Homo sapiens*** at Wookey Hole fig. 5.29
Croatia			
Krapina		1899–1905	Neanderthal
England			
Gough's cave		1901	*Homo sapiens*
	Knipe	1905	***Pithecanthropus*** fig. 5.34
Germany			
Ehringsdorf		1907	Neanderthal
Mauer		1907	*Homo heidelbergensis*
France			
Le Moustier 1		1908	Neanderthal
La Chapelle-aux-Saints		1908	Neanderthal
	Boule	1909	***Neanderthal***, Chapelle-aux-Saints fig. iii
La Ferrassie 1		1909	Neanderthal
Combe Capelle		1909	Homo sapiens
La Ferrassie 2		1910	Neanderthal
	Keith	1911	***Neanderthal***, Chapelle-aux-Saints fig. iv
La Quina		1911	Neanderthal
La Ferrassie 3 & 4		1912	Neanderthal
Le Moustier 2		1914	Neanderthal
	Knight/Osborn	1915	***Neanderthal***, Le Moustier fig. v

So, for much of the period covered by Moser in chapter 5 the database of human origins was very thin indeed. As for the reconstructions, they too take some time to get going (Table 1). For example, it is interesting to see that in Thomas Huxley's influential essay *Man's Place in Nature* of 1863, which championed human evolution, the Neander valley skull found in 1857 is illustrated as a scientific specimen, an engraving akin to Frere's rendering of the Hoxne handaxes. No place here for imaginative reconstructions of our ancestors. Probably because the archaeology of stone tools dominated in this early phase it was sufficient just to make the living prehistory argument to flesh out the finds.

Among those early finds perhaps the most remarkable is Eugene Dubois' discovery at Trinil in 1891 of the famous skull cap which was first christened *Pithecanthropus erectus* and later changed to *Homo erectus*. Dubois was searching for the physical evidence to prove the German scientist Haeckel's theory that humans passed through an ape-man stage (*Pithecanthropus*) and that this probably occurred in Asia. This countered Darwin's earlier view that we should look to Africa for the human cradle. It is also remarkable because, as Moser shows, *Pithecanthropus* got a full reconstruction in Henri du Cleuziou's book (figure 5.27) *before* any fossils which could fit its description were discovered, and then another by Gabriel von Max (figure 5.28) soon after its announcement. What you have to ask yourself is whether Dubois' discovery was really necessary to paint the later picture? Haeckel had long before proposed a stage in human evolution which he called the speechless ape-man (*Pithecanthropus alalus*); von Max provided the image (figure 5.28) to fit the theory.[15]

Visual theories: which sex made the past?

So what were these artists basing their reconstructions upon? It certainly was not a great deal of hard evidence for either the use of stone tools or the anatomy of early humans. Rather it was the artistic tradition of showing primitives. When it came to portraying the sexes in human evolution the evidence was even less substantial than that available to show the differences between fossil species, based on theory or finds.

A rare early glimpse is provided in Worthington Smith's delightful *Man the Primeval Savage* of 1894. This is a richly illustrated account of his own remarkably astute observations of flint implements in Bedfordshire, England. He never found any early human remains. I reproduce here (figure i) his frontispiece, which combines the classic iconography of primitiveness in a well-posed family group of Pre-Raphaelite demeanour and hairstyles; their handaxes lie at their feet and a Hercules-derived club is to hand. This is a very different image from Max's speechless ape-men (figure 5.28) which appeared in the same year (but then these were British savages). Elsewhere in the book Smith even has female flint knappers, a visual proposition in an oft-repeated scene which almost no one else has countenanced.[16] His little

Figure i. A Stone Age Family. Drawing by Worthington G. Smith for his *Man the Primeval Savage*, 1894, title page.

family sketch tries harder than most to incorporate the archaeology he knew so well and his group does not fit readily into those half-dozen scenes which Moser has identified as iconic. As a result, it is both more interesting and more difficult to place.

Smith was something of a one-off among the early illustrators. Usually, as I pointed out above with my head count of males and females in two children's books, the males dominate. Neither was this limited to scientific images. By the last decade of the nineteenth century the pace of reconstructions was growing rapidly. Different traditions were also emerging, including E.T. Reed's famous *Prehistoric Peeps* drawn for the satirical magazine *Punch*. These cartoons are almost exclusively male dominated. They also appeared in 1894 and poked fun at knock-kneed politicians dressed up in skins, wielding clubs and battling with dinosaurs at funfairs.[17] Fred Flintstone and Barney Rubble need look no further for their ancestors.

However, the depiction of the sexes in human origins is no joke. Instead it is a vivid reminder of how visual images communicate ideas which, once proposed in this medium, are very difficult for an historical discipline to shift. These images can owe little to archaeological endeavour and scientific analysis and instead everything to those visual threads which have a long history in the European view of the world. I once sat through a technical conference paper at the Royal Society on the genetics of human evolution only to have the lecturer summarize the complexity of his scientific argument by showing a Gary Larsson cartoon. I have to wonder at moments like that if science is all, theoretically, that it is cracked up to be.

The depiction of gender in these images of early humans has been thoroughly examined by Stephanie Moser,[18] Diane Gifford-Gonzalez,[19] Linda Hurcombe[20] and Erica Hemming.[21] Gifford-Gonzalez, by studying eighty-eight reconstructions of Crô-Magnon life, has highlighted major differences in where the sexes are placed in the frame. She compares the positioning of three common Stone Age types. Her sample of Madonna-with-Child (you will find a good example in figure 5.20) were fairly evenly split between fore-, middle- and background. By contrast, the Man-the-toolmaker images (e.g. figure 5.35), which she describes as usually 'a jovial fellow pounding stone on stone in a fashion more suitable to blacksmithing than to stone flaking', hog the foreground in a commanding 95 per cent of all cases.[22] The remaining 5 per cent are in the middleground. Her third example, Drudge-on-a-hide, shows a woman on her knees scraping an animal hide with a stone tool. It is a common image in twentieth-century reconstructions of Stone Age life (yes, there was one in my schoolboy textbook). It evokes a Victorian scullery-maid scrubbing the floor. Unsurprisingly the Drudge-on-a-hide hardly ever appears in the foreground.[23] This visual message hardly needs spelling out: women's work is unimportant and of lower status than the males' tool-making. Gifford-Gonzalez concludes:

> By inserting such evocative symbols from mainstream Western art traditions, artists allow the schemata to tell pre-existing, gendered tales of heroism, motherhood and drudgery to the enculturated western viewer.[24]

Here is a theory of the past portrayed in visual activities. Once we are aware of its existence it is very easy to trace its roots in western art by following successive interpretations of the Madonna-and-child image by male artists. Please note, there are no female artists in Moser's book because in the period she deals with this was an entirely male-dominated profession. Women artists still remain underrepresented in this field of scientific-based imagery just as they continue to be a small minority in academic departments and the scientific community generally.

Using the illustrations in the chapters below I traced the following lineage where the Madonna-and-child image is used not as a religious subject but rather as a way of demonstrating ancient times and that sense of the 'Other' lying outside civilized society.

1483	Figure 3.2
1500	Figure 3.8
1616	Figure 4.7
1660	Figure 4.17
1861	Figure 5.24
1870	Figure 5.20
1905	Figure 5.35

Making a similar proposition about the respective roles of the sexes from archaeological data would be much more complicated. Neither would it carry such a clear message about the respective contribution of each sex to human evolution.

The power of these images to convey an unstated idea, which would be difficult to prove with archaeological data, is neatly shown with a variant on the Madonna-and-Child image. I call this At-her-Master's-feet. Here the male is invariably foregrounded, standing, gazing purposefully into the distance/future and holding on to a tool or weapon. All of this indicates his active participation in the course of human evolution. By contrast the female is in the middle- or background, rarely holding anything except a child, usually naked and either supine or sitting, often with an adoring look. Now, compare figure 5.34, produced in 1905, with a diorama from *Préhistorama Museum*, created in the early 1990s (figure ii). All that has happened in the intervening ninety years is that the female's place in history, as indicated by her posture, seems to have slipped. For all the advances in archaeological data, methods and interpretation the message from the popular image remains unchanged.

Visual theories: ancestral capabilities

A good deal of discussion about human origins centres on what our ancestors could do. Could they make tools, speak, live in large social groups, hunt, make fire and so on? The arguments are complex, the data often ambiguous and so the push to show it, rather than tell it, is strong. I want to give one example which Moser has examined in detail elsewhere.[25] This concerns the public image of Neanderthal people, which is important to me because Palaeolithic archaeology is not just about discovery and description. It is also about interpretation and explanation.

Figure ii. Diorama of Palaeolithic life. Display by Eirik Granqvist for *Préhistorama Museum*, early 1990s, Ardèche, France.

It is a fascinating period not because it deals with people and objects which are fabulously old in a *Guinness Book of Records* sort of way. It fascinates because it is our only sure route, backed by evidence, to explore an alternative vision of humanity. The people we describe, and their actions which we interpret, are in many ways so similar, yet in many others so different from what we find familiar and comfortable. We remain impoverished in our understanding of the human project unless we try to understand them on their own terms which means by what has survived of their societies.

This is never going to be an easy task and images have provided a shortcut to analysis and reasoned argument based on evidence. Of all our fossil ancestors Neanderthal people have been subject to the most shortcuts.[26] They have either been placed firmly within the human lineage or expelled from it. Neanderthals, as one of the largest samples of fossil ancestors, have been the constant touchstone for this debate in literature, archaeology, cinema and the static image. They lived between 250,000 and 27,000 years ago in what is now Europe and the Middle East. They have become, however, a universal icon for the psychological investigation of ourselves that ranges from the glee of H.G. Wells, who had our Crô-Magnon ancestors exterminate them, to the sadness of William Golding, who saw their demise as a dark day for humanity.[27] The scientific debate is no less forthright and divided. Neanderthals are proposed either as the direct ancestors of modern Europeans or as a population which was replaced in that continent between 40,000 and 27,000 years ago by people who came from Africa. I favour the latter, the recent African origin model, as the best interpretation of the evidence. Just recently it has received to many people's mind convincing evidence in the form of DNA extracted from the bones of the original Neander skeleton which confirms it (Table 1).[28]

Direct genetic comparison of fossils with modern populations was of course undreamt of by earlier archaeologists. What they dreamed of was finding fossils to demonstrate the reality of human evolution. In terms of the Neanderthals, one year can be singled out, 1908, which was of key importance for both archaeological and fossil discoveries. But just as important as the discovery in that year of a near-complete skeleton in the cave of La Chapelle-aux-Saints in the Corrèze Department of France were the visual representations of that find.

The first image (figure iii) is a classic case of character assassination. It appeared in the French newspaper, *L'Illustration*, in 1909 and was claimed as an 'accurate reconstruction of the Prehistoric cave-man' when it was reproduced one week later in the *Illustrated London News*. The artistic details had been sanctioned by the leading French palaeontologist of the day, Marcellin Boule, and for many years his magisterial account of the skull and skeleton was regarded as a scientific *tour de force* of fossil anatomy.[29] His conclusion that Neanderthals had no part in our ancestry chimed well with the opinion of the three clerics who had dug up the skeleton and brought it to him for analysis and adjudication.[30]

But not everyone agreed. In particular Boule's counterpart in England, Sir Arthur Keith, commissioned a reconstruction of the same skeleton

Figure iii. The Neanderthal from La Chapelle-aux-Saints. Drawing by Kupka, *Illustrated London News* February 1909, pp. 302–3.

which appeared in the *Illustrated London News* in 1911 (figure iv). Boldly titled 'Not in the "Gorilla" stage', Keith's illustration was clearly flinging down the gauntlet to the Frenchman and even gilding the lily somewhat by showing the man wearing a necklace for which there is no evidence at all. The move, artistically, from Mugger-waiting-behind-a-rock to Toolmaker-by-the-fire-of-progress could not be more dramatic.

Which image and theory prevailed? The answer was emphatically Boule's. Keith eventually abandoned his reconstruction and the theory it enshrined and instead pursued the false trail laid in 1912 by Hinton and Dawson, the Piltdown hoaxers. Moreover, I think the events of the First World War which shortly followed were also set against Keith's image. The carnage of that war stripped away the veneer of civilization and revealed an older moral ancestry that people wanted to expel, ignore or blame on someone else. The values commonly ascribed to Neanderthals were part of that process. They are nicely summed up in a specially commissioned picture by the American palaeontologist, Henry Fairfield Osborn (figure v). Painted by Charles R. Knight, it appeared in 1915 and has been widely reproduced ever since. So widely that it eclipsed the two earlier images and these remained unremarked until republished by Moser in 1992. I can remember when she showed them to me how surprised I was that the palaeontological arguments found their most dramatic expression visually, rather than in scientific texts. It was on seeing Boule and Keith's reconstructions of the same evidence side-by-side that I realized just how important it was to take the visual language of archaeology seriously. It was only after the Second World War that Boule's anatomical conclusions were shown to be wrong and a complete rehabilitation of Neanderthals took place. But not before the damage to their public image was irrevocable.

Figure iv. A revised view of the Neanderthal from La Chapelle-aux-Saints. Drawing by Amadée Forestier, *Illustrated London News* May 1911, pp. 778–9.

What lies ahead?

So this is why these images are important to someone like me, a Palaeolithic archaeologist. I can dismiss them, ridicule them, laugh with them, tear my hair out about them, try to change them, but I cannot ignore them. They are both liberating and blinkering. They are very much a part of the Old Stone Age landscape, powerful visions about what it was like and why we should be grateful we no longer live like that.

Figure v. Neanderthals at Le Moustier in the Dordogne. Drawing by Charles R. Knight for Henry Fairfield Osborn's *Men of the Old Stone Age*, 1915, pl. 1.

Moser's book now lets all of us return to similar visual encounters with the past, whether in childhood or adulthood, and provides us with a means of understanding a part of that experience, enabling comprehension of why such images are important rather than trivial in investigating the past and an appreciation of how we participate in and contribute to a collective representation of times and places none of us can ever visit yet which, for reasons of forging identity and defining communities, we deem important. And finally we can achieve a recognition of how we borrow from the past to make the present in our own, recycled image.

But previously I rashly promised to draw a lesson from this investigation of our visual language and ask if fresh images are possible or will these reconstructions always be varnished with old theories and preconceptions? Well, the short retort that Palaeolithic archaeology could do with its cubist revolution would be one answer, but a rather unsatisfying one as I do not currently see our Braque or Picasso.[31]

My answer is, emphatically, that we can harness the power of these images to promote our understanding of the Palaeolithic world and all our wonderful ancestors. Stephanie Moser points out time and again in her chapters what we must do to make that possible. There will be no fresh images until we finally abandon the idea that the study of human origins is a celebration of progress. We have done that in many of our words on the subject but we have not yet done it in the images we employ. We have not done it precisely because we have not seized them by the scruff of their theoretical necks, as Moser has done here, and shaken them until their origins are laid bare. Gabriel de Mortillet in 1867 declared that the Palaeolithic demonstrated the 'great law of the progress of man'.[32] Popular accounts, such as van Loon's in 1922, provided a visual image of how that could be conceived. My schoolboy textbook *Looking at History* was also a self-confessed story of progress, and we are constantly surrounded by pictures of marching timelines that continue to tell the familiar story of technological change linked to posture, brow ridges, clothes and, of course, males. There are other stories to tell. Diversity and difference, for example, require their own imagery if they are to be incorporated into our discussions of human experience, whether of half a million years ago or yesterday. It is time to continue the critical assault on the image of the past, while acknowledging that our visual language remains one of the most potent means of scientific communication that we have.

Introduction

For many centuries people have been producing illustrations of primitive human-like beings who were thought to have lived in the far distant past. The vast number of such pictures reveals that one of the most natural and fundamental of human desires is to know where we as a species came from. The question of our origins and the way in which we became distinctively human is a subject that has found visual expression in a diverse range of media. Indeed, an interest in how our first human-like ancestors may have looked has resulted in the production of many paintings, sculptures, book illustrations and museum displays. Many of the visual images that exist were produced in conjunction with the establishment of prehistory as a discipline in the late nineteenth century. Since then research has yielded many important findings concerning the origins of our species, generating considerable public interest in the remote past. This interest has been sustained by the continued production of pictorial reconstructions of ancient ancestors for illustrated magazines and books on human evolution. Such images provide us with a glimpse into unimaginably distant times, introducing new fossil relatives as they are discovered in various parts of the world. These pictures are important because they represent the attempt to make sense of our ancestry – to explain where we came from, how we first lived, and what we looked like. Over the last century scientific reconstructions of the earliest hominid ancestors have served a critical role in bringing our most dimly perceived past into the realm of human understanding.

Despite the fact that pictorial reconstructions have been and continue to be a fundamental means of communicating ideas about human origins, we have been reluctant to examine the role that they have in conveying a sense of the past.[1] Essentially, these images have been taken for granted. They have been seen as unproblematic and self-explanatory rather than as complex documents which draw on a range of pictorial devices in order to create meaning. The major reason why reconstructions have been neglected as a subject worthy of study is that they have been perceived as divorced from the 'serious' practice of science. For many scientists these hypothetical artistic representations are considered simply as popular presentations used to brighten up books, or educational devices used to facilitate understanding for the non-professional.[2] However, this assumption reflects a great misunderstanding of science and the way it functions. In particular, it fails to recognize the central and powerful role of visual representation in science. Visual representation is not only crucial to the communication of scientific discoveries and ideas, it is also a central component of the scientific process, playing a role in the production of theories about scientific phenomena. Pictorial reconstructions are a major part of the representation of archaeological ideas about the past and are worth studying because they reveal how our sense of most distant times is inherently a visual one. Furthermore, an historical overview of this visual tradition demonstrates how a vision of human antiquity existed long before the scientific discovery of it took place. Images inspired by mythological, religious and historical views of the past have existed since the classical period and although speculative rather than scientific, they have had a fundamental impact on more recent images.

My research on visual reconstructions began with an investigation of the scientifically based images produced from the late nineteenth century to the present.[3] In examining this history I focused on pictures manufactured in association with the discovery of skeletal remains and prehistoric sites, documenting how the images reflected contemporary research developments. While I was aware that pre-scientific or speculative images of the past existed, I did not credit them with having a significant role in shaping the more recent images, which are based on systematic study and the excavation of new data. However, on closer examination I realized that the sources of influence for reconstructions went further and further back in time and that it was possible to find precursors for them in a vast array of diverse visual traditions going back to antiquity. It thus became clear that the scientifically based illustrations were heavily dependent on a visual language that was already established.[4] Thus, my objectives in this book are to look more closely at the images of the past that were generated before scientific study of the past was undertaken and to evaluate how these have influenced their scientific successors. This aim relates to Wiktor Stoczkowski's argument that scientific theories concerning the past have been informed by earlier speculative ideas.[5] In describing a speculative prehistory that existed before the scholarly discipline emerged, Stoczkowski shows how prehistoric people were *invented* long before they were actually *discovered*. He then suggests that by forgetting the old 'figmentary prehistory', we deprive ourselves of understanding the 'conditioning to which our imagination is subject'.[6] This argument applies to the visual perception of the past in the sense that if we do not acknowledge the earlier images we will fail to appreciate how our ideas of the past have evolved. Thus, this book presents a survey of ancestral imagery, from classical times to this century, bringing alive the old visions and examining how they remain within us.

This book tells the story of how reconstructions were first introduced to portray a vivid subject-matter on which little was known, and how many centuries later they were enlisted by prehistorians as a vital element in the establishment of their new discipline. However, before embarking on this story some discussion is devoted to the role of visual representation in science. Chapter 1 briefly outlines the history of scientific illustration, revealing how various sciences began to create their own visual languages from around the sixteenth century. The process by which scientific illustrators created visual conventions that were distinctive to their disciplines is then discussed and the major characteristics and conventions of scientific images are analysed. This discussion of the nature of scientific illustration introduces many of the themes that are raised throughout the book, focusing as it does on the use of visual devices to express ideas and concepts.

The second chapter examines the visions of human creation produced in antiquity. While the topic of human prehistory did not attract empirical investigation in classical times, there was a general philosophical interest in the nature of archaic life and some basic schemes of evolution were proposed. Philosophers, poets, and historians of the Greco-Roman world created a vivid mental picture of life before 'civilization'. While no illustrations of these evolutionary schemes survive, a number of iconographic traditions communicated the idea of a primitive or prehistoric existence. The iconography of Greek mythology, where particular figures were rendered according to distinct visual attributes, laid the foundations for the imagery of ancestors. Also important were the classical depictions of 'barbarians', or the other races thought to live in distant lands. Such iconographic traditions were the first step in the creation of a visual language for representing a sense of the remote human past.

Chapter 3 discusses notions of the distant past created in association with early Christian representations of Genesis, where Adam and Eve were depicted as the original ancestors of humankind. Biblical iconography became a profoundly important source for illustrations of the past and remained so until the late nineteenth century. Ideas about the primeval past were also conveyed in association with medieval ideas about the different states of human society and about non-Christian peoples. A number of iconographic traditions, including the imagery of the Marvels of the East and of the wildman of the woods, contributed to the visual image of what it meant to be primeval and prehistoric. With the Renaissance came an explosion of artistic and illustrative traditions, providing yet another source of visual ideas on human origins. An explicit iconography of prehistory emerged when the Greco-Roman theories about human origins were illustrated in the printed books of the 1500s. Finally, Renaissance artists contributed to an iconography of human origins when they portrayed classical myths of human development. While all these visual representations were hypothetical, they nevertheless provided a clear idea about what the distant past was thought to be like. A lack of scientific data on prehistory certainly did not prevent or inhibit people from providing detailed and vivid portraits of our ancestors.

Not long after the Renaissance more accurate pictures of the past were constructed. Chapter 4 looks at the contribution of antiquarians to an iconography of prehistory in the sixteenth and seventeenth centuries, revealing how the imagery of European ancestry played a role in further developing the conventions for depicting our first ancestors. Early portraits of the ancient inhabitants of Europe are important because they show how ethnological imagery and studies of ancient sites increasingly informed reconstructions of the past. However, more important was the construction of a visual 'type', in the form of the ancient Celtic warrior, which came to influence the image of our first ancestors as prehistoric warriors. This stereotype became common in travel accounts, costume studies and then later in pictorial history.

The introduction of the first scientific images of prehistory in the second half of the nineteenth century is documented in chapter 5. These pictures were based on the discovery of fossil data and contributed to the acceptance of the fact that humans were truly ancient. Such images were also important in making the theory of human descent from the apes comprehensible. These revolutionary ideas needed to be expressed in familiar and essentially visual terms before they could be understood. Working in collaboration with artists and engravers, science writers sought to establish a new vision of the Stone Age, but their illustrations drew heavily on the familiar icons of classical, early Christian, medieval and Renaissance imagery.

Chapter 6 looks at the representation of early prehistory in the visual arts, the print media and in museums in the late nineteenth and early twentieth century. It was around this time that prehistory became a popular theme in history painting, particularly in France, and pictorial reconstructions became commonplace in the leading illustrated magazines of the day. The role of museums in manufacturing visual representations is discussed with reference to the creation of murals for display, and finally, the formation of a specialist industry in the production of reconstruction drawings is examined. The chapter concludes by considering the work of the major artists who went on to develop the reconstruction genre as a special class of scientific illustration from the 1960s to the present.

Several points need to be made regarding the scope of this study. First, discussion is limited to two-dimensional images such as vase paintings, wall paintings, illuminated manuscripts, book illustrations and works of art on canvas. Although the focus is on paintings and engravings this does not mean that these are thought to be superior to other arts media. Indeed, the representation of the past in three-dimensional forms, as in sculptures, architectural features and museum dioramas, is equally vast and worthy of investigation.[7] The rationale for focusing on the two-dimensional representations is that these provide sufficient and clear examples of the iconographic traditions being discussed. Secondly, this study does not comprise a comprehensive catalogue of reconstructions; rather, representative examples have been selected from the various illustrative traditions. Thirdly, the focus is on traditions of representation in western Europe. This is not meant to suggest that there is an absence of illustrations of the past from other parts of Europe and, indeed, from other cultural traditions. The reason for the focus on western Europe is that it is here that we see the greatest proliferation of images produced in association with the rise of science.

The nature of this study also merits clarification. There are many difficulties associated with examining a wide range of different iconographic traditions over time and the presentation of an overview of such a very large and complex subject has its own particular problems. For instance, no image is produced in a vacuum and ideally each should be considered within its own temporal, regional, intellectual and socio-political context. However, the extent and range of this study means that it is impossible to do justice to all of the contexts in which each illustrative tradition arose. In tracing the persistence of iconographic themes over the centuries it became apparent that each image considered served different needs, addressed different questions and solved problems specific to the historical context of the time. Although aspects of continuity in visual traditions from many periods of history are chronicled, the intended implication is not that there was one long homogeneous and continuously evolving tradition that neatly and inevitably led to the production of scientific images of prehistory. Furthermore, in tracing the roots of the scientific iconography of prehistory, it is important to acknowledge that the motivation for reconstructing ancestors has varied over time. Not all visual traditions reflect a concern with prehistory, or indeed with the past. There were numerous agendas and motivations, including the concern to understand the present state of humanity, the demonstration of cultural superiority, the outlining of the difference between humans and animals, the revelation of the difference between different races, and the bringing to life of creatures reported in travel accounts. In many ways the pictures presented here do not tell a story about the growing interest in the past as much as they show us humanity's interest in other peoples and places.

Finally, this is not a survey of ideas and how they are visually represented, but rather, a survey of images and how they communicate and construct ideas. This distinction is important as it differs from the traditional historical approach to dealing with the study of the past. Put simply, the objective here is to treat images as the primary documents rather than as the by-products of scholarly work. This aim is based on the premise that visual documents can be just as informative as written text when dealing with the perception of remote time. Another important founding assumption is that images have played a fundamental role in the development of ideas, not simply in representing them. At this point it is worth stating the power of imagery in constructing knowledge. The central perspective underlying this book is that images are important because they have the capacity to *make* knowledge. Much has been written on this feature of images but a recent quotation by Thomas Mathews is particularly apt. Considering early Christian imagery and the creation of an iconography of Christ in the fourth and fifth centuries, he writes,

> Images are not neutral; they are not just stories put into pictures. Nor are they mere documents in the history of fashion. Images are dangerous. Images, no matter how discreetly chosen, come freighted with conscious or subliminal memories; no matter how limited their projected use, they burn indelible outlines into the mind. Often images overwhelm the ideas they are supposed to be carrying, or dress up with respectability ideas that in themselves are too shoddy to carry intellectual weight. Images not only express convictions, they alter feelings and end up justifying convictions.[8]

Thus, this study is not a history of research or of the different intellectual traditions pertaining to an understanding of prehistory. It is a study in iconography, where visual images are analysed in terms of their symbolic content and the meanings they convey. The investigation therefore focuses on the content or subject of the images rather than their form, which has involved the identification and classification of motifs relevant to notions of distant time. More specifically, the iconic elements and pictorial motifs of the illustrations are analysed in terms of what they communicate about the topic of human origins. Although the emphasis is on the informational rather than the aesthetic quality of the images, it is important to note that the didactic component of the pictures is often shaped by artistic conventions and that these are taken into account where relevant.

Several themes and arguments underlie and emerge from this study. It is argued that images have been a way of dealing with the problem of human ancestry and that what they have essentially done is bridge the vast gap between the past and the present. Furthermore, we have represented the past with the aid of visual symbols and have come to understand the past through a limited iconic vocabulary.[9] Despite the vast accumulation of scientific knowledge regarding prehistory over the last century, our basic images of human origins have actually changed very little. It is also clear that the set of visual symbols or icons that have been created for communicating a sense of the remote past were established long before prehistory ever became a discipline. The explanation for the persistence of age-old visions regarding our beginnings lies partly in the power of illustration. Once translated into images, ideas about prehistory were difficult to replace. Indeed, the early visualizations of prehistory have maintained a stubborn grip and it has been almost impossible for the scientific approach to dismantle some of these traditions of representation. This, as we shall see, has been a perpetual problem for many sciences since the Renaissance. The importance of the pictures is that they show how empirical data have not really had the power to challenge some of the speculative visions of the past. While it is true that there have been some significant changes in ancestral imagery, such variations have generally been restricted to the details and not to the actual meaning underlying the images. Rather than devaluing or undermining the power of science to revolutionize our understanding of human origins, this study of pictures serves to put such developments in perspective. By demonstrating that the scientific understanding of human evolution owes much to mythological, religious, and historically inspired artistic traditions, this study emphasizes how, in Stoczkowski's words, pictures can give us the 'pleasure of understanding the conditioning to which our imagination is subject'.[10]

CHAPTER 1

The Artist's Eye and the Mind of Science

The rise of science in the sixteenth century brought many advances in the understanding of the natural world and the place of humans within it. One of the major results of the scientific revolution was the creation of new visual modes of representing phenomena, reflecting how art came to play an important role in the process of observing and describing scientific specimens and concepts. Indeed, the sixteenth century is characterized as a period when science and art joined together to provide accurate observations of nature and culture. It was as a result of this union that illustration emerged as a force that would become integral to the scientific understanding of the world. While Renaissance art was critical to the emergence of scientific illustration, two other factors contributed to its rise. First was the production of the printed book, and second was the impact of travel in the New World.

Both art historians and historians of science have documented the fusion of art and science in the early Renaissance.[1] The invention of linear perspective and the illusion of depth had an important impact on the way scientific phenomena were studied and a number of leading artists of the day played a critical role in the development of science.[2] As Walter Herdeg has argued, it was during this time that the role of artists changed from that of a 'delineator of the palpable to that of a conceptualiser giving form and substance to highly theoretical constructs'.[3] So it is in association with the Renaissance that artists became teachers and that the genre of scientific illustration was born. Illustration became firmly established as an essential part of scientific communication, serving not only to describe phenomena, but also to explain the place and purpose of such phenomena in the world. The story of how illustrations became an important feature of scientific works is one in which scientific, religious and aesthetic traditions are all combined.[4] Furthermore, the history of the involvement of artists in documenting scientific phenomena is highly complex, and as Bernard Smith argues, 'it would be profoundly misleading to assume that this increasing use of art for the conveyance of relating scientific information operated as a direct, unilinear process by which error and illusion were cast off and the truth progressively revealed'.[5]

The emergence of scientific illustration is also intimately connected with the rise of the printed book in the late fifteenth century. During this time the manuscript tradition and the scribes and illuminators of the medieval period were gradually replaced by printed books.[6] Accompanying the advent of printing were technological changes associated with the production of images. Improvements in the production of woodcuts, engravings and etchings meant that illustrations were more readily adopted as a means of presenting information. As a result of their increasing usage, images started to acquire their own identity as an important component of the book.[7] The first illustrated books were produced in the late 1400s, a major example being the *Buch der Croniken* or *Nuremburg Chronicle* of 1493, which featured numerous woodcuts illustrating biblical history, the marvels of the east, and European topography in the form of maps and views of towns.[8] By the early 1500s many distinct traditions of book illustration were beginning to emerge, particularly biblical illustration.[9] However, at this early stage the quality of engravings was not high and few scholars recognized the educational value of illustrations.[10] Indeed, many humanists explicitly discredited the use of pictures in texts.[11] Despite this, schools of illustration grew up in the great publishing centres of Europe, often influenced by the traditions of painting in the region. Next to the Bible the major illustrated text of the 1500s was Ovid's *Metamorphoses*. The focus on the Bible and the classics reveals, as Lucien Febvre and Henri-Jean Martin observe, that the aim of the illustrated book in the sixteenth century was to 'make real and comprehensible the different episodes in the life of Christ, the prophets and the saints, and to give some reality to the demons and angels who disputed for the souls of sinners, and also to the mythical and legendary personalities familiar to the men in that age'.[12] Encouraged by the didactic potential of illustrations, as demonstrated in these religious and mythological texts, some scientists started to include illustrations in their books. The rapid improvements in the quality of images in the 1500s were another incentive. For instance, the increasing naturalism in the style of illustrations, which stemmed from developments of naturalistic representation in Renaissance art, meant that images became less schematic and more useful in the observation of phenomena.

The emergence of scientific illustration was also associated with European travel and, in particular, the recording of the New World in the 1500s. It was in the late fifteenth century that artists started to accompany European expeditions to foreign lands. In 1483 the Flemish artist, Erhard Reuwick, went to the Near East as part of Bernhard von Breydenbach's pilgrimage to the Holy Land. As a result of this Reuwick produced a series of illustrations of peoples, places and animals for Breydenbach's book *Peregrinatio in Terram Sanctam* (Journey to the Holy Land) of 1486. These illustrations show a concern for recording scientific phenomena and an interest in producing visually striking images. As David Bland states, the result of this expedition was the 'first truly topographical book with the first attempt to illustrate the thing at the moment of seeing'.[13] Artists were subsequently enlisted as vital members of expeditions to the New World. While the earliest illustrations of native American Indians appeared in Columbus' *Letter* of 1493, it was not until 1505 that images with a degree of accuracy were produced.[14] Within a number of decades the visual image became a critical part of the scientific recording of the new lands, featuring in atlases, encyclopaedic works and travel accounts. This culminated in the 1580s with John White's drawings of the Virginian Indians, in which a comparatively high level of scientific accuracy was finally achieved.[15]

These advances and developments resulted in the adoption of illustrations as didactic aids in scientific treatises from around 1530. Early examples include the botanical treatises or herbals, notably Otto Brunfels' *Herbarum vivae icones* of 1530. This book was distinguished by its use of original plates based on direct observation of specimens, as opposed to copied illustrations from earlier books. Another important example was Leonhart Fuch's *De historia stirpium commentarii* of 1542. In Fuch's book the value attributed to the image was revealed by the fact that he included portraits of his draughtsman and blockcutter. Fuch is also attributed with being one of the first scientists to emphasize the educational importance of the image:

> The woodcutter Veit Rudolf Speckle, by far the best in Strassbourg, has so ably carried out in carving the design of each picture that he seems to compete with the painted for glory and victory. But though the pictures have been prepared with great effort and sweat, we do not know whether in the future they will be dammed as useless and of no consequence and whether someone will cite the most insipid authority of Galen that no one who wants to describe plants should try to make pictures of them. But why take up more time? Who would in his right mind condemn pictures which can communicate information much more clearly than the words of even the most eloquent men . . . those things that are presented to the eyes and depicted on panels of paper become fixed more firmly in the mind than those that are described in bare words.[16]

It was not long before zoological works started to incorporate accurate illustrations of specimens.[17] Notable among these was Conrad Gesner's *Historiae animalium* of 1551 and *Icones Animalium* of 1553, which included some illustrations based on direct observation. However, as was typical of many early scientific treatises, Gesner combined his new images that were based on observation, with more speculative classical and medieval images, which were based on verbal descriptions and mythological ideas. While the early illustrations for botany and zoology raised the potential of visual aids, it was in the field of human anatomy that the potential of illustrations for both recording and explaining phenomena was fully realized. While Leonardo da Vinci's and Albrecht Dürer's work was paramount for the understanding of human anatomy, it was the publication of Andreas Vesalius' *De Humani Corporis Fabrica* in 1543 that signified the true beginnings of visual education in science. With its striking illustrations of the internal structure of the human body, this text not only secured the development of anatomy as a scientific discipline, but also established the place of illustrations in science.

Many historians of science have discussed the impact of Vesalius' illustrations, with their great concern for accuracy in the representation of the human body.[18] However, the success of the illustrations not only stemmed from the realistic rendering of anatomy, but also resided in the artistic elements of presentation. As Jonathan Sawday has noted, art was as much the dynamic behind the act of representation as was science itself.[19] For instance, an important aspect of the Vesalian illustrations was the way in which the specimens, stripped of their skin and with detached body parts, were rendered in classical poses and placed in landscapes with ruins.[20] Pictorial conventions such as these revealed the extent to which scientific illustration depended on the visual arts. The use of motifs from classical art, for instance, served to elevate the visual qualities of the images. However, the impact of artistic conventions was more than simply decorative, and ultimately served to shape the meaning of the image. The postures, gestures and backgrounds made the dead flayed bodies appear vibrant, active and almost living. Furthermore, the calmness of a rural landscape with picturesque ruins softened the reality and impact of the fact that the illustrations portrayed grotesque mutilated figures, who were often featured holding their own hanging muscles.[21] The function of such pictorial details, where corpses were involved in their own self-demonstration, was also to communicate the complexity of the body and its meaning in the universe. For instance, the ruins in the background suggested a process of decay also affecting the human body. Vesalius' figures thus not only represent the important relationship between artistic and scientific elements, but they also demonstrate how scientific illustrations gained their power by placing specimens in a visual context.

Throughout the 1600s the new scientific disciplines began to develop their own traditions of illustration. This development involved the creation of pictorial conventions or canons for presenting particular specimens or concepts. Certain aspects of scientific imagery became standardized as a communal language that could be understood by the professionals in the field. In addition to botany, zoology and anatomy, astronomy also started to formulate its own visual language.[22] Of critical importance was technological illustration or the imagery of machinery, which some have argued laid the foundations for the emergence of genuinely scientific illustration.[23] However, the new traditions of scientific illustration did not simply replace the older non-scientific traditions of representation; rather, they incorporated many features of the old into the new. Historians of scientific illustration have shown how the emblematic and allegorical elements, the artistic conventions and the visual concepts from pre-scientific traditions maintained their hold and powerfully influenced the supposedly 'new' scientific illustrations.[24] This alliance between art and science continued throughout the eighteenth century. Developments in natural history illustration saw new areas of visual representation emerge, notably the illustration of fossils, topographic, geological and archaeological imagery. These areas of illustration emerged in association with the increasing number of scientific voyages in the 1700s.[25] Travel accounts were no longer just characterized by their illustrations of plants, animals and peoples, but by more accurately rendered topographic pictures, detailed illustrations of geological features and pictures of ancient monuments and ruins.[26] This scientifically inspired imagery was influenced by the visual arts and, in particular, by traditions of landscape painting popular at the time.[27]

It was around the late 1700s and early 1800s that the relationship between the visual arts and science began to change. As science gained its power over the production of knowledge, connections with the subjective world of art were increasingly rejected. Scholars of the natural world and other scientific domains wanted to construct an essentially scientific or objective way of viewing phenomena. They wanted to create a distinctively new language of visual representation in which the aesthetic appeal of an image came second to its informational content. Background decoration and other artistic elements were considered extraneous, compromising the status of images as truly authentic documents of real phenomena. A clean break from the past was promoted and the borrowing of motifs from art was scorned. Scientists now sought to establish their own illustrative vocabularies which did not draw on previous traditions of representation. This can be clearly seen in anatomical illustration where the practice of including backgrounds was heavily criticized and subsequently abandoned as a convention.[28] Such concerns reflected the professionalization of scientific communities and were also part of a wider strategy to attach authority to scientific interpretations of the natural world. Scientific illustrations thus became increasingly abstract, particularly for the biological and medical sciences.

The nineteenth century saw the introduction of a number of new approaches in scientific illustration. The biological sciences, with their illustrations of the cellular and microscopic components of human and animal forms, provided major new perspectives on the living world, as did palaeontological, geological and geographic illustration, which rendered the earth's interior and ancient landscapes in detail.[29] Perhaps the most important development in scientific illustration at this time was that it was now also designed for popular consumption. This can be seen in the increasing numbers of science texts devoted to a non-professional audience. Again, developments in book illustration partly facilitated this rise, which was also related to changing social and economic conditions, such as improved education and increased literacy levels.[30] Public demand for educational works on science engendered new types of scientific illustration. No longer were illustrations designed to summarize and simplify scientific concepts; they were now designed to dramatize information or make it entertaining. One type of illustration that achieved this better than any other was the reconstruction drawing, introduced to communicate palaeontological and geological discoveries. Such illustrations reconstructed ancient landscapes and extinct species from fossil remains and ancient strata. They differed from all previous types of scientific illustration in the sense that they were based on the interpretation of fragmentary material rather than on the observation of existing phenomena. Scientific reconstructions were distinguished by the fact that they had a greater imaginative or hypothetical content than the more established types of scientific illustration. Furthermore, at a time when scientific illustrations were becoming increasingly abstract and diagrammatic, these illustrations stood out because they used a highly naturalistic style. Finally, reconstructions were extremely effective as didactic aids because they presented new scientific data within a genre of representation familiar to their readership.

Research on reconstruction drawings in geology and palaeontology has revealed their special contribution to the history of these disciplines.[31] Martin Rudwick, in his book *Scenes from Deep Time*, has demonstrated the central place of these pictorial reconstructions in making the discovery of a vast earth history comprehensible. He shows that the power of these reconstruction drawings in introducing new fossil ancestors and in bringing the deep past to life was such that scientists overlooked their imaginative or hypothetical status, and readily used them as part of their repertoire of explanatory aids. Thus, while such illustrations became popular as a key way of communicating disciplinary findings to a non-professional audience, they were also designed for professional consumption. Soon after geology and palaeontology had initiated this tradition, prehistoric archaeology adopted the pictorial reconstruction to promote an understanding of human origins and life in the Stone Age. It is here that the story of how scientific reconstructions of prehistory were produced begins. Before embarking on this story, however, it is important to outline the characteristics and conventions of scientific illustration, as these raise many of the central themes of the book.

The characteristics and conventions of scientific illustration

As a result of the growing interest in the social dimensions of science, historians of science have become concerned with the role that the visual plays in communicating scientific ideas.[32] Scientific illustrations have finally started to attract attention, after having been neglected as a medium of communication in science for many years. This lack of interest in scientific illustration is best accounted for by Samuel Edgerton, who states that art historians have only looked at scientific pictures when they are produced by geniuses like Leonardo, 'otherwise, they consider the genre remarkably inimical to creativity, a mere prostitute to someone else's ideas'.[33] Furthermore, historians of science have treated pictures as 'afterimages' of verbal ideas, failing to recognize how scientific illustration is a unique form of pictorial language with its own 'grammar and syntax'.[34] Recent research on the role of illustration in science has challenged the common conception that pictures are simply provided to 'brighten up' the text and that they are peripheral to the arguments being presented by authors. Not only do images bring concepts to life, lend weight to ideas and crystallise arguments, but they constitute a powerful rhetorical tool that features highly in the repertoire of explanatory aids employed by scientists.[35] Thus, pictorial devices have been reconceptualized as resources for the actual practice of science. A growing number of historians of science have reflected on the creation of their own disciplinary iconographies, where visual conventions communicate and, indeed, define their subject. Historians of physics, maths, chemistry, medicine, zoology, astronomy, botany, geology, palaeontology and archaeology have all identified a set of basic canons that illustrators utilize when conveying particular scientific concepts and principles.[36] Furthermore, they have begun to examine the specific historical contexts in which disciplines constructed their own visual languages. An important realization, as Martin Kemp has argued, is that the 'characterisation of the role of representation in science cannot be adequately achieved without a close study of how illustrations actually functioned in their particular historic environments'.[37]

Current thinking about the use of imagery in science has highlighted three general features of scientific illustration and its role in the practice of science. First, pictures play a role in constituting scientific theories. This concept is significant because it suggests that images contribute to the formulation of ideas rather than simply being representations of them. Furthermore, it suggests that scientists actually think in terms of visual images. Second is the idea that scientific illustrations can embody theoretical ideas not explicitly stated in the text. In this sense images can convey the ideological positions or political viewpoints of the illustrator, the commissioning author, the scientific community and the wider social and cultural community. As James Ackerman has argued, the significance of the scientific image was that 'it not only could reinforce the author's written statement but could *itself* be the statement'.[38] The third general feature of scientific illustrations is their persuasiveness. Scientifically inspired images are persuasive because they provide us with a much clearer and more direct understanding of phenomena than is communicated via verbal text. This feature raises the issue of how images communicate differently from text. Images rely on devices such as the visual symbol or icon, which is used to communicate an idea. The appeals made to our understanding by visual symbols in images are completely different from those of text. The advantage of images is that they can convince us of new ideas or theories because they present them according to a set of familiar pictorial elements that have been assembled in a familiar compositional format. Furthermore, images affect us in a subconscious way, and we tend to absorb them in an instant without realizing just how much they have shaped our thoughts. As Stephen Jay Gould has argued, 'iconography comes upon us like a thief in the night – powerful and remarkably efficacious, yet often so silent that we do not detect the influence'.[39] Finally, scientific illustrations are persuasive because they have the ability to make theories for which evidence is limited seem credible. For instance, pictures can fill in the gaps in a theory with small details such as a background scene. These details have been described by Greg Myers as 'gratuitous', in the sense that the 'squiggles and splotches that do not seem relevant to the claim the picture illustrates have their own significance, as part of what makes the picture seem continuous with our own world'.[40] Illustrations can convince us of theoretical standpoints when sufficient data may be absent because they can subsume evidence into a visually appealing display. As Nicolaas Rupke states, 'illustrations may be a means to express beliefs for which concrete proof is lacking and as such they can be used as instruments of persuasion, rather than argumentation based on evidence'.[41]

In addition to these general traits there are a number of more specific characteristics and conventions of scientific illustrations. A major characteristic of scientific illustrations is that they have a harmonizing role, whereby new evidence is presented according to established traditions of representation. An example of this can be seen in early zoological illustration, where an image of a 'man-ape' was reproduced in Conrad Gesner's comprehensive work on animals. Gesner, who aimed to depict the animal species according to objective observation, simply copied Reuwick's illustration of a mythological creature that Reuwick himself stated he could not identify.[42] Another instance of this was when the notable anatomist Nicholas Tulp replicated an illustration of 'Homo sylvestris' or an anthropoid ape in his book on anatomy, which was clearly an anthropomorphic impression.[43] Furthermore, scientists did not refrain from producing illustrations of the mythical creatures thought to live in remote countries, even when their existence was disproved. This not only reveals the extent to which the ancient writers were considered the ultimate authorities, but demonstrates how iconographic traditions maintained their influence in spite of the rise of science.

Scientific illustrations make use of pictorial motifs from the visual arts to represent scientific phenomena and these often shape the meaning of the image. Sometimes it is not so much the informational content of the image as its conventions and context which give it its meaning. This, as we saw earlier, is demonstrated in early anatomical illustrations where background landscapes and poses were integral to the overall message of the image. Another later example of this characteristic is Bernhard Siegfried Albinus' *Tabulae sceleti et musculorum* of 1747, in which dissected bodies are portrayed in meticulously rendered pastoral landscapes, in scenes with classical architecture and alongside exotic animals. Such was the prominence given to the backgrounds that Albinus himself justified their function, stating that they 'not only . . . fill up the empty spaces of the tables and make them appear more agreeable; but likewise that . . . the light and shades of the figures might be preserved and heightened, and the figures themselves appear more raised and rounded'.[44] The backgrounds were thus thought to make the figures more 'realistic' or three-dimensional. Beyond this, the backgrounds also served to counteract the horror of human dissection by placing specimens in a picturesque, narrative and familiar context.

A third characteristic of scientific illustrations is that key images are recycled in other publications and in many different contexts. The selection of particular images, which are then copied in other texts, leads to the formation of visual icons, or well-known images. Such images acquire a meaning beyond their initial purpose, often becoming associated with an idea or landmark in the history of science.[45] The criteria according to which images are selected for recycling varies. On the one hand, images are often chosen because they are the first published impression of a species or phenomena based on first-hand observation. However, they were also chosen because they were visually striking or easy to copy. A problem with the recycling of iconic images is that they retain their popularity and continue to be reproduced even when new data are found. An historical example of this is Dürer's engraving of a rhinoceros of 1515. This image, based on other people's sketches rather than on direct observation, was copiously reproduced in works of natural history, no doubt because of its striking visual qualities, but also because it was the first image of such an animal to be circulated in Europe. Even when images become scientifically outdated they continue to be published. While this is partially due to the fact that it is cheaper for publishers simply to copy or reproduce images already in existence, it also reflects how certain images have become so familiar that people are subconsciously unwilling to replace them with a new version. Example of this are Vesalius' illustrations of the human body. Even when new knowledge on the interior of the body was published, people continued to copy Vesalius' images rather than update them.[46]

In addition, it is important to note that scientific illustrations serve many other roles beyond simply describing new phenomena. Though constructed for scientific purposes, illustrations often have an underlying social agenda, which may be related to the class, race or gender of the producers of the illustration and to the specific historical circumstances in which it is produced. An example of this can be seen in early ethnographic imagery, which did not function simply to describe what other races looked like, but also to legitimize the process of colonization.[47] The emphasis on cannibalism in depictions of the Indians encountered in the New World, for instance, justified the subjugation of peoples who were thought to live such a primitive and savage existence.[48] In early anatomical illustrations the symbolism of the images reflected the extent to which religious thinking shaped the perception of the human form. Jonathan Sawday has highlighted how important religious didacticism was in the production of anatomical images, arguing that the imagery of 'sacred anatomy' exerted a powerful hold on the devices and forms of representation by which the body interior was understood.[49]

A central question associated with scientific illustrations is that of accuracy. Scientific illustrations are commonly assumed to be distinguished by the fact that they are based on observation or objective methods of study. However, the concept of 'accuracy' comes in many different forms, meaning different things for different scientific disciplines, and being problematic within individual disciplines themselves. For example, many early scientific images that were termed 'accurate' because they were based on observation were actually derived from verbal accounts, written reports and rough field sketches. Furthermore, many 'first-hand' illustrations were actually based on sketches provided by others and were thus copies of original illustrations rather than being drawn from actual specimens.[50] Many illustrations compile features from a number of specimens into one image. Relevant here is James Ackerman's discussion of the difference between mimetic and didactic imagery, where the former seeks to reproduce individual specimens with their own idiosyncrasies and imperfections, and the latter seeks to represent a type or class of object so as to reveal its distinctive forms most clearly.[51] This latter strategy can be seen in palaeontological illustration, where skeletal fragments from a number of specimens are combined to provide a complete type specimen or image of a species.

Where reconstructions of ancient life are described as accurate, the implication is that an extinct dinosaur or hominid really looked as it does in the illustration. However, what accuracy actually means here is that the illustrator has used an understanding of anatomy and a set of skeletal remains to inform the reconstruction. Similarly, accuracy in early ethnological images is problematic. It implies that a good physical likeness of a cultural group has been achieved, but what accuracy often means in this context is that the material culture in the image is authentic.

The concept of accuracy in scientific illustration is also selective. Specimens or phenomena are simplified by emphasizing their meaningful features and ignoring their unimportant ones. Indeed, Herdeg asserts that the significance of a scientific drawing is 'perhaps best assessed by the fact that all trivialities are eliminated from it'.[52] Accuracy is further qualified for those illustrations that compress information by placing different species, for example, into a single illustration. The objective to make illustrations effective didactic tools and to convey as much information as possible often results in their becoming unnatural representations. Again, this is a feature of palaeontological imagery where it is common to see many different species of animals and plants placed together in the same scene, most of which would never have coexisted in this manner.[53] It is also a problem in ethnographic imagery where figures are shown carrying out a range of activities which in reality may have occurred at different times of the day, week, month or year, and not necessarily in the same location.[54]

Finally, and perhaps most importantly, scientific illustration has an iconographic dimension upon which it depends in order to communicate ideas effectively. This iconic element of scientific imagery refers to two different processes. First, illustrations utilize established icons that signify an idea, emotion or state of being. These icons, with their recognized meanings, are incorporated into pictures to convey a general message or idea. Secondly, particular details may be highlighted, simplified or repeated, leading to the creation of a vocabulary or symbolic language particular to an individual science. Examples of this can be seen in all areas of scientific illustration, where imagery gradually becomes more simplified over time, making frequent use of a set of icons. A critical aspect of the iconographic dimension of scientific illustration is this process of simplification, which serves to restrict or limit knowledge. Furthermore, the idea that many of these frequently depicted icons have been inherited from earlier visual traditions implies that scientific illustration has retained many elements from the more speculative traditions of understanding. This, together with the simplifying role of imagery, suggests that the iconographic dimension of scientific illustration plays a role in the maintenance of ideas over time. It is this aspect of scientific imagery which is at the heart of this book.

CHAPTER 2

Mythological Visions of Human Creation

Philosophers, scholars and artists of the classical period created a general vision of primeval life that continues to influence our perceptions of the past. Communicated in striking visual terms, classical ideas about animal-like primitive creatures have remained remarkably persistent. The Greco-Roman notions of the distant past were primarily inspired by creation myths, but in addition to these mythological schemes there were a number of iconographic traditions that conveyed a sense of an archaic human existence. These traditions were associated with the representation of particular mythological figures, imagined creatures and other races, and are of critical importance in understanding the iconography of prehistory because they provide the major visual icons for communicating the distant past.

The topic of the ancient past was not of great academic interest to classical scholars, who were more concerned with recent and contemporary history. Indeed, there exists no major recognized work on prehistory in the classical literature.[1] The obvious explanation for this lack of interest was that evidence of prehistory had not yet been recognized as such. For instance, Pausanias' *Description of Greece*, written in the second century AD, referred to the discovery of huge fossil bones, the remains of mammoths and other extinct animals.[2] However, these were not interpreted as evidence of a remote prehistory; rather, they were thought to be the bones of giants. The other reason why prehistory was not pursued as a scholarly subject was that there were established creation myths and stories which accounted for the emergence of humanity. Therefore, despite the lack of scientific work on prehistory, there was a significant treatment of the subject within myth, where writers elucidated on life in more distant times in the context of their treatment of other subjects. A number of Greco-Roman writers described primeval life in their national histories, geographic descriptions, cosmological studies, poems and epic stories. In these works, descriptions of primitive life were typically used as a point of comparison with the present rather than representing a genuine interest in the past. Such mythological schemes served as a vehicle for highlighting current problems with 'civilized' society. Thus, many classical writers referred to notions of prehistory in the context of describing life before knowledge of the arts and the construction of cities.

Classical schemes of human evolution

The poet Hesiod was one of the first writers of the western tradition to provide an explanation of our human beginnings. This was outlined in *Works and Days*, written around the eighth century BC, which was an account of Greek cultural history. Here Hesiod presented the legend of the Five Races or generations of the world, in which the successive races of humankind are described.[3] First was the Golden race, who were peaceful and happy, living in a natural state without hardship. They were succeeded by the Silver race, who represented a deterioration in that they were inferior physically and morally and they began to fight with one another. Third was the Bronze race, who represented a further decline in that they became violent and began to eat flesh. Fourth was the race of Heroes, who did not represent a further deterioration in culture, being noble and righteous. They were followed by the Iron race, who were savage, libidinous and cruel. With this final race of humanity there was a complete physical and moral decline. The Five Races scheme, with its metallic ages, incorporated elements from other creation myths, especially Babylonian, Persian and Asiatic ones.[4] The symbolism of the metals is important in that it embodies a sense of cultural evolution, later to become a fundamental feature of scientific schemes of prehistory. However, cultural evolution was certainly not the underlying theme of Hesiod's scheme. His scheme was one of degeneration, in which the most distant past was conceived of in the most positive light and the most recent past was considered to represent a decayed state. Thus, in the Five Races legend, history was characterized not by progress, but rather by decline.

Hesiod's vision of human degeneracy informed successive schemes of the past and became a popular concept in Greek and Roman literature, where it was commonly known as the five ages of humankind. Many Greek writers used it for their own purposes, incorporating ideas of a Golden Age or original state of primal innocence into their treatises on history, astronomy, geography and agriculture. For example, in the fourth century BC Dicaearchus wrote about the evolution of human culture from the Golden Age to his own time in his *Life of Greece*, Aratus described an early Golden Age in his *Phaenomena* and Plato highlighted the virtues of primitive life in *Protagoras*.[5] With the Roman scholars the concept of a Golden Age became even more popular, and major authors of the time used it in their poems and epics. Most notable was Ovid's detailed account in *Metamorphoses*.[6] Another important example was Virgil's description of life before tilling, which was introduced in his *Georgics*.[7] The legend of the ages provided not only a basic chronological framework of human evolution, but also a compelling vision of early life. When printed classical texts were first illustrated in the fifteenth and sixteenth centuries, this legend provided one of the major visual themes.

An alternative to Hesiod's scheme was outlined by those who argued that human evolution was characterized by progress rather than decline. The major proponent of this view was the Greek poet and philosopher Lucretius, who, in his *De rerum natura* of the first century BC, developed the idea that history was characterized by gradual social and technological advance. Emphasizing the brutal and primitive nature of our beginnings, Lucretius informs us that the first humans were little different from beasts. His description of life in primeval times is so detailed and compelling that we feel we are actually witnessing it:

> Yet the human race was hardier then by far
> No wonder, for the earth was hard that formed them
> Built upon bigger and tougher bones within,
> Bowels and flesh sewn tight with well-strapped muscles,
> Not easily overcome by heat or cold
> Or by strange diet or bodily decay.
> For many revolutions of the sun
> They led the life of the pack, like beasts that roam.
> There was no ruddy farmer to steady the plow;
> Unknown were iron tools to till the fields,
> How to plant out new shoots, or from the tall trees
> Prune away the branches with the hook.[8]

Thus we learn that the first ancestors were born of the earth, and that they were large, muscular and strong. They did not live as couples, but rather lived like animals in a pack. The skills of working the land were unknown to them, as was the knowledge of metals and the ability to grow and maintain crops. Lucretius continues,

> What the sun and the showers bestowed, what the earth created
> Of its own doing, satisfied their hearts.
> Often they met their bodies' needs by feeding
> From the acorn-copious oak, and the berries you see
> Ripen in winter, wild strawberries, purple-red,
> Rose bigger and more plenteous from the earth.

Many other foods the flowering fresh earth bore,
Hard fare, but ample, for wretches born to die.
And springs and rivers called them to quench their thirst,
As now from the mountains clear cascades of water
Draw from afar the thirsty animals.
Those rovers found and dwelled in the sacred groves
Of the Nymphs, wherever the rush of a good deep brook
Spilled over to wash the wet and slippery stones,
The slippery stones, and trickled over the moss,
Or where streams sprung up bubbling from the fields.[9]

It is thus suggested that the first race created nothing, as they were content with what the earth provided for them. Furthermore, no investment was made in building a better life because they knew of nothing different. The needs of the first born were thus very simple, being purely those of the body, such as hunger and sex. We learn that their diet of berries and other fare was rough, but that such a diet was satisfactory for such primal beings. With comments such as these, Lucretius is telling us that these ancestors deserved their primitive life because they had no aspirations for improvement. To satisfy their thirst they wandered, like animals, in search of a mountain spring, and it was in the woods that they stayed. This description of a nomadic life, driven purely by the search for food and water, emphasizes how these creatures had no attachment to a particular place, and thus lacked a sense of territorial identity.

They had no foundry skills, no use for fire;
They didn't know how to clothe themselves with skins
But lived in the wild woods and the mountain caves,
Stowing their dirt-rough limbs among the bushes
When driven to flee the wind's lash and the downpour.
They could not recognise the common good;
They knew no binding customs, used no laws.
Every man, wise in staying strong, surviving,
Kept for himself the spoils that fortune offered.
And in those forests Venus brought lovers together.
Mutual desire might win a woman over,
Or the man's violent strength and reckless lust,
Or a present: wild strawberries, nuts, or the choicest pears.[10]

Ignorance of metalwork, fire and how to make garments set these creatures firmly apart from the inhabitants of civilized Greece. They were so primitive that they did not even know how to protect themselves with skins. The description of their life in the 'wild woods' and the caves of the mountains is particularly evocative, reinforcing their remoteness and desolation. That they are said to have had 'dirt-rough limbs' suggests that they did not even know how to clean themselves. Awareness of morals, of a sense of right and wrong, of a notion of how to identify themselves with customs and of a means of structuring their life through laws is completely absent. Individuals thought only of themselves; they did not share or give to others. Male and female were united not by love but by lust, and if the desire to unite were not mutual, the male would use violence or a bribe to get his way.

> Trusting the marvellous strength of their arms and legs
> They harried and pursued the woodland beasts
> With stones for hurling and bludgeoning-clubs; they killed
> Many; a few they hid from in their dens.
> When the night caught them, just like bristly hogs
> They flopped their uncouth limbs to the earth, naked,
> Rolling about them a thatch of leaves and branches.
> Nor did they wail for the day or wander the fields
> To search for the sun, in fear of the shades of night,
> But silently they waited, tombed in sleep,
> Till the red torch of the sun brought in the light.
> They'd grown used to seeing, from when they were little,
> Darkness and light give birth to each other forever,
> And so they took it as a matter of course
> And didn't worry that eternal night
> Would steal the sunlight away and seize the earth.
> Poor souls, this worried them instead; wild beasts
> Would terrorise their rocky dens, they fled the charge
> Of the froth-snorting boars and the lions swift and strong;
> Trembling, they yielded in the dead of night
> Their leaf-strewn bedding to those savage guests.[11]

With their powerful bodies and using stones and clubs, the ancestors could chase and kill animals. It is not clear whether they ate the animals they caught, but since they did not know how to make fire or utensils, they would have had to rip the raw flesh with their hands. Although depicted as hunters, they were not always superior to the animals, and on many occasion they fled in fear of the larger beasts. When night fell, just like pigs they fell to rest in a nest of leaves. Familiar with the pattern of night and day, they did not fear that the night would never end. Rather, they would fear animal attacks and the loss of their makeshift bedding.

With these words a most powerful vision has been created. Although physically strong, the first humans remain pitiful creatures who possess no redeeming qualities. Lucretius continues for several pages, masterfully creating a grand narrative of the gradual advance of culture. He emphasizes the acquisition of the most basic traits of civilization, when people started to make huts, use fire and sew skins for clothing. The institution of marriage was then introduced, neighbours were joined in friendship and the first signs of speech appeared. Soon after, our ancestors learnt to cook, weave, domesticate animals, plant crops and make music. Like Hesiod, Lucretius describes the different stages of evolution in terms of metals. However, unlike Hesiod, he outlines specific cultural and technological achievements in association with their discovery. For instance, with bronze they tilled the soil, and with iron they made tools and weapons. Finally, the life of the soil-bred dwellers of the woods was quickly forgotten; Lucretius states, 'So acorns came to be hated; so the strewn beds of mounded grass and foliage were abandoned; and clothing made from pelts fell into contempt'.[12] The critical point to make about Lucretius' verbal description is that it provided such a strong visual statement on the past. The image of hairy animal-like savages who lived in forests and who then acquired skins and learnt how to make fires is vividly 'painted' for us, albeit in words.

Lucretius' progressivist or evolutionary model of human origins was, like Hesiod's account, endorsed and elaborated by other writers. In the first century BC, for example, Diodorus Siculus, in his *Bibliotheca historica*, describes our first ancestors as leading a rude and brutish life, wandering up and down in the fields, feeding upon herbs.[13] Other writers developed Lucretius' model by highlighting certain events as critical in the evolutionary process. Vitruvius, in his *De architectura* of 27 BC, emphasizes the pivotal role played by fire in human evolution. While Greek legends claimed that Prometheus introduced fire to humans, Vitruvius argued that humans had discovered it from an accidental forest fire. He informs us that it was as a result of discovering fire that people learnt to come together, to socialize and thus acquire speech. With these skills, humans then learnt how to construct dwellings and lead a domesticated family life. Like Lucretius, Vitruvius explains in detail the manner by which this process took place

> The men of old were born like the wild beasts, in woods, caves, and groves, and lived on savage fare. As time went on, the thickly crowded trees in a certain place, tossed by storms and winds, and rubbing their branches against one another, caught fire, and so the inhabitants of the place were put to flight, being terrified by the furious flame. After it subsided, they drew near, and observing that they were very comfortable standing before the warm fire, they put on logs and, while thus keeping it alive, brought up other people to it, showing them by signs how much comfort they got from it. In

that gathering of men, at a time when utterance of sound was purely individual, from daily habits they fixed upon articulate words just as these had happened to come; then, from indicating by name things in common use, the result was that in this chance way they began to talk, and thus originated conversation with one another. Therefore it was the discovery of fire that originally gave rise to the coming together of men, to the deliberative assembly, and to social intercourse. And so, as they kept coming together in greater numbers into one place, finding themselves naturally gifted beyond the other animals in not being obliged to walk with faces to the ground, but upright and gazing upon the splendour of the starry firmament, and also in being able to do with ease whatever they chose with their hands and fingers, they began in that first assembly to construct shelters. Some made them of green boughs, others dug caves on mountain sides, and some, in imitation of the nests of swallows and the way they built, made places of refuge out of mud and twigs.[14]

Vitruvius then goes on to detail how the primitive hut evolved into the first building, thus marking a major advancement in human culture. Again, the point to make here is the extent to which a pictorial statement on the past was being made. With the detailed descriptions provided by the classical writers, we can almost see our ancient forebears standing before us.

There were thus essentially two explanatory schemes for the early stages of human life. While Hesiod's legend of the Five Races suggested that human life had gradually deteriorated to a state of chaos, the progressivist views of Lucretius envisaged cultural and technological progress over time. Both schemes referred to the adoption of cultural inventions such as the plough, the ship, weapons and buildings, but one saw these inventions as representing a disjunction from the simplicity of life and for the other they signified advancement. These two different perspectives have been described as primitivism and anti-primitivism.[15] While the primitivist view was nostalgic and glorified a simple idyllic existence, the anti-primitivist view appreciated the advances technology had brought. It is the latter that is most closely aligned with the development of scientific views of prehistory. Within the context of classical thinking however, the anti-primitivist view was tied in to wider debates about the nature of progress in Greek society, where people were reflecting upon their current state of existence.

Anti-primitivist ideas were conveyed in other creation myths and in stories about particular regions of Greece. For instance, in the Pelasgian myth, the first man, Pelasgus, sprang from the soil of Arcadia and was followed by others whom he taught to make huts, feed upon acorns and sew pigskin tunics. Arcadia, a central area of the Peloponnese, was seen as a place of great antiquity, representing the type of existence people led before cities were built. Indeed, Arcadians were claimed to be the oldest inhabitants of the Peloponnese and the history of these people is the story of attaining civilization, where the hut came before the house, skins came before woven garments and acorns before the cultivation of grain. Classical descriptions of the first inhabitants of Arcadia emphasized their primitive state: Aristotle, for instance, claimed that they were barbarians and Apollonius Rhodius stated that they lived on acorns in the mountains in an age before the deluge. Finally, Pausanias tells the story of how Pelasgus made huts for the people and weaned them from eating grass and roots.[16] Thus, like Lucretius' account, stories of Arcadia parallel the theory of human development from a savage state. As Simon Schama has commented, 'in an unexpected way, then, the Greek myth of Arcadian origins anticipated the theory of evolution in its assumption of continuities between animals and men'.[17]

The classical writers addressed the topic of archaic human life by constructing an elaborate mythology that described it in a colourful and compelling way. Alain Schnapp has talked about the 'seductive capacity' of these models, which were described with great creativity and inventiveness.[18] I would argue that the seductive capacity of these models lay in their inherently visual nature, and that it was the ability of the classical writers to construct vivid mental images which led to their success. The mental images took hold in the consciousness of Greco-Roman people because they appealed to the imagination and to their basic fears and thoughts about creatures and races from distant lands. While classical ideas about the original ancestors provided a general visual image of prehistory, it is in the pictorial representation of mythological stories and figures, imagined creatures and other races that we see the roots of an iconic vocabulary for defining the past.

The iconography of Greek mythology

In Greco-Roman art there are numerous examples of how painters and sculptors sought to convey a figure's primitive, wild or non-human status by highlighting certain pictorial motifs. A brief survey of some aspects of Greek vase painting demonstrates that classical artists created pictorial formulae for portraying creatures and peoples thought to be non-Greek and thus non-civilized. In the illustration of particular myths or stories and of certain mythological figures we see a set of key icons emerging. Such icons were readily adopted for depicting figures with non-Greek attributes, playing a major role in symbolizing primitiveness and the distant past.

Of all the figures in Greek art, the hero Herakles is of the greatest importance in the creation of an iconography of human prehistory. Indeed,

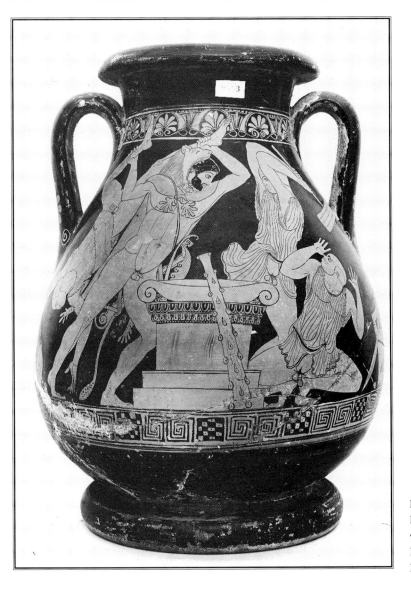

Figure 2.1. Herakles fighting Busiris' servants. Red-figure vase painting by the Pan Painter, *c.* 470 BC. Athens National Museum, No. 9683.

the iconography of this hero continues to shape the representation of prehistoric forebears today. Herakles embodies many of the qualities of primitive humans: he is naked and is frequently shown in combat with monsters and wild animals. More significantly, however, Herakles is defined by two basic icons – a club and a skin. His club is a rudimentary and primitive weapon, distinguished by its knotted and rough appearance. His skin is that of a wild lion and is roughly tied round his neck. Hundreds of images of Herakles show him with these features, reflecting how the skin and the club became imbued with symbolic meaning, serving to identify him as a primitive warrior. Figure 2.1, of Herakles fighting the Egyptian servants of the King Busiris, demonstrates the emphasis placed on these icons. Even though he is not using his club, it is included in a prominent place in the foreground of the image, as an integral part of his identity. Alongside stones or rocks, the club represents the most primitive form of defence. A remarkably unsophisticated weapon, it demonstrates a closeness to nature. It is for this reason that prehistoric ancestors have been similarly signified by the possession of such an implement. The skin, which testifies to Herakles victory over the Nemean lion, also denotes closeness to nature and an uncivilized status. This symbolic dimension was quickly appropriated as a means of communicating primitiveness. The detail of securing the skin by tying the paws around the neck was another motif to represent primitive peoples, demonstrating their inability to sew garments, which, as we saw with Lucretius, was singled out as a key step in human progress.

Other aspects of Herakles' physical appearance and his postures are also important: his nakedness, his hairy beard and his stance, with club raised ready to strike his victim. Together all these these attributes emphasize the primal quality of his existence. As well as symbolizing primitiveness, Herakles' nakedness communicates his powerful and heroic status. Holding the raised club is significant because it is an active pose, a pose quickly appropriated to portray prehistoric ancestors confronted with wild beasts. Specialists in the iconography of Herakles have emphasized the important symbolic dimension of his features. For example, Rainer Volkommer has shown how in earlier representations Herakles wore armour, but that this became simplified and standardized to the skin and the club to convey the essence of the mighty figure.[19] Furthermore, as Beth Cohen has pointed out, Herakles' club and lion's skin convey his raw physical strength: the animal skin was worn by figures associated with nature or the uncivilized wilderness in Archaic Greek Art, and the symbolic meaning of the club derives from its use against wild beasts.[20]

In addition to Herakles, there were a number of other mythological figures that represented a primitive kind of existence. Of particular importance were the giants, who were frequently depicted in Greek vase painting. Beyond its evolutionary associations, Arcadia was also known as the place where gigantomachy, or the great battle between the gods and giants, took place. Representations of this myth, which was popular at the end of the fifth century BC, provide some of the first visual ideas of prehistory. In figure 2.2, which depicts the gigantomachy, we can see the giants preparing to storm Olympos, where the gods are preparing for battle. The giants, wearing leopard skins and holding large rocks, clearly represent an uncivilized stage of development, standing in marked contrast to the gods, who have horses and elaborate armour. Paolo Arias has described this vase painting as the 'most haunting

Figure 2.2. Gigantomachy. Red-figure vase painting by the Pronomos Painter, *c.* 400 BC. Museo Archeologico Nazionale, Naples, No. 2883.

picture of the gigantomachy we possess', and I would suggest that it is the use of such simple and striking pictorial motifs that lends to the drama of the image.[21] The primitive status of the giants is signified by their simple weapons, their nakedness and their skins. Indeed, Jane Henle has described the giants as 'cavemen', because of their animal skins and rocks.[22] A significant change in the representation of the giants is noted by Thomas Carpenter, who comments that they were initially depicted as warriors with shields and helmets, but were then transformed into cavemen or wildmen.[23] This transformation reflects how the visual attributes of nakedness, rocks and skins took on a symbolic meaning. The gigantomachy myth had originally been about the dethroning of the gods, but later it came to represent the triumph of civilization over barbarism. The iconography shows how barbarism was effectively symbolized by a simple set of pictorial motifs.

Other mythological figures with a primitive or prehistoric dimension were those characterized by their closeness to nature and the animal world. Pan, Polyphemus, centaurs, Amazons, Artemis, satyrs and maenads were all identified with wild landscapes such as forests, which in themselves signified a primeval place. Such figures were symbolic creatures who represented life on the edge of humanity. While they all had distinctive historical functions and experienced changes in representation, some of these figures had a half-human, half-animal status, which was suggestive of earlier stages of human existence. Of particular significance was Pan, the pastoral god from Arcadia. With his human body and arms, a goat-like head and a tail, Pan was a shaggy creature which lived among the mountains, caves and rocks. In figure 2.3,

Figure 2.3. Persephone and Pans. Red-figure vase painting by the Pentalica Painter, *c.* 460 BC. Boston Museum of Fine Arts, No. 01.8032.

which shows two Pans with Persephone, his distinguishing features are nakedness, an animal-like head and lustful behaviour. All of these conveyed his alliance with the animal world, yet his comfortable presence in the human world. As Philippe Borgeaud has argued, Pan embodied the metamorphic borderline between humans and animals.[24] Beyond his physical attributes, Pan was identified by his homeland and the landscape that he inhabited. Arcadia was perceived as ancient and his habitat as wild country far from the city. Both reinforced his primal and somewhat uncivilized status.

Polyphemus, the one-eyed Cyclops described in Homer's *Odyssey* who is known for trapping Odysseus in his cave, can also be seen to represent a primitive stage of evolution. Identified by his long wild hair, nakedness and savage behaviour, Polyphemus was a giant who lived on a distant island and inhabited a cave. Figure 2.4, which depicts the blinding of Polyphemus by Odysseus, shows how the primitiveness of this creature is visually conveyed. His hair and his beard, which are long, together with his nakedness and size set him apart from the other figures who have short hair and are clothed in tunics. Again the homeland and habitat of this figure contribute to his status on the boundaries of humanity.

Centaurs, the half-human half-horse creatures often featured fighting their enemies the Lapiths, also represented the wild and bestial aspects of human nature. Depicted in art brandishing boughs, hunting, or being violent, lustful and drunk, the centaurs led a primitive kind of existence. Like giants, they were often featured wearing skins and using rocks as weapons. In figure 2.5 two centaurs are fighting the Lapith Kaineaus. The centaur on the left is wearing a skin, while the one on the right is naked; the left-hand figure uses a rock and the naked one a stick as a weapon. Their primitive dress and weapons function to separate them from the sophisticated equipment and armoury of the Lapith. Again like Pan and Polyphemus, centaurs lived alongside nature rather than in cities. Coming from Thessaly on the outskirts of Greece, they were perceived as characters from a remote, pre-human past. As Page du Bois has commented, centaurs demonstrate the Greek ambivalence about nature and the prehistory of humanity.[25]

Figure 2.4. The blinding of Polyphemus. Black-figure vase painting, *c.* 520 BC. Museo Nazionale di Villa Giulia, Rome.

Figure 2.5. Centaurs fighting the Lapith Kaineus. Red-figure vase painting by Polygnotos, *c.* 440 BC. Musées Royaux d'Art et d'Histoire, Brussels, No. A134.

Figure 2.6. Amazonomachy. Red-figure vase painting by the Eretria Painter, *c.* 420 BC. Metropolitan Museum of Art, New York, No. 31.11.13.

Also on the outskirts of Greek society were the Amazons, the race of women warriors who came to help the Trojans fight the Greeks and who became known as 'avatars of the outdoors'.[26] In terms of their iconography it is significant that they were often featured wearing Persian trousers, reflecting how the Athenian defeat of the Amazons was used as a parable for the war between the Greeks and Persians. However, this also shows how pictorial attributes were used to signify their 'otherness' and difference from civilized Greeks. In figure 2.6, which shows the Amazonomachy, the Amazons are shown fighting the Greeks with stones, axes and spears. Their decorated trousers and tunics, which are imitations of Persian garments, have the appearance of animal skins. As with many of the other figures associated with a primitive status, the Amazons came from outside Greece. Their homelands were described as being on the edge of the world, which signified that they were from a distant, less-evolved culture and that they came from a zone representing the frontier between civilization and savagery. William Tyrell has commented on the Amazonian habitat as a bestial realm inhabited by wild creatures, stating that 'less a place than an idea, it expresses spatially the breakdown of difference, of the categories used to define culture and to distinguish it from bestiality below and divinity

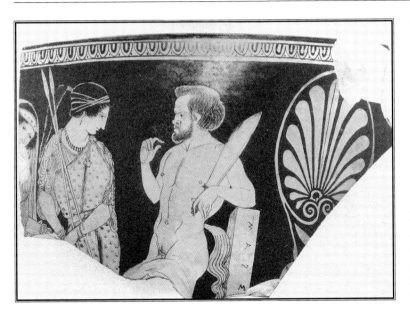

Figure 2.7. Artemis with Marsyas and Hera. Red-figure vase painting from Lucania, *c.* 400 BC. Metropolitan Museum of Art, New York, No. 12.235.4.

above'.[27] Thus, the Amazons, like the giants, gradually acquired pictorial attributes that communicated the essence of their status in Greek society.

Artemis, the twin sister of Apollo, is another important character among the mythological figures that conveyed primitiveness and antiquity. Defined by Homer as the 'Mistress of Beasts and all Wild Things', Artemis was a hunter who was defined by her animal skin. Represented in figure 2.7 with Marsyas and Hera, Artemis is wearing a leopard-skin garment tied at the shoulder. Maenads, the followers of Dionysus, were similarly depicted wearing animal skins, signifying both their closeness to nature and their prowess as hunters of wild beasts. Finally, satyrs, the attendants of Dionysus, also show how the concept of barbarism became equated with prehistoric life. Satyrs were often depicted as naked, barely covered by animal skins, and like Pan were associated with wilderness and nature. As inhabitants of the countryside, they were symbolic of life in pre-urban Greece. However, as Andrew Stewart notes, the satyr's domain was 'more a bizarre distortion of city life than a simple inversion of it'.[28] In figure 2.8 a satyr at the return of Hephaistis to Olympos is wearing a simple skin draped over his shoulder. This in itself is enough to signify his position outside Greek society.

The iconography of many mythological figures, among them those discussed above, played an important role in Greek thought, in the dialogue about what it meant to be Greek. Barbarians and animal-like creatures were excluded from the definition of Greek identity, and often primitive humans were connected with them. For instance, in *Aeneid* Virgil refers to the environment of the primitive forebears as the homeland of wood divinities, and Ovid, in *Fasti*, states that the ancient Arcadians worshipped Pan. In tracing an emergent iconography of prehistory it is important to note the changing representation of mythological figures in Greek art, where defining characteristics were not instituted immediately but were developed as the identity of the figures became symbolically significant.[29] Associated with this was the creation of a set of pictorial motifs that came to symbolize primitiveness, notably nakedness, animal-skin garments, rough weapons such as clubs and stones and animal characteristics.

Figure 2.8. Satyrs in the return of Hephaistos to Olympos. Red-figure vase painting by the Kleophon Painter, *c.* 430 BC. Hirmer Verlag, Munich, No. 2361.

Greek geography and the perception of other races

Classical ideas about peoples living in other lands provide us with another source of evidence as to how a sense of the primitive was visually constructed. In his study of ancient geography, James Romm has shown how the Greeks correlated historic time with geographic space, locating the earliest stage of evolution beyond the edges of the earth and postulating progressively more primitive social development outside their Mediterranean hearth.[30] Thus, the further away, the more primitive and prehistoric people became. India and Ethiopia in particular were perceived as places where time stood still and where strange races of great antiquity had survived untouched by civilization. The first major Western source of ideas on other races was Herodotus, who, in the fifth century BC, described over fifty different human cultures in his *Histories*. Many of the distant races described by Herodotus were understood in terms of primitivist thought, being seen as noble savages who led a paradisiacal life. Other races were seen as monstrous, taking on a semi-human and grotesque form. While both had physical attributes relevant to the perception of prehistory, it was the monstrous races who provided the richest source of inspiration on the topic.[31] From the first century AD the existence of strange races living in remote parts of the world became a topic of great interest to encyclopediasts and synthesizers. With these writers, however, the emphasis was on the bizarre and strange customs of foreigners. Pliny the Elder, for instance, assembled the observations of writers such as Herodotus, Megasthenes and Ctesias on the monstrous races in his *Historiae Naturalis* of 77 AD.[32] In a chapter on 'Remarkable racial bodily configurations' Pliny describes creatures who had eyes in the centre of their foreheads, backward-turning feet, dog-heads, hairy bodies, dog's teeth, snakes for ears, lion's heads and oxen feet. Some of the figures from Greek mythology were adapted and included in this array of monstrous races, such as the giants, pygmies, centaurs and satyrs. While no classical pictures of the monstrous races survive, the verbal descriptions provided such inspiring material for visual representation that they became a popular visual theme in the illuminated manuscripts of the medieval period (see chapter 3).

Artists of antiquity also presented notions of a less evolved and more primitive existence in their depictions of other cultures. In his study of Greek images of non-Greeks Brian Sparkes has shown how images of the Egyptians, Scythians, Ethiopians, Thracians and Persians all served to emphasize the cultural achievements of Greece by portraying other races as barbarians.[33] These peoples were portrayed not only with different clothing and accessories, which were in themselves seen as primitive and uncivilized, but with facial and bodily differences. While nudity tended to be a major distinguishing feature separating Greeks from barbarians, trousers instead of togas and beards instead of clean-shaven faces were also important pictorial devices. The visual treatment of the Persians, as uncivilized people with beards and in strange garments, was particularly significant. In figure 2.9, which shows a Persian warrior with raised hands, we see how dress is used to distinguish foreigners from Greeks. Not only is he wearing trousers as opposed to the Greek toga, but the spots on his garment resemble those seen on animal skins. The depiction of Egyptians in the painting of Herakles fighting Busiris' servants (figure 2.1) provides another example of how cultural difference was visually presented. Physical traits are used to distinguish foreigners, in this case the negroid features, baldness and circumcision of the Egyptians.[34] Ethiopians are depicted with exaggerated facial characteristics and distinctive afro-style hair, as in figure 2.10 showing Memnon and his

Figure 2.9. Persian warrior. Red-figure vase painting, *c.* 460 BC. Museum for Kunst und Gewerbe, Hamburg, No. 1981.173.

Figure 2.10. Memnon and squire Amasis. Black-figure vase painting by Exekias, *c.* 540 BC. British Museum, London, No. B209.

squire Amasis.[35] Furthermore, the two Ethiopians both hold clubs and one a basic shield. Their simple weaponry stands in contrast to the large shield of Memnon and his elaborate helmet and spear.

The various elements of classical iconography discussed here were all produced in their own specific historical and political contexts, but in general they all related to Greek and Roman ideas about city versus rural life, and civilization versus barbarism. Such images were part of the much wider Greek construction of 'barbarians' who were defined simply by their lack of Greek characteristics.[36] The Greek notion of barbarity as a universally anti-Greek attribute arose in the fifth century, and the art of the time reflects this perception of other cultures. It was also a strategy by which increasingly urbanized peoples coped with the peoples who maintained a traditional rural existence. Images of other cultures and non-urban peoples in art thus endorsed the city dwellers' claims to superiority over the pastoral life and illiterate peoples. While they did not have an explicitly historical dimension, the images show how the people living on the fringes of civilized life were perceived as following an ancient and outmoded type of lifestyle.

As early as the classical period the roots of a visual tradition for depicting prehistory were established. In seeking to convey cultural and geographic distance and difference the Greeks and Romans used a set of pictorial attributes that effectively separated 'outsiders' from them. These pictorial attributes designated mythological figures with a wild status, such as Herakles, Polyphemus, Artemis and maenads, and mythological figures with an animal status, such as Pan and satyrs. They were also used to denote enemies such as the Giants, the Amazons and the Persians, and foreigners such as the Egyptians and the Ethiopians. All were figures of opposition and as such were defined by attributes conveying their lesser cultural status. In this sense icons functioned to demonstrate inferiority, and a simple set of icons quickly became symbolic of wildness and primitiveness. In terms of the iconography of prehistory, the significant feature of these icons was the way in which they conveyed temporal as well as spatial difference.

CHAPTER 3

Religious and Secular Visions of Human Creation

Human evolution was not a topic of interest to early Christian thinkers, who rejected pagan mythology and the idea of human progress from a savage state. The rare examples of interest in humanity's original condition are outlined by George Boas in his survey of early Christian and medieval thinking on primitivistic and anti-primitivistic thought.[1] He discerns a tension between the idea of regression and that of progress; the major difference in early Christian and medieval thinking was that progress was not associated with cultural development but rather with religious and moral improvement. The development of the arts, which had been a major theme of anti-primitivist thought, was not emphasized in Christian thought. New visions, or ancestral images, came with the illustration of biblical history, the major new framework for understanding human creation. It was around the fourth century that Christian iconography began to replace the images of the Greco-Roman pagan gods, with humanity's beginnings now being portrayed in pictures of Adam and Eve. Biblical history provided a model for images of prehistory in the sense that it encompassed the major framework for understanding the evolution of the earth and the appearance of humans. However, the Bible was also a major source of influence in that it followed a narrative framework. As Stephen Jay Gould has remarked, biblical illustration forms the basis for prehistoric art as chronological pageantry.[2]

It was the biblical story of Genesis, or more particularly, the story of the creation and the fall of Adam and Eve, that inspired artists and book illustrators to produce numerous images of early human life. Pictures typically focused on Adam and Eve beside the tree of knowledge in the

Garden of Eden, their expulsion from their paradisiacal homeland and their labours in the wilderness. In many ways the life of Adam and Eve in the Garden of Eden resembled the descriptions of the life of the Golden race in the Five Ages of Hesiod. Like the people of the Golden race, Adam and Eve did not need clothes, shelter or weapons because there were no threats to their life. While the Creation and the Golden Age were both very popular as visual themes, the biblical story was more prolifically illustrated throughout the early Christian and medieval period. Similarities between the classical and biblical schemes can also be seen in the story of the expulsion from Eden, which led to a degradation in the life of the first couple, and the model of Hesiod, which embodied the concept of regression from an early idyllic state. Like the classical myths about early forebears who sprang from the earth, the biblical story of human creation had great visual potential. Greek mythology differed from the Bible in its filling the past with strange animal-like creatures and monstrous races, whereas Adam and Eve and the first animals were all perfectly formed.

The fact that the Bible inspired endless visual representation reflected the belief that the illustration of biblical stories aided the spread of Christianity. As André Grabar notes, there was a didactic purpose to this imagery, in that it revealed God's forgiving nature and his kindness to those who had faith in him.[3] The proliferation of biblical imagery also indicates how powerful the Bible was as a statement on human history. An integral part of its success in making and communicating this statement was the way in which artists highlighted key iconographic themes. These themes provided people with a way of making sense of their past and their own place in the world. Some of the iconographic features of religious art were later associated with the secular imagery that contributed to the perception of distant times. For instance, medieval imagery of the monstrous races in the East and the iconography of the wildman were particularly important in creating a stereotype of a wild and bestial ancestor. Early Renaissance painters and book illustrators also contributed with their visual translation of Lucretius' evolutionary views. By the 1500s a clear and defined set of icons was being employed to communicate a sense of humanity's remotest existence. While it built on classical iconography, this set of icons was expanded and clarified by early Christian, medieval and Renaissance artists.

Biblical imagery and the iconography of Genesis

Surveys of biblical illustration have outlined the basic iconography of human creation as stated in Genesis, where Adam and Eve are typically featured next to the tree of life in the Garden of Eden.[4] In general, such scenes evoked a sense of the primitive past, with naked figures living close to nature without technology or the arts. However, the nakedness of Adam and Eve signified their lack of vice rather than primitiveness, and the Garden of Eden was cultivated. So it was not until their expulsion from Eden that we see Adam and Eve depicted in a truly primitive state. For it was after they had sinned that they learnt to cover themselves and that they were banished to a hard world. The imagery of the expulsion was important in symbolizing the human struggle to gain salvation. It is here that we see artists creating visual icons to emphasize the predicament of humanity.

The earliest images of Adam and Eve appear on the paintings in the Rome catacombs and provide an image which was to shape profoundly all subsequent visions of human antiquity. In the Catacomb of the Via Latina, dated to the middle of the fourth century, there are paintings of the expulsion of Adam and Eve from the Garden of Eden, which is a new scene in funerary art. Antonio Ferrua notes that they are already in 'tunicis pelliceis' or coats of skin.[5] This pictorial detail is symbolically important because it signifies their rejection by God. In figure 3.1, another painting of Adam and Eve below the expulsion scene, we can more see clearly their dress and situation in the landscape. Here Adam and Eve are grieving, or in a melancholy pose. The landscape behind them is a country one with grasses and shrubs and they are sitting on a rocky knoll. Thus they are in a pastoral landscape outside the Garden of Eden. The skin garments and the landscape, which are so critical in signifying their status in the eyes of God, also convey primitiveness. Ferrua refers to the introduction of visual topics such as the expulsion, stating that because these scenes had not yet become a fixed canon in the minds of the artists they were treated with a certain freedom.[6] In the Bible we are told that Adam and Eve make their own garments from fig leaves, and therefore the decision to represent Adam and Eve in animal-skin garments was an innovative step, making use of an icon that had already carried some meaning in classical times. From this point on the attribute of the animal skin was used to symbolize the passage of Adam and Eve from Eden to expulsion and, above all, their regression to a primitive state. There are many examples of this icon in medieval art.[7]

The scenes of Adam and Eve labouring after their expulsion are also important. It is here that Adam is represented as a digger toiling on the land and Eve as a nurturer raising infants. That Adam is featured working the soil signifies that the land beyond Eden was not cultivated. It also signifies Adam and Eve's regression to an early state, where they have to fend for themselves in wild and desolate surroundings. The iconography of Adam using a spade to dig the earth is important because it shows how an implement is used to define him and his plight. We have seen how implements had similarly been used in classical iconography, where stones and clubs, for instance, symbolized the status

Figure 3.1. Adam and Eve grieving. Early Christian painting from catacomb of the Via Latina, Rome, mid-fourth century. Cubiculum B, left-hand arcosolium.

Figure 3.2. Adam and Eve.
Woodcut from *Nuremburg
Chronicle* 1483, pl. IX.

of the figure being represented. The primitive existence of Adam and
Eve in the labouring imagery is reinforced by the fact that Adam often
wears a fur garment. In his analysis of medieval depictions of Adam as a
labourer, Michael Camille has commented on the icons of the spade and
the animal skin. Referring to the stained glass panel in Canterbury
Cathedral, which is dated to *c.* 1180, Camille describes Adam as wearing
a '"primitive" animal skin'.[8] Thus, while the focus of the image is on the
figure digging into the earth, the icon of the skin reinforces the
meaning of this activity. Many other representations of Adam and Eve
labouring utilize this motif to the same effect. In figure 3.2, for
example, we can see Adam dressed in a shaggy fur garment as he digs
the earth. Eve, with a cloth draped over her, suckles her infant.
Underneath her cloth, however, Eve also appears to be wearing a fur
garment. The symbolism of the fur garment provides the rationale for

the whole scene. The skins represent what it is that Adam and Eve seek to redeem themselves from – an animal-like state in which there is no place for the respect of God. The primitive and rocky landscape in which the couple are situated emphasizes their remoteness from civilization and the life of the city. The other point to note in the labouring imagery is the standardization of gender roles. The representation of the division of labour in this way was to become a dominant theme in the imagery of human ancestry.

Beyond Adam and Eve other biblical figures were important in the iconography of prehistory. Notable were the traditional Old Testament prophets, such as St John the Baptist and Elijah, who were frequently shown wearing coats made from skins or coarse camel's hair.[9] The point to make about this pictorial attribute was that it did not signify that these figures were in a primitive state; rather it revealed their connection with the wilderness. In this context it is important to note that in Christian thought the wilderness had a symbolic meaning beyond being a primitive place. Most significantly, it was a place where prophets hid from the danger of cities; the city as well as being a place of culture was also a place of war, and thus dangerous. The issue of city versus wilderness is important in Christian thinking. While the wilderness was a place of primitiveness, it was also a place where miracles occurred and where healing by saints and monks took place.[10] Another biblical figure who conveyed a sense of the distant past was Esau, the brother of Jacob. Esau is described as being hairy all over and is frequently depicted as a wildman.[11] The description of his physical appearance as hairy relates to his status as a hunter who lived in the wild. It also relates to his being the forefather of the Edomite nation, who may have been perceived by the Israelites as hunters.

In conclusion, the iconography of Adam and Eve before and after their expulsion from Eden is important in the iconography of prehistory. When they are in Eden they are naked; when they have sinned they are covered with garments. In art these first garments were made from either fig leaves or skins, both being extremely primitive and indicating their closeness to the wilderness and their isolation in the world. Above all, the garments symbolize their degradation from a superior state, emphasizing that they now need to be protected from the elements and that they have to fend for themselves. The landscape element is also important in that the representation of deserts, wilderness and forest settings evoked a primeval atmosphere. In representations of Genesis in Christian iconography visual icons signifying primitiveness were maintained from classical times and appropriated for the biblical context. Once incorporated into biblical scenes the familiar icons of skins, rough implements, shaggy hair and desolate environments began to take on their own specific meanings, but in essence they communicated the same general message.

Medieval visions of the monstrous races of the East

Early Christian and medieval thinkers did not have as much interest in other races as did the Greeks and Romans. Generally, the other races thought to live in distant lands were described as naked, with no agriculture, no iron, no fire, no clothing and no arts. However, from the third century AD there were a few writers, such as Solinus, who continued the tradition of recording ethnological diversity initiated by Herodotus. While some races were thought of as non-Christian savages, other races such as the Brahmin of India were seen as Noble Savages. Thus the two traditions of primitivist and anti-primitivist thought continued side by side as they had in the classical period. However, there was a difference between classical and Christian primitivism: in the former savages had nothing, and in the latter they possessed luxuries. This is evidenced in the stories of the Earthly Paradises, where a great wealth in jewels was described. In this context the noble savages were admired not so much for their morals but because of their natural marvels. The subject of the marvels of the East attracted visual treatment in the medieval period and, like Greek depictions of other races, made an important contribution to the iconography of prehistory.

Inspired by the vivid descriptions of the monstrous races of the East by the Greco-Roman authorities, medieval scribes produced illustrations of strange creatures with half-human and half-animal features. These appeared in a number of medieval manuscripts but are best known from the earliest text on the subject, *The Marvels of the East*, which was produced around the eleventh century.[12] Thought to derive from a European archetype, this picture-book was based on travellers' accounts of the classical period and Pliny's synthesis.[13] It is an important example of quality illustrations in a secular manuscript, containing more secular pictures than any other manuscript of the period.[14] Rudolf Wittkower believes that the images themselves derived from a large stock of classical models.[15] Characterized by its striking illuminations of the monstrous creatures thought to be living in places such as India and Ethiopia, the *Marvels* constitutes a primary source for the iconographic representation of prehistory.

Among the many images of monstrous races in the *Marvels* are a number of creatures which are defined by prehistoric motifs, for example the 'cynocephali' or dog-headed creature, the men with hair to the ground, the cannibalistic giants, the 'homodubi' or half-man half-donkey, the 'donestre' or lion-headed creatures, bearded women and women with hair to their heels and boar's teeth. In figure 3.3, which presents the race of long-haired men, is a naked figure with hair to the ground eating a fish. Clearly his hairiness and nakedness define his primitive status. The fact that he eats a raw fish also suggests that he is ignorant of the

Figure 3.3. Long-haired man. Manuscript illumination from *Marvels of the East*, eleventh century, Cotton Ms. Tiberius B.V. British Library, London, fol. 80a.

knowledge of cooking and is thus little different from the animals who hunt. A depiction of the race of huge men with legs that were 12 ft long and bodies that were 7 ft wide (figure 3.4) shows a giant devouring a man. He is characterized by his hairy spine and arms, his nakedness and his dark skin, all which emphasize his status as a primitive and animal-like creature. Timothy Husband has commented on the hairy spine of this figure, stating that at this stage body hair was not a predominant feature and that it was not until the twelfth century that hairiness became a pictorial convention associated with savage behaviour.[16] While this may be true, long hair and rough beards had been used to signify a wild, unkempt and primitive status from classical times. The giant's dark skin is another important feature that would later become a critical way of signifying a prehistoric status for newly discovered ancestors. In figure 3.5, which features the *homodubi*, we can see how the club is used to signify a primeval status. While the half-human half-animal status of this race was its distinguishing trait, the illustrator has added the icon of the club to reinforce its primitive nature. In figure 3.6, which presents the race of bearded women, we see a figure wearing a skin loincloth made from a horse hide. This race of hunters was thought to use tigers and leopards as hounds. The long hair, beard and the skin garment of this figure are all critical in defining its status. Finally, all of the above examples inhabit a stark landscape which is mountainous and rocky. This feature serves to emphasize their remoteness or existence on the outskirts of civilized life. And while all the figures are presented as races who existed in the far distant reaches of the world, they are also implicitly presented as existing in far distant time.

Figure 3.4. Cannibalistic giant. Manuscript illumination from *Marvels of the East*, eleventh century, Cotton Ms. Tiberius B.V. British Library, London, fol. 81b.

Another important feature of the *Marvels* illustrations is the way in which they are rendered. Each figure and its surrounding landscape is presented almost schematically, with a simple dark outline and little detail. The sheer simplicity and lack of pictorial depth emphasize the iconic dimension of the images. Mary Campbell comments on the iconographic quality of the illustrations, noting how they lack the 'gratuitous detail of more mimetic art and as a result convey little information, and much meaning'.[17] The point is that the figures did not need to be detailed because their meaning was clear and could be understood by the audience. These strange races had a symbolic meaning in Christian thought in the sense that they embodied all the characteristics of non-Christians. Christian thought emphasized the purity of the species, and these illustrations clearly represented 'deformed' aberrant beings. Thus, the intention of the images was not so much to provide a detailed description of coexisting races but to communicate the plight of non-Christians.

Many images of monstrous races subsequently appeared in the encyclopaedic descriptions of the world, which were popular from the

Figure 3.5. The Homodubi. Manuscript illumination from *Marvels of the East*, eleventh century, Cotton Ms. Tiberius B.V. British Library, London, fol. 82b.

twelfth to the middle of the fifteenth century. In these illustrations we see a tendency toward more detailed representation of the races. While this reflects changing trends in art it may also reflect the influence of a scientific approach, where a concern to depict phenomena accurately was emerging. A good example is the picture of Ethiopian races in *Le livre des merveilles de ce monde* (The book of marvels of the world) from around 1460 (plate 1). Here, many different races are depicted together in a landscape which is characterized by caves, rocks, mountain peaks and cliffs. Among the array of creatures are two men wearing shaggy garments and standing in front of a cave eating lizards, four strange dragon-like creatures, the Blemmyae or race with their heads in their chest, robed men interacting with a dog-like creature, a large bird with horns, naked men, a king-like figure, a hairy naked figure with large ears, a naked hairy giant and two female figures, one with hair reaching the ground and the other with horns. Behind them in the distance is the city Heliopolis of Egypt, a clear contrast to the rocky and mountainous terrain they inhabit. Amid all the characters in this picture, one seems to stand out. The hairy figure in the centre with a club over his shoulder represents the emergence of a new character on the scene. He is the caveman or wildman, a major addition to the cast of monstrous races, who was known as the *troglodyte*. This new type of race is distinguished by its hairiness and the possession of a club. While it may represent the classical attempts to define the anthropoid apes, it can also be seen as representing a medieval contribution, whereby certain features from other races were appropriated and used to create a more generic monstrous race.

Figure 3.6. Bearded Woman. Manuscript illumination from *Marvels of the East*, eleventh century, Cotton Ms. Tiberius B.V. British Library, London, fol. 85a.

A number of scholars have documented the representation of monstrous races in medieval imagery, notably Rudolf Wittkower and John Friedman.[18] Both have examined the changing attitude towards the races and the significance that they had in defining the nature of humanity in Western Christian thinking. What their research has shown is that the monstrous races were essentially characterized by their difference or their opposition to humans. These non-Christian and primitive creatures lived outside the city, in caves, woods, or in the mountains, and they possessed a basic set of primitive physical traits. What defined them was their uncivilized status, and while they were thought to exist in the present, in many ways they were also seen to represent the past. Sharing many of the attributes of classical mythological figures, the monstrous races constituted an important source from which images of human origins were constructed.

The imagery of monstrous races remained remarkably consistent throughout the medieval period. While increasing travel to the East did diminish the belief in their actual existence, the images themselves were never wholly discarded. Many areas of the East became known as a result of the Crusades and pilgrimages to the Holy Land, but travel literature of the fourteenth and fifteenth centuries, such as the Marco Polo manuscripts and *Mandevilles Travels*, retained the iconic pictures of monstrous races.[19] Furthermore, the pictorial tradition of monstrous races retained its grip on European imagination even when travels in the New World cast serious doubt on the existence of such creatures. It seems that the iconography of human-like figures with an array of anatomical aberrations fitted comfortably with the early depiction of cannibalistic and savage North Americans. As Friedman has argued, the 'myths of the monstrous races, though geographically obsolete, were too vital to discard. They provided a ready and familiar way of looking at the native people of the New World'.[20] The power of these images to survive must be seen in the context of Christian thought, where they functioned as useful vehicles for defining non-believers. However, they also persisted simply because they were so visually compelling and ingrained in peoples' consciousness. Indeed, what had made the monstrous races so believable was the fact that they were brought to life in illustrations. Their existence was reinforced by the fact that the original illustrations were copied and reproduced in numerous different contexts, becoming more authoritative every time.[21] Thus the new scientific knowledge resulting from geographic and navigational studies did not kill off the monstrous races, but rather kept them alive. As Mary Campbell has commented, 'when new knowledge did arrive it was easily enough corrupted into older images'.[22]

An important development that had an impact on the perception of the monstrous races was the emergence of the sciences of anatomy and zoology in the 1500s. These disciplines placed a premium on the accurate description of the human form and animal species based on first-hand observation of phenomena. They thus challenged the authority of the classical texts and raised many questions about the descriptions of monstrous races. However, despite this concern for careful recording and observation of humans and animals, the imagery of monstrous races was still endorsed by scientists of the time. As Wittkower has shown, the races continued to live on until the 1700s, often in pseudo-scientific dress, as scientists attempted to harmonize textual traditions with factual observation.[23] This is most clearly indicated by the fact that the imagery of the monstrous races became aligned with the emerging iconography of the apes. An key example of this alliance was Conrad Gesner's *Historiae animalium*, which combined illustrations based on observation with images of imaginary creatures. The monstrous races were thus not completely and neatly replaced, but rather evolved into something different. Gradually, however, the monstrous races were replaced in illustrations by the exotic peoples of the New World, a new source of icons for defining prehistoric existence. More significantly, perhaps, they became fused into one general stereotype of the hairy naked wildman of the woods.

The wildman of the woods

The medieval iconography of the wildman constituted a profoundly important visual source on primitive life. The wildman was first depicted in art in the mid-thirteenth century and became very popular in the second half of the fourteenth century. Although an imaginary creation, it was the closest that medieval scholars came to understanding humanity's primeval beginnings. Thought to have come from the mountains of central Europe, the wildman was a naked hairy figure with both human and animal traits, who lived in the forest, without knowledge of metals or agriculture, eating berries, acorns and the raw flesh of animals. Clearly, the wildman had taken on many features of the monstrous races and the primitive forebears outlined by the classical authors. This can be seen in the classic portrait of a wildman (figure 3.7) which highlights the distinguishing characteristics of hairiness, nakedness, a club and a hollowed-out tree trunk for a home.[24] The actual notion of a wildman can be traced to the Babylonian epic of Gilgamesh, where the character Enkidu was featured as a hairy creature who lived outside the city. More generally, however, we can see in the wildman the influence of classical and early Christian iconography; for example he is suggestive of Herakles in that he is typically depicted with a club. The significance of this figure for understanding human prehistory has already been raised by Richard Bernheimer who claims that in many ways the life of this creature 'resembled that which we now attribute to the raw beginnings of human cultural existence in the Stone Age'.[25]

While ideas about the wildman clearly derived from classical sources, this figure was not perceived in medieval thought as the primal ancestor described by Lucretius. It thus lacked a scholarly basis, being confined to the realm of folklore, legends, epics and romances. Essentially, the wildman had an unclear status in medieval thought – there was confusion over his position in God's creation. Since medieval thought emphasized the purity of all the species, the wildman could not be conceived of as a half-evolved human, or as a stage in the progression of humans to civilization. Despite this, its visual attributes carried a powerful symbolic meaning relevant to the perception of prehistory. The emphasis on its hairy state, for example, signified a primitive animal-like status. As Husband states, with the wildman 'hairiness became a universal cipher for violence, primitiveness, and remoteness'.[26] Nakedness was also critical in communicating barbarity and, as Friedman comments, was a 'sign of wildness and bestiality – of the animal nature thought to characterise those who lived beyond the limits of the Christian world'.[27] The club also signifies primitiveness and indicates that 'men who carry clubs are ignorant of chivalric weapons and the military customs of civilised westerners'.[28] Finally, the cave

Figure 3.7. Wildman of the woods. Drawing accompanying the 'Ballade d'un homme sauvage', *c.* 1500. Ms. fr. 2366. Bibliothèque Nationale, Paris, fol. 3v.

home symbolized the wildman's existence outside humanity, showing how this creature was too primeval to live in cities.

Medieval thinkers did not give the wildman an explicitly historical dimension, but they did perceive it as representing a condition of humanity. That this condition could be perceived as the first prehistoric stage of human life is suggested by some visual images of the wildman produced in the late fifteenth century. In a painting attributed to the French artist Jean Bourdichon, *L'homme sauvage ou L'Etat de nature* (The wildman or the natural state), the wildman is placed in the context of society (figure 3.8). He is presented outside his cave home, with a wildwoman and infant seated at its entrance. The picture clearly draws on religious iconography, with the wildman standing in a pose much like that of St John the Baptist, and the female appearing much like Eve in the Genesis imagery. Equipped with his club the wildman confronts the viewer with a direct gaze. This painting gains much of its significance from being the first in a set of four images, each of which portrays one of the four states or conditions of society: the wild, the poor, the working and the noble. Grete Ring has labelled the painting of the wild condition 'The Primitive man (the troglodyte)', which suggests that it represented not simply a condition of society but also an earlier stage of evolution.[29] Clearly, primitivistic thinking has informed this painting, in that the wild couple look content with their life. A ballad accompanying the painting reveals the role of the wildman in nostalgic thinking of the time:

I live according to what Nature has taught me –
Free from worry, always joyously.
For mighty castles, grand palaces I do not care.
In a hollow tree I make my home.
I do not delight in fancy food
Or in strong drink.
I live upon fresh fruit alone,
And so I have, thank God, enough.

I drink clear water, fresh and pure,
Just when I'm thirsty, never otherwise.
I amuse myself by day and when night falls
I quite wisely eat my evening meal.
So I have no cause to fear
That anyone would do me harm, since I have wronged
Not a single creature under heaven.
And because of that, I have, thank God, enough.

I have no need for fancy clothes.
My hairy coat protects me well enough
So that I fear neither heat nor cold.
I don't want to sleep in a soft bed,
Because I learned all during childhood
To lie down simply in a patch of grass.
And so I have, thank God, enough.

When the weather turns to rain
And the wind blows hard
I tell myself it can't go on
Too long like this,

Figure 3.8. *L' Homme sauvage ou L' Etat de nature*. One of four loose-leaf illuminations attributed to Jean Bourdichon, *c.* 1500, Miniature no. 90. École Nationale Supérieure des Beaux-Arts, Paris.

And thus I rise above it.
I comfort myself and live in hope
That soon the sun will shine again,
And because of that, I have, thank God, enough.

Prince, what good is it to live so proudly
And to plunder just to lead a pompous life,
When at the moment of one's death
A shroud alone will be enough.

Thus the wildman rejects the grand life, testifying to the value of a simple existence where a diet of fruit, a hairy coat and a bed of leaves are enough. The painting by Bourdichon can therefore be seen as a statement of social disillusionment, where the wild condition fares better in comparison to the noble one.[30] While the states of society are not presented as chronological in the series of paintings, the picture of the wild couple implies a historical dimension. The iconography of the wildman thus played an important role in debates about the early state of humanity, addressing the question of whether it was 'golden' or barbaric. Essentially, this kind of wildman iconography represents a continuation of primitivist thought transformed in the Christian context.

With travel in the New World in the 1500s and the discovery of new races the depiction of the wildman, like that of the monstrous races, decreased. However, it still survived in many parts of Europe, particularly in Germany, where an iconography of early folk life saw the wildman stereotype adapted to portray an ancient German existence. Again, the imagery showed a remarkable facility to be harmonized with new ideas and discoveries.

Book illustration and the engravings for Vitruvius

In the 1500s engraved illustrations started to become a key feature of printed texts, which had been produced from the late 1400s. The most lavishly illustrated books were Bibles and classical texts. David Berkowitz argues that the woodcut attained its 'highest level of artistic achievement in the book art of the mid-16th century', when 'artists and woodcutters rapidly evolved a new vocabulary of expression'.[31] The beginnings of this development can be seen in the illustrations for the *Nuremburg Chronicle* of 1483, which included numerous biblical and historical images.

With the Renaissance came a revival of interest in the works of the classical scholars and many of the key texts from antiquity were printed in the major centres of Europe. Initially the humanist scholars did not approve of illustrations, and most of the classical texts, when first

printed, were devoid of any woodcuts.[32] However, this soon changed and
a number of classical texts became well known for their illustrative
themes. Two such texts were Ovid's *Metamorphoses* and Vitruvius' *De
architectura*. To some extent the immense popularity of these texts
reflected a revival of interest in classical myths about life in earliest
times, a theme which is discussed in detail in Arthur Ferguson's study of
Renaissance thought on the topic of prehistory.[33] While Ovid's
Metamorphoses became a favoured text for illustration in the sixteenth and
seventeenth centuries, when artists and engravers produced many prints
of the four ages (gold, silver, bronze and iron), of greater importance for
the emergence of a scientific view of prehistory was the publication of
illustrated versions of Vitruvius' book on architecture.[34] Vitruvius'
manuscript was the only surviving work on architecture from antiquity,
and while it had been copied in the middle ages, it was not until the
fifteenth century that it became a major source for the Renaissance
rebirth.[35] The first edition of 1486 was printed without woodcuts, but
in 1511 an illustrated version was printed with engravings. In this
edition a woodcut depicting the invention of fire was included among

Figure 3.9. The discovery of
fire. Engraving for *M. Vitruvius
per iocundum solito castigatior
factus . . .*, 1511. Venetiis,
fol. 13r.

Figure 3.10. The discovery of fire. Engraving by Cesare Caesariano for *Di Lucio Vitruvio Pollione de architectura libri dece . . .*, 1521, Como, fol. 31r.

the illustrations (figure 3.9). This image established a basic iconographic theme which was reproduced in many subsequent editions of the text and which has become a core motif in the iconography of modern prehistory. In it a group of people clothed in skins have gathered around a fire in a forest clearing. This basic composition was elaborated in 1521, with the production of an edition of the text by the Italian architect Cesare Caesariano. Caesariano was a member of the artistic circle dominated by Leonardo da Vinci and Bramante, and his edition is characterized by its high-quality woodcuts.[36] Two illustrations of prehistoric life are presented in association with Vitruvius' chapter on the evolution of the primitive hut. The first represents the coming together of people after they have discovered fire (figure 3.10). The group of naked people gathered around the large flames are engaged in conversation and other social activities, such as breaking up wood, eating and tending to the fire. In the background a group of people and

EX PRIMA MVNDI HOMINVM AETATE AEDIFICATIO · MVLTI ENIM AB
ANIMALIBVS EXEMPLA VITAE CONSERVAME Q̃ IMITATI SVNT & C̃

Figure 3.11. Building the first huts. Engraving by Cesare Caesariano for *Di Lucio Vitruvio Pollione de architectura libri dece . . .*, 1521, Como, fol. 32v.

some animals are fleeing the forest fire. These people have not yet learnt to tame fire; thus they stand in contrast to the group assembled near the fire who are acquiring the basic knowledge needed to develop civilized society. In the second woodcut people are engaged in the process of building their homes (figure 3.11). On the left is a completed square structure as described in detail in Vitruvius' text. Behind it is a similar structure which is occupied by a family. To the right is a more primitive type of hut, which became common in biblical imagery later in the century.[37] In the foreground the most humble of all structures is being built, a hollowed-out cave. On the one hand this image may represent a general communal scene where people have learnt to cooperate and work together, yet on the other it may represent different modes or stages of human existence. Whatever the intention, the general message is one of primitiveness – the garments are rudimentary, the landscape is wild, and sticks and rocks serve as the only tools.

These two images, of the forest fire and the building of the first hut, stand out among the rest of the illustrations in Caesariano's book, which are detailed geometric and architectural drawings. The fact that the topic of humanity's primitive existence was chosen for visual depiction attests to its potential for graphic reproduction and, following the publication of Caesariano's images, many other versions of the scenes were created. In 1522, for example, a simple woodcut featuring figures around a fire appears in another Italian edition of *De architectura* (figure 3.12). With this image we can see how the visual theme of fire as a civilizing force has become simplified into an iconic statement. In subsequent editions of Vitruvius' book some new elements are introduced but the essence of the picture is retained. In the French edition of 1547, for instance, the forest fire scene makes even more clear the separation between those who control fire and those who do not, by depicting the former wearing skin garments, while the latter are completely naked (figure 3.13). Furthermore, some of the fire-

Figure 3.12. The discovery of fire. *M.V. de architectura libri decem . . .*, 1522, Florentiae, fol. 26v.

Figure 3.13. The discovery of fire. Engraving by Jean Goujon for *Architecture, ou Art de bien bastir . . .*, 1547, Paris, fol. 15r.

Figure 3.14. Building the first huts. Engraving by Jean Goujon for *Architecture, ou Art de bien bastir . . .*, 1547, Paris, fol. 15v.

controlling humans are wearing animal-head helmets reminiscent of Herakles. These symbolized the status of some ancestors as primitive warriors and, like the primitive tents, became a popular motif in other iconographic traditions.[38] In the illustration of the building of the primitive hut, men are breaking up rocks in order to make bricks rather than hollowing out a cave (figure 3.14). There are also notable changes in the German edition of Vitruvius of 1548. In the fire scene, for instance, a man from the woods is lighting a stick from the fire, and the families in the foreground are eating fruit (figure 3.15). In the image of the primitive hut, the figures carving out a cave are naked and there is a different, more complex type of hut in the background (figure 3.16).

The Vitruvian imagery had an important impact on the iconography of prehistory, not only in the sense that it was the earliest imagery devoted to the subject of prehistory, but also because it provided such a contrast to the previous paradisaical imagery of the past. It signified a scientific edge in the imagery of the past, contributing to the slow replacement of the medieval images of the grotesque and wondrous.[39] Although these illustrations present concepts outlined by the classical

Künstliche verzeichnung wie man sich vermůt/die aller ersten Menschē ge=
lebt/vnd durch erfindung des fewrs in gemeinschafft vnd freundtliche beywo
nung komen/vnd die sprach der redt sich vnter jnen erhaben hat.

Figure 3.15. The discovery of
fire. Engraving for Vitruvius
Vitruvius Teutsch . . ., 1548,
Nürnberg, fol. LXIr.

authors, they incorporate the style and artistic conventions of the Renaissance and some Renaissance artists went further in developing the primitivist and anti-primitivist vision of the ancient writers.

The visual arts and the classical revival

The publication of classical texts in the late medieval and early Renaissance periods provided much inspirational material for artists. A number of artists were inspired by the different ages of humanity as defined through the metals and, although the majority of painters chose the primitivist vision of human origins as an artistic theme, the anti-primitivist vision was dramatically brought to life by the Italian artist, Piero di Cosimo. The distinguishing feature of the visual arts and their treatment of the theme of human origins is the rich symbolism of expression. Indeed, as we have learnt from Ernst Gombrich, Renaissance art was characterized by its symbolic dimension, where artists made use of symbols that conveyed readily understood meanings.[40]

Figure 3.16. Building the first huts. Engraving for Vitruvius *Vitruvius Teutsch . . .*, 1548, Nürnberg, fol. LXIIv.

The primitivist vision of human origins was portrayed by the German-born painter, Lucas Cranach, who depicted progressive deterioration in accordance with Hesiod's scheme. Painting around the beginning of the sixteenth century, Cranach included pictures of prehistoric life in his scenes from mythology and history. He chose the Golden Age as a recurrent theme in his work, being the first among northern European painters to portray the subject. His paintings of this early idyllic stage of human life feature our ancestors singing and dancing among the animals (figure 3.17). While the figures are naked, their physical appearance does not appear primitive. While they do not live in the city, the landscape, with its pretty flowers and plants, does not resemble the wilderness. There is also a cave within their enclosure, but rather than signifying their dependence on such structures for shelter, it adds a romantic feeling to the scene. We can see parallels with the imagery of Genesis, which was characterized by its paradisiacal gardens, plants and animals. This image is also biblical in the sense that the people of the Golden Age are enclosed in a walled garden reminiscent of the Garden of Eden. The general mood of the painting hardly evokes savagery; rather it is sensuous and erotic. Cranach also depicted human decline in his paintings of the Age of Silver. In one such painting the decay in human cooperation is represented by a violent scene of human aggression (plate 2). Here we see naked men hitting each other with large sticks, with an injured or dead figure on the right. On the left a man with blood dripping down his shoulder struggles to defend himself against his attacker. Seemingly oblivious to the violence, the women watch over the scene with their infants, with the exception of the female figure on the right, who also holds a stick. The physical appearance of the men is primitive, their faces

Figure 3.17. *The Golden Age.* Painting by Lucas Cranach, *c.* 1530. Nasjonalgalleriet, Oslo.

contorted and savage. The landscape is notably different from the Golden Age garden with its grass and flowers. Instead these ancestors inhabit a dark and woody landscape with stony outcrops and an inhospitable rocky overhang. As Max Friedländer and Jacob Rosenberg state, 'having reached the Age of Maturity, men begin to quarrel through foolishness and lead but a short life.'[41]

The Florentine artist Piero di Cosimo depicted the beginnings of human life in a series of five paintings produced between 1490 and 1505. While these paintings highlight several themes in human prehistory, a central motif appears to be the forest fire. The first three pictures portray the phase before humans knew how to use fire, and the last two depict life after the arts and crafts had been introduced. The series thus shows our evolution from savagery to civilization. Erwin Panofsky suggests that the paintings were part of a cycle representing the two earliest phases of human history as described by classical authors.[42] However, a more recent interpretation by Sharon Fermor argues that they were the result of three separate commissions.[43]

The first painting, simply entitled *The Hunt*, depicts the first humans, who lived like animals and did not know how to use fire, make clothes or grow crops (plate 3). It is a wild scene full of violence and frenzy, showing a race who lived a savage and selfish life, where conflicts with others was common. Bestial humans and centaurs fight animals with clubs and their bare hands. One figure in the foreground wears a garment but the rest are naked, their groins covered with leaves or furs. The leafy coverings recall biblical iconography, where Adam and Eve are shown wearing these first garments which they made to cover themselves because of their shame.[44] All the animals and figures are in active poses, with the exception of the human corpse in the foreground on the right. The artist's motivation in depicting this corpse can be interpreted in two ways. First, Piero appears to have been influenced by contemporary developments in early Renaissance painting where artists sought to demonstrate their skills in representing linear perspective and foreshortening. He may well have been influenced by Paulo Uccello's *The Battle of San Romano* of 1450, which depicts a dead warrior lying on the ground in a similar manner.[45] This was the first time that a figure had been painted in such a way and other artists must have been inspired to attempt this visual trick. The famous *Christo Scorto* by Mantegna, which shows the dead Christ in a similar foreshortening, may also have influenced Piero.[46] In a later painting by Piero, entitled *The Building of a Double Palace*, there are two similar naked corpses, revealing how he tried to perfect the technique.[47] Another motivation for depicting the dead corpse could have been that Piero was influenced by contemporary anatomical illustrations; images of dead bodies on the dissection table were increasingly being incorporated in scientific treatises on human anatomy. Or perhaps Piero was simply trying to communicate that the humans in this painting were no different from the animals which they fought.

More generally, *The Hunt* shows similarities to Antonio Pollaiuolo's *Battle of Nude Men* of 1475, which has naked men fighting each other with swords and axes.[48] Other features of the painting that demonstrate the influence of earlier visual works include the image of animals fleeing from the woods, driven out by the fire. This can also be seen in illustrations of Vitruvius discussed above. Perhaps the fire has symbolic significance in the sense that the existence of this vital tool, which is critical for human progress, appears to be ignored by the ancestors. Finally, the painting corresponds in general to Lucretius' description of the first phase of evolution, in which humans were considered to be nothing but brutes who lived alongside the animals.

In the next painting, entitled *Return from the Hunt*, people are shown unloading animal corpses from boats (figure 3.18). There is a noticeable advance towards civilization in that humans have learnt to cooperate and

Figure 3.18. *Return from the hunt*. Painting by Piero di Cosimo, *c.* 1490–1505. Metropolitan Museum of Art, New York.

get along with their own kind. Men and women embrace each other and work together, rather than living as selfish individuals. The fact that they have learnt the art of boat-building emphasizes their progress. In the background is a forest fire, which has forced animals to flee. In a very general sense the picture can be seen as corresponding with Lucretius' second phase of evolution, where humans learnt to build huts, make fires, cook, weave, grow crops, domesticate animals and live as couples. However, the picture does not show all these achievements, such as woven cloth, domesticated animals, buildings or families. The main changes that it does highlight are social interaction and technological advance.[49]

Another painting by Piero, interpreted as the third in Panofsky's cycle, can be seen as representing a further advance in human culture (plate 4). Entitled *The Forest Fire*, this picture features a landscape with humans and animals. On the right a man wearing a coat of cured leather is shepherding cows. In the background there is a house and a group of figures possibly engaged in some kind of agricultural activity. In the centre of the image is a blazing fire in the forest, which has driven out its animal inhabitants. Some of the animals fleeing the fire have human-like faces and are reminiscent of the monstrous creatures in the *Marvels of the East*. The emphasis on the animals in this picture reveals Piero's interest in unusual animals, which was inspired by the appearance of exotic animals in Europe in the fifteenth and sixteenth centuries.[50] This painting can also be seen as following Lucretius' second stage of human evolution, when our ancestors have learnt to construct huts, weave clothes and till the land.

Two more paintings by Piero are thought to address the subject of human evolution. Both feature the Greek god Vulcan, representing the

Figure 3.19. *The finding of Vulcan on Lemnos*. Painting by Piero di Cosimo, *c*. 1490–1505. Wadsworth Atheneum, Hartford.

mythological story that this god of fire was the first teacher of human civilization. The first, *The Finding of Vulcan on Lemnos*, presents the story of how Vulcan fell to earth after his parents had thrown him off Mount Olympos because he was deformed (figure 3.19). Here he is seen arriving on the Island of Lemnos, greeted by a group of nymphs. He is naked and twisted by deformity and the landscape suggests that he has arrived in an uninhabited wilderness. Virgil had suggested that Vulcan was raised by apes, but in this painting Piero has replaced the apes with nymphs, possibly because they are more artistically pleasing. In the second painting, *Vulcan and Aeolus*, we see Vulcan with Aeolus, the god of winds, who is busy instructing humans how to use fire (plate 5). On the left Vulcan is hammering out a horseshoe and Aeolus is using the bellows. Once again the focus appears to be on the fire, which draws the attention of the man on the horse overlooking the two gods. Aeolus is looking up at the man on the horse, perhaps explaining the new technology to him. In the background four figures are shown constructing a house, which comes directly from the illustrations of Vitruvius. The builders of this hut are naked, with the exception of loincloths. While one uses a metal tool, another uses a club. To the right is a family group, who are awakening, while in the centre foreground a naked man sleeps. This has been interpreted by Philip Ritterbush as representing the dawn of civilization; the sleeping man is viewed as the sleep of reason from which civilization is awakening.[51] Various exotic animals, including a giraffe and a camel, provide interesting subjects for the artist.[52] Finally, the landscape is rocky and mountainous, suggesting that this is a primitive place far from any city.

Although in a general sense these five paintings can be seen to be related, they do not appear to belong to a united set. While the first two (*Hunt* and *Return from the Hunt*) and the last two (*Vulcan on Lemnos* and *Vulcan and Aeolus*) can be seen as pairs, the third (*Forest Fire*) appears to be independent. All seem to contain elements of Lucretius, but other classical ideas are also included. The hunt scenes appear to be a vivid illustration of Lucretius, whereas the later paintings are concerned with the life of Vulcan rather than the evolution of humanity, even though some details of the paintings refer to this latter subject. A number of inconsistencies reveal that Piero did not strictly adhere to Lucretius. For instance, Lucretius argued that humans discovered technology themselves; he did not see it as happening as a result of the intervention of the gods. Furthermore, for Lucretius, technological progress was not entirely dependent on fire as is suggested in the Vulcan paintings. Fermor questions the emphasis on fire as the main theme, suggesting that Piero 'appears to be interested in a range of different facets of early life, rather than emphasising one'.[53] Essentially the forest fire appears to be a pictorial motif taken from the Vitruvius illustrations. Perhaps Piero's choice of certain elements was the result of a specific request. The fact that his view of primitive life is not consistent argues against the paintings being a unified set. In the two hunting paintings life is brutish, whereas in the Vulcan set life is innocent and simple.

Whether or not these five paintings by Piero constitute a coherent series, each brings the subject of prehistory alive. This is partially because the classical views on the subject of our origins have been translated into vivid paintings, but also results from the artist's powerful and evocative rendering of the subject. Indeed, Piero di Cosimo is described by Panofsky as having an 'extraordinary preoccupation' with primordial existence and as treating primitive life as a reality.[54] What distinguishes his work is his concern for detail, which has led scholars to emphasize the scientific quality of the paintings.[55] Furthermore, as Ritterbush has commented, 'it is remarkable that so complex a theme as the evolution of the human mind and the gradual acquisition of the arts of civilization could be dealt with in 15th century art. This accomplishment must be credited to the symbolic faculty rather than to any scientific observation of primitive man by travellers'.[56]

The treatment of human origins as a subject in the visual arts appears to have been influenced by the woodcut illustrations in the printed editions of the classical texts and the Bible. However, Renaissance artists made their own unique contribution to the emerging iconography of prehistory by adding a dramatic artistic dimension to it. Thus, by the 1500s there were already a wide range of different visual areas that contributed to the developing iconography of prehistory. It is possible to see how biblical imagery, secular illustration, engravings for classical texts and early Renaissance painting successfully conveyed the notion of historical distance by using a set of pictorial icons. These icons were used because they were quickly understood and it appears that the construction of a notion of the primitive or the prehistoric was essentially visual.

CHAPTER 4

Historical Visions of National Origins

With the Renaissance came several important developments in the reconstruction of an ancient human past. It is here that we see the first signs of a scientific approach towards understanding the life of our early ancestors. This approach was 'scientific' in the sense that reconstructions started to incorporate findings based on the recovery of artefacts from sites, or from the study of material culture in museums and collections. It essentially developed in association with the establishment of an antiquarian tradition of scholarship in Europe, which was characterized by an interest in national origins and the prehistoric past of the great European nations. As part of this interest some authors constructed visual images of the first Britons, Germans, Scandinavians and Gauls, for instance. Such images drew on classical sources, ethnological data, artefact collections and studies of ancient sites and monuments. However, illustrations of the ancient European races from the sixteenth to the eighteenth centuries were more a result of the publication of classical sources and travel accounts in the Renaissance, than of antiquarian studies of field monuments and artefact collections. This chapter looks at some of the first images of ancestors that were produced in relation to the antiquarian tradition. In particular, it explores the construction of the stereotype of the ancient warrior of antiquity, which was a central image in the iconography of early prehistory because it was intimately connected to the anti-primitivist vision.

Although antiquarian scholars were not preoccupied with the idea of a truly deep prehistoric past, their interest in tracing their national roots back to earlier times was important in stimulating research on human origins. They did not seek to represent the first humans, yet nevertheless the antiquarians and historians who illustrated their books with pictures of national ancestors played a critical role in developing the visual attributes of a more remote past. Initially a feature of costume books, illustrated travel accounts and geographic studies, these historical reconstructions gradually began to appear in national histories in the seventeenth century. The new images of ancestors were distinct from the classical and medieval images in the sense that they combined many different lines of evidence in order to construct a more accurate picture of the past.

The development of an antiquarian iconography of the past has been documented by the historian of antiquarianism, Stuart Piggott, and more recently by the art historian, Sam Smiles, both of whom have explored the construction of an archaic British past through the visual arts.[1] While Piggott laid the foundations for this subject, Smiles has achieved much in the way of establishing the features of an iconography of the past, or more specifically how the 'essence' of a nation was skilfully expressed in visual terms. Historians of the imagery produced in association with sixteenth- and seventeenth-century travel accounts, notably Paul Hulton, have also discussed the historical reconstructions of Europeans.[2] Together these scholars have shown how such images combined classical observations, ethnography and research on costume, armour, prehistoric sites and monuments into powerful visual statements. Furthermore, they have asserted that the practice of producing illustrations of early historical figures must be considered in the context of changing approaches toward the study of the past.

The late Renaissance and antiquarian images of ancient ancestors reflect how scholars were starting to use alternative sources, and especially visual rather than textual evidence, in their reconstruction of the past. This was part of a more general movement in scholarly studies, where observation and an inductive approach toward the analysis of phenomena were being promoted. It was more specifically related to the birth of classical archaeology, in which material culture was being used to understand the Greco-Roman Empire. As with the classical scholars, the new community of antiquarians no longer strictly relied on ancient texts, but rather began to use material objects and illustrations as sources. First, coins, medallions, sculptures, maps and curiosities were enlisted, and then ancient artefacts were used as evidence.[3] The story of how visual materials were used in the understanding of history is told by Francis Haskell in *History and its Images*, which traces the practice of using authentic objects to explain national history.[4] In addition to using visual materials to reconstruct particular events, some historians and antiquarians used them to create general reconstructions of the dress and social lives of past peoples. Such images were typically presented in discussions on the customs and manners of the ancient Europeans. The individuals who created these scenarios were aware of their speculative nature, but nevertheless saw them as satisfying an important need in their study of the past. Indeed, the significance they placed on these reconstructions was often revealed by their description of them as accurate portrayals, thereby reflecting a wider concern with authenticity in illustrations of history. As Elizabeth Eisenstein reports in her history of printing culture, the literati of the 1500s had a 'pedantic insistence on "correct" presentation of costumes and setting', which was a reaction to the mistakes and inappropriate uses of early woodcuts.[5]

While a number of artistic and illustrative traditions contributed to the emergence of an antiquarian iconography, it is the imagery produced in association with travel to the New World that provided the major source of inspiration. For scholars seeking to establish a history independent of Greece and Rome, the newly available pictures of the peoples of the Americas and later the peoples of the Pacific constituted a vast quarry of information with enormous didactic potential. The illustrators who were employed to produce a visual record of the people, plants and animals encountered in the new lands generated a whole new body of 'scientific' data, which could be useful in other contexts.[6] For example, the ethnological imagery was used as a comparative source for examining parallels in native American Indian life and the European past. Some innovative antiquarians even enlisted the ethnological images as evidence for inferring earlier stages of human existence. Thus, the striking image of the naked savage decorated in body paint or covered in tattoos was appropriated as a template for reconstructing ancient Europeans, especially the Britons, Germans and Gauls. The importance of antiquarian images in this context was that they marked the beginning of a more widespread acceptance of the anti-primitivist or evolutionary view of human origins. The comparison of the newly discovered Indians to ancient Europeans endorsed the progressivist model of Lucretius, where humans were thought to have moved slowly towards civilization rather than degenerating from a Golden Age.

Costume books, festivals and the Picts of Lucas De Heere

In the sixteenth century depictions of ancient European peoples were produced as part of a wider interest in the dress or costume of different nations. Important early examples of such images were produced by the Dutch painter Lucas De Heere, who created two watercolour drawings of ancient Britons. These pictures were produced when De Heere went to England as a Protestant refugee in the 1500s, staying in London from 1567 to 1577.[7] During this time he was appointed by the High Admiral of London, Edward Lord Clinton, to paint a gallery of figures representing the costumes of all nations.[8] This large volume has over 180 watercolour drawings of figures, some of which are copied from

Figure 4.1. 'Les premiers
Anglois comme ils alloyent en
guerre du temps de Julius
Cesar.' Watercolour drawing
by Lucas de Heere, 1577, from
his *Theatre de tous les peuples et
Nations de la terre* . . ., pl. 1.
Ms. 2466, fol. 60r.

older sources, and others which are taken from life. Of the eighteen
illustrations of British costume the first presents two ancient Britons
(figure 4.1). Entitled 'Les premiers Anglois comme ils alloyent en guerre
du temps de Julius Cesar' (The first English as they go to war in the
time of Julius Caesar), this picture consists of two warriors holdings
shields and swords. They are characterized by their nakedness and their
painted body decoration. While the figure on the left has lions' faces
painted on his knees and shoulders and a serpent painted on his thigh,

the figure on the right is covered by long crossing lines, a crescent on one nipple and a sun on the other. Their hair is long and has a wild unkempt appearance, as do their moustaches, which go past their chins. It is most likely that De Heere got the idea of nakedness and painted bodies from descriptions of the Picts in the classical sources. Whether he had seen and been influenced by the naked Native American Indians who were decorated in body paint is difficult to tell. However, field sketches of New World Indians may have been circulating in London at the time. Also, we know that De Heere himself had been involved in the illustration of the ethnographic peoples of the New World, as he had seen an Eskimo brought back to England by Frobisher in 1577 and then produced a watercolour drawing of him.

One of the major sources of inspiration for the portrait of the ancient Britons was the increasing illustration of different nations in early costume books. Of particular importance were the representations of the 'wild' Scottish and Irish, which were seen to portray a less civilized way of life. Of equal importance were the Renaissance festivals, pageants, tournaments and spectacles, in which the representations of different nations and historic figures provided a great source of visual entertainment. Roy Strong has documented the major events of the fifteenth and sixteenth centuries, where people dressed in the costumes of different nations, and where ancient Irish and Scottish were included as a source of comparison with contemporary Europeans.[9] An important example was the Bayonne *magnificences* of 1565 where the knights of antiquity and the modern nations went on show. Here groups were dressed as wild Scotsmen, Turks, nymphs and demons 'demonstrating the monarchs power over savages and the realm of mythology'.[10] The final spectacle in this event was the tourney between the knights of Great Britain and Ireland, which is represented in one of the Valois Tapestries hanging in the Uffizi.[11] It is important to note that in costume books and festival presentations accuracy in the representation of different nations and historic figures was not a major concern. Rather, it was the pictorial and decorative aspects of national and ancient dress that were of interest as a visual kind of entertainment. For instance, it was common to present historic figures in their ancient military dress, with the emphasis being on ornate and almost theatrical outfits. Such pictures were rarely sourced in a reliable way and, as Frances Yates has commented, the illustrations in the costume books 'tend to repeat the same types again and again rather than to make original observations'.[12]

In examining early representations of the Irish, Hiram Morgan highlights the way in which a decorative image of this nation was created and how artists used earlier images and ideas rather than working from real life.[13] He goes on to argue that the resulting series of images, 'which accreted characteristics over time', must be seen in the context of the

Renaissance world when nations were subject to generalization, misrepresentation and caricature.[14] The situation for ancient figures was exactly the same, revealing how strongly the heritage of ancestral images lies in the imaginative realm. What is also significant is that the imagery of the Scots and the Irish, which in turn went on to influence antiquarian imagery, was essentially negative.[15] When compared to the pictures of other nations, the incivility and primitiveness of these nations were highlighted. Clearly then, De Heere was influenced by an area in which a great deal of imagination was used and in which negative stereotypes were presented. Thus the supposedly military attire of the ancient Britons derives more from colourful costumes than real military dress and must be seen in the context of the flourishing tradition of picture books which drew heavily on earlier images.

The other drawing of ancient Britons produced by De Heere was done between 1573 and 1575 and appeared in a manuscript on the geography and customs of England, Scotland and Ireland, which was a gazetteer of the British Isles for refugees fleeing from war in the Low Countries.[16] The reconstruction of the ancient figures is very similar, with two naked men covered in body paint. The major differences are in the designs on the figure on the right and the fact that this figure also has a sword. A significant feature of this picture was the context in which it was placed, as De Heere included it in a series of drawings, one of which was of the monument Stonehenge. By placing the image of ancient ancestors in association with an image of a prehistoric site, De Heere was making a connection between the ancient Britons and the ruins in the landscape. However, as we shall see, it was a long time before reconstructions of historic figures were taken out of the realm of costume studies and placed in a fuller archaeological context.

The ethnologically inspired visions of Jacques Le Moyne de Morgues and John White

A major set of images of historical ancestors was produced in association with the voyages of exploration in the sixteenth century. Two expeditions to the New World have particular importance for antiquarian images, as it was as a result of these that the artists Jacques Le Moyne de Morgues and John White produced pictures of ancient Picts and Britons. In addition to illustrating the lives of the indigenous Americans, these artists also produced a number of costume drawings of different historical and national types which were probably influenced by De Heere. Indeed, there is a general similarity between De Heere's pictures and those of the New World Indians attributed to Le Moyne and White. What distinguished their work, however, was the extent to which their reconstructions were informed by the imagery of native American peoples.[17] While De Heere's earlier images of ancient Britons are important, it is Le Moyne and White who are known for establishing the genre of historical reconstruction, as it was they who produced the first major series of drawings of ancestors in which a concern for accuracy was demonstrated. Indeed, Michael Alexander describes Le Moyne as the 'first efficient artist', and Paul Hulton describes White's paintings as the first illustrations 'to which the word scientific can justly be applied'.[18] Despite the scientific status accorded to these ethnographically inspired images, they were a strange blend of art and science, combining anthropological and archaeological elements with artistic conventions. Furthermore, there is some confusion about the different roles White and Le Moyne played in establishing the genre of historical reconstruction. For instance, it is widely believed that both artists were aware of each other's work and that White's interest in depicting older nations was stimulated by Le Moyne. What is more difficult to ascertain, however, is whether White's images actually derive from a set of originals produced by Le Moyne, now lost.[19]

Jacques Le Moyne de Morgues was a Huguenot artist who accompanied the French expedition of Laudonnière to Florida in 1564. He was forced to flee back to England after the French settlement was destroyed, where he worked up his field sketches into watercolours. Although only one of his original pictures of the Indians of Florida survives, we know his work through the engravings of Theodore de Bry (see below). More recently another Le Moyne original has been discovered, an image now called 'A Young daughter of the Picts', which is thought to have been painted around 1585–8 (plate 6). This portrait of a young woman covered from head to toe in detailed representations of flowers constitutes one of the most remarkable images of an ancestor from this period, or indeed any period. The figure is distinguished by its highly elaborate body decoration, which in general can be seen as deriving from ethnological imagery where many figures have painted designs on their torsos and limbs. However, the details of this decoration are very European, the flowers being based on species known only to the western world. In addition to her body paint, the 'Young daughter of the Picts' wears a torque around her neck and waist, with a chain that connects her sword to the waist. She also holds a long spear with a metal tip. Her anatomy and posture are inspired by classical art and her hair is typical of Renaissance painting. Seeing naked women with body paint in Florida may have inspired Le Moyne to project such a vision back into the European past. However, there is a strange paradox in that Le Moyne has included in the background a village with houses, these being very different from the primitive huts of the New World Indians. Another interesting detail is the pair of figures toward the left of the picture, who, with their raised arms and swords, appear to be fighting each other. Whether Le Moyne was making a statement about the nature of ancient life with this detail is difficult to know, but what is clear is that he created a striking vision of British ancestry. Also influential in this representation were the costumes used in festival presentations. More specifically, there is a striking resemblance between the elaborate dress of the Irish footmen featured in a representation of the procession in Stuttgart in 1617 and the floral design on the Pictish woman's body. Although the Stuttgart event took place after this picture was painted, there is a possibility that there were other festivals where Irish figures wore similar dress. As Morgan notes, the rich fabrics of the Irish footmen were never used in Ireland and must be seen as visual entertainment.[20] The origin of such details is difficult to ascertain, but what seems clear is that they were artistically rather than historically inspired. Finally, until Le Moyne's image of the Pictish woman appeared it had always been assumed that White produced the set of original images that were subsequently used by antiquarians to reconstruct ancient Britons. However, it now appears that Le Moyne established this tradition, and that White's contribution was to develop it further by drawing more closely on ethnological imagery.

John White accompanied Sir Walter Raleigh on his trip to Virginia in 1585 and produced a pictorial record of the life of the Algonquian Indians and of some of the local fauna and flora.[21] In addition to his images of the people on the east coast of North America, White produced twelve drawings of people of other nations, including three ancient Picts, two ancient Britons, two Eskimos and five 'oriental' figures which were Turkish and possibly Greek. His pictures of the Eskimo (Inuit) man, woman and child, all of whom were brought to England by Martin Frobisher in 1577, were done before his ethnological drawings and demonstrate that he had an interest in illustrating different national types before he went on Raleigh's expedition.[22] It is likely that he was influenced by De Heere's portraits of the Eskimos, as they are quite similar in style. The Turkish and Greek figures probably derived from a costume book, suggesting that White may simply have been copying from originals that inspired him.[23] Similarly, the Picts and Britons may have been copied from Le Moyne. The significance of his drawings however, is that White seemed to be putting them in a different context, rather than presenting them as isolated examples. For instance, White's drawings of the ancient Picts and Britons are presented as comparative types to the other images in the collection and, as such, have been described by Hulton as 'essays in comparative anatomy'.[24]

The first drawing in John White's series of ancestors, now entitled 'Pictish Man holding human head', features a proud warrior covered in body paint, displaying the decapitated head of one of his victims (plate 7).

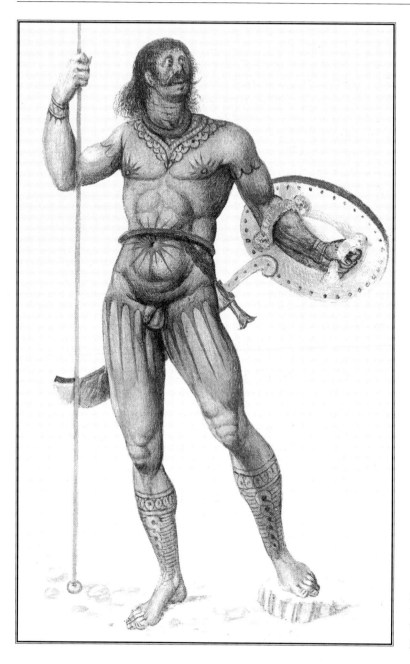

Figure 4.2. Pictish Man.
Watercolour drawing by John
White, *c.* 1585. British
Museum, London.

Several sources of influence have contributed to this scene. The reference
to head-hunting, the shield and the metal torques around his waist and
neck all come from classical accounts, especially those of Herodian and
Dio Cassius. Details of the body decoration reflect traditions in
Renaissance painting, but the idea that ancient Picts and Britons
painted their bodies was discussed by many classical writers. The

designs on the body are almost theatrical, including an owl's face on the chest, lions' heads on the stomach and legs and serpent-like creatures on the arms. Below the knees are scales suggestive of armour, and the sword is often used in fifteenth- and sixteenth-century paintings to suggest oriental and barbaric associations. The animal faces and scales are very similar to designs on ancient military costumes as represented in Renaissance art. For example, they closely resemble the costumes of the Irish knights at the Bayonne festival of 1565 as illustrated in one of the Valois tapestries.[25] Again, this reveals how some details derive from festival costumes rather than from historical ideas about military dress. The spear, with the ball on the end, represents the bronze globular spear-butts from Scotland, which were subsequently shown with all ancient Britons.[26] The posture of this figure is Mannerist, and his long hair and moustache derive from European images of the 'wild Irish'. In addition to these influences, some aspects of the body decoration resemble details of ethnological imagery. For instance, the decorations on the top of the warrior's legs look similar to those frequently depicted on the legs of the Indians.[27] For Hulton and Beers Quinn the most surprising aspect of the painting is the portrayal of this British ancestor as a naked and painted barbarian, this being 'a comparatively new idea which primarily derived from the pictures of tattooed Indians of the New World'.[28] Thus, while most of the details of the picture come from classical and contemporary artistic sources, the general image of a naked warrior can be seen as coming from ethnological illustrations.

Many elements of the first portrait are repeated in the second image in the series, now titled 'Pictish man' (figure 4.2). The major difference here is that the body decoration has been toned down and the decapitated head replaced with a spear. Other details reflect the influence of classical descriptions, such as the sword chain mentioned by Diodorus Siculus and the spear with the bronze apple on the end, as described by Dio Cassius. Again, the ornamentation is influenced by Renaissance design, but it draws much more closely on the decorations of Algonquian Indians. In particular, the decoration on the calves is reminiscent of that featured in John White's portrait of an Algonquian man, now titled 'Indian in body paint'.[29] The design on the top of the thigh of the ancient Pict duplicates the design on the lower leg of the Indian, and the decoration around the neck is also very similar. While the Indian portrait reveals an emphasis on circular designs, the Pictish images replace these with star motifs. To complete his set of images of the Picts, White produced a picture of a 'Pictish Woman' (plate 8). In addition to her detailed body decoration, she is distinguished by her long flowing golden hair, which was common in Renaissance painting and biblical imagery. On her stomach and breasts a star motif is featured, while on her shoulder and knees there appear to be monstrous beasts of some kind. Again, the design on her legs and the bands on her arms appear to be taken from White's images of Indian women.

White's historical reconstructions were closely connected to his ethnological drawings, reflecting a mixture of realistic ethnographic detail and more speculative historical creation. They are thought to have been copied from an old English chronicle, which Stuart Piggott believes was Scottish, not English.[30] These historical images are not credited with having the same authority as the ethnological ones; White certainly did not work under the same constraints when painting historical figures as he did when painting ethnological portraits. As Paul Hulton and David Beers Quinn state, White 'no doubt gave his imagination considerable freedom, uninhibited by duties to record'.[31] Despite this, White showed a concern for detail in his historical reconstructions, seeking to incorporate information from as many sources as possible. For instance, despite the stylistic aspects of the pictures, Hulton asserts that 'there are genuine archaeological elements'.[32] The point is that even though these elements come from different historical periods, the images of the Picts provided antiquarians with a specific notion of what their ancestors looked like in pre-Roman times.[33] This notion drew heavily on the Renaissance ideal of the 'warrior hero of antiquity'.[34]

Travel accounts and the engravings of Theodore de Bry

The work of Le Moyne and White became widely known when the publisher and engraver Theodore de Bry published their drawings in the first two volumes of his great series of travel accounts, *America*, which was published between 1590 and 1634.[35] The inspiration for this series was the illustrations produced in association with the French and British settlements in North America. On hearing of the existence of Le Moyne's pictures De Bry travelled from his home in Frankfurt to London in order to obtain and then publish them, but he was refused permission. Not long after, he returned to London to purchase White's drawings via Richard Hakluyt, who had been part of the Raleigh expedition. By this time Le Moyne had died and de Bry was finally successful in obtaining his drawings also. Although the French expedition, upon which Le Moyne's drawing were based, came before the English one, de Bry featured the latter as the first book in his series. According to Michael Alexander this was the stipulation of Richard Hakluyt, who had political motivations for wanting the Raleigh settlement to be published first.[36] The third major source for de Bry's series was the set of twenty-eight woodcuts of Brazilian Indians, which related the story of Hans Staden, a prisoner of the Tupinamba Indians. Of all the published accounts of European expeditions to the New

World, it was de Bry's illustrated series that was best known for its accuracy. De Bry did not select particular images or adapt field sketches, but faithfully copied all the originals as exactly as possible. As Alexander notes, 'though a *mannerist* in the heyday of mannerism . . . de Bry did not let his decorative urge overwhelm his historical integrity'.[37] However, by changing the medium from watercolour to print there is a change in emphasis caused by the heavier line and black and white contrasts involved in printmaking.[38] This change in emphasis gave the figure an iconic status as a portrait of the past.

De Bry is well known for his publication projects in the seventeenth century, his workshop being characterized by an interest in narrative techniques and serial illustration.[39] In the series of travel accounts comprising *America* the image had primary status, above that of the text. Indeed, the engravings were the central means for telling the story of how the New World Indians lived, and how they fought with the colonists. In the first book of the series, which presents an account of the Florida expedition, a complete set of engravings based on White's originals is followed by a new section which includes engravings of White's drawings of the Ancient Picts and Britons. Titled 'Som picture of the Pictes which in the olde tyme dyd habite one part of the great Bretainne', this section consists of five figures, which de Bry tells us were given to him by White. However, there is some confusion over whether de Bry used a set of originals produced by Le Moyne instead of White's to produce the engravings of historical ancestors. While de Bry stated that the engravings were from White's drawings, only two of the five engravings are close to White's originals. Again, this could mean that de Bry copied all the pictures from Le Moyne, or that White copied Le Moyne's originals for the engraver. That Le Moyne is the original author appears to be indicated by the fact that instead of reproducing two Pictish men and one woman, as appear in the White originals, de Bry presented two Pictish women and one man, with one of the female figures clearly based on Le Moyne's 'Young daughter of the Picts'. However, whoever the author of de Bry's engravings was, it was this publisher and engraver who gave the figures a fuller context than had been previously provided. He did this by giving each picture a long descriptive caption, and also by adding backgrounds to the pictures.[40] De Bry emphasized the status of his engravings as accurate documents by prefacing his label for each one with the phrase, 'The true picture of . . .'. This accuracy was further enhanced by the careful listing of each detail in the image on an adjoining page. For example, the caption for the first engraving reads,

In times past the Picts, inhabitants of one part of Great Britain, which is now named England, were savages, and did paint all their body after the manner following. They let their hair grow as far as their shoulders, saving those which hang upon their forehead, which they did cut. They shaved all their beard except the moustaches, upon their breast were painted the head of some bird, and about the nipples were the beams of the sun, upon the belly some fearful and monstrous race, spreading the beams very far upon the thighs. Upon the two knees some faces of lion, and upon their legs as it had been scales of fish. Upon their shoulders griffins heads, and then they had serpents about their arms. They carried about their necks one iron ring, and another about the mid of their body, about the belly, and hanging on a chain, a cimitar or Turkish sword, they did carry in one arm a target made of wood, and in the other hand a pick, of which the iron was after the manner of a Lick, with tassels on, and the other end with a round ball. And when they had overcome some of their enemies, they did never fail to carry away their heads with them.[41]

The significance of captions such as these is that de Bry is presenting an interpretation of the image. Essentially he is informing us that before they became civilized, British ancestors were as savage as the New World Indians. With regard to the backgrounds, the landscapes and structural features served to give the figures a sense of historical time and place. Thus both text and background transformed the illustrations from being costumed figures in an artificial setting to being real ancestors who had lived in the past.

The resemblance between the original paintings and de Bry's engravings is very close. For instance, apart from a few details, such as the addition of a spear and another decapitated head in the foreground, the engraving 'The true picture of one Picte' closely matches White's drawing (figure 4.3). Despite this, de Bry's engraving does not have the theatrical or wild quality of the original. The second engraving, representing a woman Pict, also closely matches White's third drawing, except that she lacks the decoration on the face. Figure 4.4 is the third engraving, which has been closely copied from Le Moyne's elaborate painting. Although the same level of detail could not be reached with the representation of the flowers, an attempt has been made to replicate the decoration accurately.

The significance of de Bry's engravings for the development of an iconography of the past cannot be overemphasized. Art historians have highlighted his part in forming a visual conception or ideal type of the American Indian; however, in addition to this, de Bry played a critical role in creating the visual archetype of the ancient European warrior.[42] He did this by taking a set of what were essentially costume studies and providing them with a meaningful historical context. De Bry created the stereotype of an ancient Celtic ancestor for an important reason,

Figure 4.3. 'The true picture of one Picte.' Engraving by Theodore de Bry, from his *America*, 1590, pl. 1.

namely to make sense of the ethnographic images that were the focus and reason for the whole *America* series. De Bry himself stated that with these images he aimed to demonstrate that the Britons once looked like and lived in the same primitive manner as the peoples living in the New World. At this point it is perhaps worth referring to de Bry's inclusion of an extra decapitated head in the image of the Pictish man (figure 4.3). As Stephanie Pratt has argued, 'perhaps more than the body ornament or tattooing, the practice of defacing the dead human body, allied as it was to the practice of cannibalism, was the underlying link to be made between the figures of the Pict and the Indian'.[43] Whether de Bry added

Figure 4.4. 'The true picture of a yonge dowgter of the Picts.' Engraving by Theodore de Bry, from his *America*, 1590, pl. 3.

the extra head to reinforce his point about the barbaric nature of Indian life or as an extra decorative touch, it is impossible to know. What is clear, however, is that de Bry's images established a firm link between ancient Britons and American Indians via visual reasoning. Indeed, according to Piggott it was de Bry who was responsible for making the 'ethnographical comparison which was to influence all subsequent antiquaries', and which 'completely altered the view of the ancient Briton'.[44]

The process by which the indigenous Americans became exemplars for the ancient European past is beyond the scope of this study. However, in this context it is important to note that this process demanded profound interpretative leaps, and that the images played an absolutely critical role in facilitating this. Verbal accounts, for instance, would not have had the same impact or power in convincing antiquarians of the similarity between Indians and Picts. As Thomas Kendrick has argued, 'exactly in what way Red Indians became a pattern for ancient Britons is not known, but the important links were the pictures of the tattooed Indians, and the idea that an ancient Pict, a painted man, must have looked very like such an Indian'.[45] Today the impact of de Bry's engravings is still strong, and this no doubt stems from the combination of drama and detail. As we saw in the preceding chapters, the role of the visual in making a connection between people living in far distant lands and ideas about human antiquity was not new. Essentially what de Bry had done was to make this connection more real.

Fundamentally, the importance of de Bry's series of engravings resides in the fact that the figures would become stereotypes to be reproduced in many other texts. This point has been made by Pratt in relation to the ethnographic images, whereby an iconic type of the North American Indian was created.[46] De Bry's engravings also became a quarry for artists and illustrators reconstructing prehistory. Indeed, the creation of a Celtic stereotype based on these sixteenth-century engravings has persisted until this century.[47] Part of the appeal of de Bry's stereotype lay in its status as an accurate document.[48] Historians of scientific illustration have shown how original engravings, claimed to be based on observation, became icons and were continually reproduced in other texts.[49] This also appears to be the case for the historical reconstructions, where the impact of producing the first 'scientific' representation of a phenomenon was such that once it was created it was very difficult to replace. Furthermore, as historians of the monstrous races imagery have shown, even when new scientific discoveries were made the original images were not revised; in some cases, even when they were revised, subsequent texts would continue to go back to the earlier stereotype. This is also the case for the de Bry engravings. They had such authority and such a memorable visual meaning attached to them that people were reluctant to change them. Significantly, de Bry's engravings were produced when the tradition of antiquarian scholarship was not really established. By the time that studies had been carried out on the material culture, sites and field monuments of ancient Europe, it was too late to create a new image of the ancient Briton because the 'ideal type' had already become established. Indeed, as Smiles has argued, 'with scant archaeological evidence available to contest or supplement the classical accounts it is evident that once an adequate visualisation of their several descriptions had been achieved it would be difficult to improve or displace it'.[50]

The historical reconstructions of Le Moyne and White were firmly integrated into the antiquarian tradition with the work of John Speed, who used de Bry's engravings to illustrate his *History of Great Britaine* of 1611.[51] Speed used the pictures to show how the ancient Britons were distinguished by three critical features, 'nakedness', 'staining and colouring' and 'cutting, pinking and pouncing'.[52] The pictures were central to the argument he made in his chapter on physical appearance, which is best conveyed in his own words:

> It may seem hereby, that these originals of particular nations were not much unlike that first beginning of the universal prosemination of Mankind, when our first parents innocently walked in naked simplicity.[53]

Here the national ancestors of Britain are described as following a way of life that would have been shared by the first humans on the earth. Beyond situating the Britons so deeply in the past, Speed further secured the ideal type of a Briton by presenting a figure of a Pict on the title page of his book *Theatre of the Empire of Great Britaine*, also published in 1611.[54] By placing a single figure labelled 'A Britaine' in the prominent position on the page, above portraits of a Roman, a Saxon, a Dane and a Norman, Speed created a powerful visual stereotype. Equipped with his spear and a shield, a skin cloak and iron chains, this naked ancestor becomes established as the generic representative of the race.

Despite the remarkable persistence of Speed's iconic stereotype, not everyone was convinced by this historical ancestor. Aylett Sammes, in his *Britannia antiqua illustrata* of 1676, criticized Speed for providing a composite picture of a Briton. He comments,

> as for those fancies of Mr. Speed, according to which he hath modelled the cuts of the naked Britains, where he brings in the maid, with flowers and herbs, and painted curiously on her body, whereas married persons were pounced with the stamps of all sorts of ravenous beasts, I shall omit them.[55]

Sammes objected to the way in which Speed had compressed all the classical observations into one general image, stating that Speed makes 'no distinction of the times of his authors writing, but huddles up a rhapsody of their manners without the due consideration of the diversity of the circumstances of the Britains were in'.[56] Furthermore, according to Sammes, Speed's costume of body paint and tattoos was taken up long

Figure 4.5. 'The sculpture of an Ancient Britain, representing the habits of the people in those times.' Engraving for Aylett Samme's *Britannia antiqua illustrata*, 1676, p. 117.

after they were called Britons.[57] In order to correct Speed's vision, he presents an alternative image of the ancient Britons (figure 4.5). This new image depicts a person of the Bretanick Islanders, who lived in the Forelings or Scyllies, where metals abounded. Following Strabo's description of such peoples, Sammes shows this figure wearing a black garment, a side coat to his ankles and holding a stave. He then states that 'these are the Silures of who Tacitus writes . . . differing from the rest of the Britains in their swarthy countenances, by which he reckons them to be of a Spanish original'.[58] The point of the picture is to show that not all inhabitants of ancient Britain were savages who went naked and brandished spears. Indeed, Sammes argues that, despite the black hair and swarthy complexions of these people, they were of a 'gentle and kind disposition, of a fair and honest behaviour, simple and sincere in their conversation, and generally the Britains, by most authors are so set out'.[59] It is, however, interesting to note that while Sammes reacted so strongly to Speed's stereotype, he participated in the creation of yet another one, that of the ancient Druid. Indeed, his classic picture of the long-bearded Druid has been of equal importance in the iconography of British ancestry.[60]

While Sammes' reconstruction was justified by him as the more authentic vision of the ancient Briton, it was de Bry's and Speed's image of the ancient Briton that retained its grip on the antiquarian imagination. Before the construction of this stereotype of an ancient warrior, antiquarians had been very resistant to the concept of a primitive prehistoric past. The new idea of the ancestors as savages was tolerated in part because they were depicted as brave warriors, but it was also accepted because of the appeal of the imagery on title pages such as Speed's. Indeed, soon after Speed's history with its illustrations was published, antiquarians began to produce vivid verbal descriptions of the earliest inhabitants of Britain. In 1612, for example, Samuel Daniel was comparing ancient Britons to North Americans in his *The First Part of the Historie of England*. When describing how the Britaines before Caesar were divided into a multitude of petty regiments without entire rule of combination, Daniel stated 'as now, we see all the west world (lately discovered) to be, and generally all other countries are, in their first and natural free nakedness, before they come to be taken in, either by some predominant power from abroad, or grow to a head, within themselves'.[61] By the mid-1600s it was common to compare the two cultures, this being epitomized in Thomas Hobbes' famous comment of 1651 in *Leviathan* that the life of primitive humans was like that of American Indians. However, it was John Aubrey's colourful description of 1659 that finally firmly established comparative ethnography in the study of Britain's past.[62] While the British antiquarians, such as John Aubrey and William Camden, refrained from using visual imagery to reinforce this point, other writers used the de Bry images of ancient Picts in a visually comparative context.[63] A key example was in Père Joseph Lafitau's *Moeurs des sauvages Amériquains comparées aux moeurs des premiers temps* (Manners of savage Americans compared to the manners of first times) of 1724, where ancient Picts were depicted alongside American Indians with similar body decoration.[64]

The historical reconstructions of ancient Britons attained a scientific status because of their association with accurately rendered ethnological illustrations. However, the status of the ethnological illustrations as accurate documents was clearly problematic and warrants some discussion. While the details of clothing and material culture in the portraits of the Indians may have been accurate, the body form, the facial features and the poses were not. De Bry was precise in the sense that he paid close attention to material culture and did not attribute items from one cultural group to another, but the stylistic and artistic components of the pictures prevented them from being totally reliable representations. For instance, rules of composition controlled the depiction of figures in their settings and conventions from portraiture shaped the way individual figures were rendered. There were other distorting elements as well, a major one being that some details of material culture were taken from European prototypes.[65] Although the concern with details of material culture signified an important change in the representation of distant forebears, the colour, the facial expressions and the theatrical postures all contributed to the nature of these images as artistic statements rather than scientific illustrations. Furthermore, they fulfilled functions beyond the purely scientific. While scholars of antiquarianism have celebrated the introduction of archaeological details and scientific elements in the ethnologically derived reconstructions, we must remember that the scientific component was in many ways secondary to other interests, these including, for instance, the desire to produce visually dramatic pictures. As we have seen with other traditions of scientific illustration, the pictures introduced scientific realism through the means of artistic conventions.[66]

The wider significance of the reconstructions in travel accounts consists in their creation of a new vision of history, distinct from that presented in the ancient texts. However, as Anthony Grafton has observed, 'the substance of that vision, ironically enough, often came from the very ancient writers whose supremacy it denied'.[67] This paradox is also reflected in the early images of ancient Britons, where in many ways the ethnological data simply confirmed the arguments of the classical authors.

Geographical studies and Philip Cluverius' ancient Germans

Not long after de Bry published the Le Moyne and White illustrations of ancient Picts, a number of European antiquarians engaged in reconstructing the life of their ancient ancestors. This was done in the context of producing national histories, regional histories and wider geographical studies. An important example is the remarkable series of twenty-six engravings of ancient life in Philip Cluverius' *Germaniae Antiquae* of 1616. This series of images was important because it was the first systematic rather than incidental visual record of antiquity. Born in

Poland, Cluverius went to Leiden University, where he initially studied law and then took on historic, antiquarian and geographic studies. After travelling widely in Europe, Cluverius returned to Leiden to assimilate his observations on geography and history, becoming well known as a founding father of historic geography.[68] *Germaniae Antiquae* was one of his first major publications and in it the life of the tribes of ancient Germany was described. It was in association with this book that he received the title of 'Geographus Academicus'. and an honorary professorship at Leiden. He then undertook studies in Sicily, Italy and the isles of Sardinia and Corsica, which resulted in *Italiae Antiquae*, published the year after he died in 1624. The popularity of these two major works at the time was indicated by the fact that translations of both were produced in French and German. The popularity of *Germaniae Antiquae* in particular was, no doubt, due to the large folio engravings of ancient ancestors in their regional dress.

Figure 4.6. Ancient Germans. Engraving from Philip Cluverius' *Germaniae Antiquae*, 1616, fig. 2.

The portraits of the ancient Germans in Cluverius' study were primarily based on the classical authors' descriptions of the Germans. Cluverius, who must have instructed the engraver, used Tacitus' *Germania* as his main source, a translation of this text being provided at the beginning of the book. Tacitus' study of the life and customs of the German tribes was widely available when Cluverius produced his text, being the key source for German historians at the time.[69] Cluverius begins his book by outlining the customs of the ancient Germans, documenting the Greek and Roman descriptions of the race. He then describes the customs of the tribes on both sides of the Rhine, discussing in turn the other parts of Europe described as 'old Celtica', which included Illyricum, Germania, Gallia, Hispania and the British Isles. He challenges the idea that the name *Celtica* was applied to Gallia alone and presents a theory, based on the writings of Moses, that the great-grandson of Noah, Aschenazes, settled in all Celtica with his sons and grandsons after the flooding of the world. Thus the first father of the old Celts was Aschenazes and the Celtic races were all one and of the same family, sharing a universal language.[70] Cluverius devotes much discussion to the appearance of the various Celtic tribes, judging this from the sources and his own observation. He argues that from central and north-western Europe going north, people got taller, whiter and more blonde-haired, until, in the far north they changed to a darker skin colour and stunted growth occurred.

That the primitivist tendencies of Tacitus are celebrated in Cluverius' *Germaniae Antiquae* can best be seen in the images, which present a race of proud and strong peoples. Indeed, Tacitus' description of the early Germanic tribes is brought to life in the engravings, where the ancestors are shown living a primitive yet heroic life. Regional variation among the tribes is communicated by the different garments, structures and weaponry. In general, the images reflect Tacitus' claim that the primary activity of the ancient Germans was warfare, as emphasis is placed on showing the various warriors and their arms. In addition to the classical sources, Cluverius and the engraver were influenced by folklore and imagery of life in the woodland regions of Europe. This is demonstrated by the close association of the figures with wild forest-like landscapes. The extent to which author and engraver were influenced by the ethnologically inspired images of White and Le Moyne is difficult to establish, but it is probable that they came across one of the many translations of de Bry's series while working in Leiden or travelling through Europe.

The title page of Cluverius' book is similar to Speed's, with idealized 'types' of ancient Germans. There are two figures, a male and a female, both of whom are naked with the exception of the loose cloaks hung over their shoulders, as described by Tacitus. The male, who wears a lion's-head helmet, has a spear with a decapitated head on the point in one hand. In his other hand he holds another mutilated head. Both figures are not tattooed or painted like the ancient Picts of Le Moyne and White, but they do resemble their portraits in that the ancient Germans, like the Celts, are depicted as savage warriors. The first set of twelve images in *Germaniae Antiquae* features portraits and social scenes, corresponding to chapters on the lives, customs, religion, habitations and costume of the ancient Germans. Following this series is another set of nine pictures of pairs of male warriors, a fortification and a battle scene, which corresponds to a discussion of the military nature of these people. Whereas the first set uses garments to indicate the regional distinctions among the race, the second set focuses on armoury and weaponry to show tribal variations. Both sets suggest the existence of primitive and more 'civilized' tribes, and they do this simply by depicting the latter with more elaborate garments and weaponry. There are also some differences in the depiction of their general physical appearance, where the more primitive types have stockier bodies. Despite the sophisticated dress and arms possessed by some tribes, the primitive lifestyle of the ancient Germans is emphasized by the nakedness of many figures and the lack of structures or urban dwellings. This reflected Tacitus' observation that the peoples of Germany 'never live in cities and will not even have their houses adjoining one another. They dwell apart, dotted about here and there, wherever a spring, plain, or grove takes their fancy'.[71] This can be seen in figure 4.6, which shows two naked warriors standing naked alongside a tree. Equipped with the most rudimentary of weapons these ancestors only partially cover themselves with skins of animals they have slain. In figure 4.7 some changes have been incorporated which may signify either regional variation or slight cultural advance. Here two warriors lean on a fence

Figure 4.7. An ancient German family. Engraving from Philip Cluverius' *Germaniae Antiquae*, 1616, fig. 8.

Figure 4.8. Ancient German warriors. Engraving from Philip Cluverius' *Germaniae Antiquae*, 1616, fig. 16.

and a woman sits holding her infant. Not only are their skins less shaggy but they are held together with a thorn or bone. In the background is some kind of building or structure. Subsequent engravings show further variation in hairstyles, garment designs and weaponry. For example, figure 4.8 features two warriors with swords and spears, elaborate animal-head helmets and a type of shoe. The figure on the right, with his large knotted club, strongly resembles Herakles. Figure 4.9 also features two warriors, this time with antlers and goats' heads for their helmets. Again, the iconography of Herakles has greatly influenced the engraver. Despite the emphasis on details of dress and weapons, these aspects of the pictures have become subsumed or secondary to the more general depiction of primitive life. One easily forgets the different types of woven cloaks, cloak fasteners and undergarments, but clearly remembers the forest settings, the large sturdy bodies, the nakedness, the animal skins and the decapitated heads.

Figure 4.9. Ancient German warriors. Engraving from Philip Cluverius' *Germaniae Antiquae*, 1616, fig. 17.

Two scenes stand out in the whole series of illustrations because they focus on the social life of the community as opposed to the dress and armoury of individuals. In figure 4.10, we see a group of ancient Germans inside a large wooden structure. This appears to be based on Tacitus' description of German dwellings as being made from rough-hewn timber.[72] While some are eating, others are cooking and engaging in conversation. The figures are either naked or partly covered with fur cloaks. An important component of the image is the addition of domestic items such as the small tables upon which their food is placed, the baskets and pots. Again, despite such details, the impression or feeling one gets from the image is one of primitiveness, where Tacitus' comments about the nakedness and dirtiness of these people, who live together on the same earthen floor, are emphasized.[73] In figure 4.11 we see a religious scene in which people are engaged in some sort of ritual involving a large bull. These people appear to be more advanced: they now have clothing as opposed to wearing skins. Above all, however, these people are distinguished from the others by the fact that there is an apparent social hierarchy, within which some have attained elevated status as priests or leaders. These two images of social life are significant because an attempt has been made to go beyond the general physical appearance of the ancient ancestors in order to show how their ways of life differed from those of the present.

As well as being shaped by the classical sources, Cluverius and his engraver's images were influenced by wildman iconography, forest imagery and ethnographic illustrations. As Simon Schama has noted, it was around this time that an 'entire genre of sentimental ethnography developed, especially in southern Germany, in which it was increasingly difficult to distinguish between the cleaned-up wild men and the

Figure 4.10. An ancient German domestic scene. Engraving from Philip Cluverius' *Germaniae Antiquae*, 1616, fig. 13.

various ancestral Germans embellished from Tacitus'.[74] Cluverius could also draw upon the traditional imagery of German folk life, which in itself was a blend of wildman iconography, biblical imagery and local mythology. Parallels with ethnological imagery can be seen in some of the details. For instance, the hooves tied around the neck and the animal-head helmets appear in the set of images of Brazilian Indians produced in 1555–6 by André Thevet and, in particular, in his volume of engraved portraits from 1584.[75] Furthermore, the formula of depicting two figures walking side by side with their heads turning towards the viewer appears on some of the early maps featuring ethnographic peoples.[76] Cluverius would not only have seen such ethnographic images in the books and great atlases produced as a result of navigation trips, but also may have encountered one of the many exhibitions of living American Indians in Europe.[77]

Finally, there is an irony in the Cluverius images as there was with de Bry's pictures of the ancient Picts. On the one hand the authors of such texts emphasized the barbaric and uncivilized lifestyle of their newly discovered ancestors. On the other hand, however, when these ideas were translated into visual images, the ancestors acquired a dignified status. This is achieved artistically, in the sense that the postures, gestures and facial expressions of the figures convey an authority and strength. Thus, in a way, the pictures actually defied the text, recasting the ancestors as a

Figure 4.11. An ancient German religious scene. Engraving from Philip Cluverius' *Germaniae Antiqua* 1616, fig. 14.

race of heroic peoples. While Cluverius intended to emphasize the savage lifestyle of the early Europeans, the engravings add another dimension, capturing in visual terms a primitivist view of the past.[78] This inconsistency is a fundamental characteristic of all antiquarian imagery, revealing the troubled and confused thinking on the state of early life. Authors like Cluverius and his illustrator, like many other people of their time, would have considered questions about whether early human existence was idyllic and worth aspiring to, or whether it was degraded and primitive. This tension, which had been evident in classical writings, remained strong in Renaissance thought and was at the heart of attempts to reconstruct national origins.[79] However, the distinctive contribution made by the imagery was the icon of the ancient primitive warrior. This icon of the savage but heroic warrior was a useful tool for projecting back into the more distant eras of human existence.

Regional histories and Johan Picardt's ancient Dutch

Other European authors and engravers constructed images of their ancestors that were not so dependent on the classical sources. Notable among these was the Dutch antiquary Johan Picardt, who published a

Figure 4.12. The ancient giants of Drenthe alongside a monument. Engraving from Johan Picardt's *Korte beschryvinge van eenige Vergetene en Verborgene Antiquiteten*, 1660, fol. 22/3.

series of pictorial reconstructions based on folklore about the local monuments in Drenthe, an old province of the Netherlands. These illustrations, by an unknown illustrator, appear in his book *Korte Beschryvinge von eenige Vergetene en Verborgene Antiquiteten* (Short description of several forgotten and hidden antiquities) of 1660, which was a study of the large megalithic burial monuments (known as *'unebeds*) in the provinces and countries between the North Sea, and the rivers Yssel, Eems and Lippe. Picardt was a minister in Drenthe, who had, like Cluverius, studied at the University of Leiden, and was the first Dutch scholar to produce a study on prehistoric monuments.[80] Indeed, his interest in the ancient sites of his province was exceptional in Dutch antiquarianism during the seventeenth century, the scholars of the time being more interested in the remains of the Romans and the Batavian natives during the Roman occupation.[81] Focusing on the 'civilized' history of their fatherland, Dutch antiquarians were not concerned with the prehistoric monuments found in the backward, rural province of Drenthe. Picardt, however, celebrated the prehistoric past of the province and wrote a book expressing local pride in the megalithic monuments. The reconstructions of the ancient people of Drenthe were thus produced in a different context from the ethnologically inspired images of Le Moyne and White, and the classically inspired images of

Cluverius. Picardt's images are important because they are early examples of reconstructions produced in association with stories about archaeological sites. Again, the extent to which Picardt may have been influenced by Le Moyne and White's drawings, de Bry's and Speed's engravings, and Cluverius' images is difficult to ascertain. Picardt cites Cluverius and Tacitus as sources at the beginning of his text, which suggests that perhaps Cluverius' images provided the inspiration for a series of pictures.

As with Cluverius' book we do not know whether the illustrator was a well-known engraver or the nature of the instructions given. One can assume, however, that the illustrator followed Picardt's objective, which was to illustrate life in association with the monuments. Included among the ancient ancestors who inhabited the province are giants who were thought to have built the megalithic structures still surviving in the landscape. This view was not unique to Picardt; it was a traditional belief that had been maintained by other European antiquarians. What Picardt contributed, however, was a detailed visual image of ancient life in the province of Drenthe. Furthermore, he may also have been giving life to theories about human descent from the giants, since around the time that he produced his book, other scholars were illustrating how humans had evolved from the giants. Athanasius Kircher, for instance, featured an image of giants in his book *Mundus Subterraneus* of 1665.[82] As Kircher's work was very influential in scholarly thinking of the time, perhaps his images influenced Picardt.[83]

The illustrations in Picardt's series contain a number of themes, including the construction of stone monuments, burial, ritual and general social scenes. In the first illustration there is a group of giants standing alongside a large monument, pointing towards it in a way that could be interpreted as conveying ownership (figure 4.12). Their size, which is comparable to that of the monument, also suggests that they made it. The monument is rendered in the popular style for depicting prehistoric ruins at the time. For instance, it is reminiscent of John Aubrey's illustration of Stonehenge from the 1660s.[84] In the foreground of the picture a giant seated on a rock is devouring a small person or human. Figure 4.13, the second illustration, features a burial scene, where people raise their hands and look to the sky as if in prayer. The raised funeral pyre with a corpse lying on it is situated in a forest, suggesting a primeval mourning ritual. The appearance of these shaggy giants and human onlookers has elements of Cluverius, such as the cloaks, clubs and hair. Following this is a scene showing giants engaged in the construction of a stone monument (figure 4.14). On the left giants carry the boulders and on the right they lay them in place. The figure on the right appears to be directing the construction process, while small people, apparently incidental to the scene, stand below him. In the

Figure 4.13. A funeral scene in the ancient province of Drenthe. Engraving from Johan Picardt's *Korte beschryvinge van eenige Vergetene en Verborgene Antiquiteiten*, 1660, fol. 32/3.

background is another monument that appears to be completed. These three pictures appear in a chapter discussing the large stones found in the area. The fourth picture in the series portrays a fur-clad couple standing at the top of a hill overlooking what appears to be some sort of town, with people in a grid-like structure (figure 4.15). It is difficult to tell exactly what this layout represents, as some squares incorporate houses and tents, while others contain only groups of people and wagons. The objective may be to present an ancient fortification system as the picture appears in a chapter on fortresses and walls in the area.

Figure 4.16 shows two large mounds, one of which has a female figure standing at a door. Below her are a group of worshippers and lying on the ground is an assortment of skulls, both human and animal, suggesting that some kind of sacrificial ritual has taken place or that these people are cannibals. This image of a female figure in a mound is derived from folk stories about local women with powers who demanded offerings from the people.[85] Presented in a chapter on the 'living places' of the 'white women', the focus of the image is again the association of the ancestors with the ancient monuments. In the sixth scene we see a

Figure 4.14. Giants constructing a stone monument in the ancient province of Drenthe. Engraving from Johan Picardt's *Korte beschryvinge van eenige Vergetene en Verborgene Antiquiteten*, 1660, fol. 32/3.

Figure 4.15. A fortified township in the ancient province of Drenthe. Engraving from Johan Picardt's *Korte beschryvinge van eenige Vergetene en Verborgene Antiquiteten*, 1660, fol. 42/3.

detailed view of a tribe of giants living in the forest (figure 4.17). This appears in a chapter on the nature, life and manners of the inhabitants of the region. The men have animal-head helmets, large wooden shields and animal hooves tied around their necks. This picture pays much more attention to the details of the figures. For instance, many of the figures wear the pointed shoes similar to those shown in Cluverius' images, and the high pony-tails of the figures on the right and the animal-head helmets look very similar to the depictions of early Germanic tribes. Other influences can be seen in the thatched structure in the background, which looks like the primitive hut in Caesariano's edition

Figure 4.16. The living places of the 'white women' in the ancient province of Drenthe. Engraving from Johan Picardt's *Korte beschryvinge van eenige Vergetene en Verborgene Antiquiteten*, 1660, fol. 46/7.

of Vitruvius and the home of Adam and Eve in de Bry's frontispiece to *America*. This picture of a tribal group also has adapted elements of ethnological imagery. For example, Picardt appears to have been influenced by images from the Dutch voyages in the Straits of Magellan, 1599–1624, as the pictures of the peoples encountered here are very similar to his naked figures wearing furs.[86] Finally, the seated female figure who turns her head is very similar to the female figure in Cluverius (figure 4.10) and in the German edition of Vitruvius (figure 3.15). This iconic image of a nurturing woman comes from early biblical illustrations. The final scene in Picardt's series accompanies the chapter on the ancient pagan religion of the region (figure 4.18). Here a central Druid-like figure is holding a large knife in one hand while he raises his other hand over an altar. Below him are figures praying, while in the background helmeted figures stand with their spears. A significant detail is the depiction of artefacts on the ground including a jug, an axe, a knife and a plate or shield. These were not based on excavated implements but were copied from earlier images. The image is similar to Cluverius' scene of devotion and sacrifice (figure 4.11), where the artefacts on the ground and the posture of those in prayer are almost identical. The repetition of such details reveals how pictorial devices took on an iconic status and were copied by others to convey particular meanings.

The distinctive feature of the series is the presentation of a primitive pagan lifestyle, as indicated by the large giants with their long hair, animal-skin garments and clubs. As in Cluverius' pictures, where attention was paid to minutiae of dress and armour, the details of the monuments in Picardt, including the stone structures and mounds, are

Figure 4.17. The life and manners of the ancient people of Drenthe. Engraving from Johan Picardt's *Korte beschryvinge van eenige Vergetene en Verborgene Antiquiteten*, 1660, fol. 50/1.

far less memorable than the image of the club-wielding tribes who live in the forest. While they did not have the same cultural and historical dimension as did the images produced in association with the classical descriptions, some aspects of the pictures do suggest tribal difference and change. Most important, perhaps, is that with Picardt's pictures we can see how the illustrations of ancestors had been taken out of the realm of costume studies and the representation of exotic races. Rather than being based on classical accounts they were now connected to the ruins and monuments in the landscape. From this point on, the archaeological dimension of the past started to assert itself in the imagery of human antiquity.

National histories and Joseph Strutt's ancient Britons

Beyond geographical and regional studies, it was in national histories that illustrations of the early inhabitants of Europe were more widely produced. This not only reflected the growing interest in writing national histories, but demonstrated how authors and editors were starting to illustrate their books with pictures of historical characters, events and monuments. It was around the late eighteenth century that increasing concern for accuracy in such illustrations arose.[87] Like the images of Cluverius and Picardt, these historical images drew on a range of sources, including classical texts, folklore, ethnology, contemporary art, heroic literature and archaeology. In tracing the use of images to illustrate history, one important individual stands out.

Figure 4.18. Ancient religious practices in the ancient province of Drenthe. Engraving from Johan Picardt's *Korte beschryvinge van eenige Vergetene en Verborgene Antiquiteten*, 1660, fol. 66/7.

Joseph Strutt played a major role in establishing illustration as a component in the understanding of history, striving to produce accurate reconstructions of past life by using all the available material on the manners, costume and ancient monuments of historical peoples. Noting the inaccuracies in the representation of dress, armour and weaponry in historical illustrations, Strutt aimed to improve the quality of reconstructions of the past in history books. While Strutt does not really get acknowledged in histories of antiquarian scholarship, his work is briefly discussed by Francis Haskell in his study of the role of images in explaining history.[88]

In 1774–6 Strutt wrote *Horda-Angel-Cynnan, or, A compleat view of the Manners, Customs, Arms, Habits, &c of the Inhabitants of England . . .*, in which he presented 150 illustrations of the costumes and armour of the English from the arrival of the Saxons. In 1777–9 he produced *The Chronicle of England; or, a compleat history, civil, military and ecclesiastical, of the ancient Britons and Saxons . . .*, in which there was an equally vast number of illustrations of British history and monuments. Included among them are two reconstructions of ancient European ancestors, one of the ancient Britons and the other of ancient Germans. In terms of his layout, Strutt appears to have been influenced by Robert Henry's *History of England* of 1771, which proposed a new outline for presenting British history. This outline, which marked a departure from traditional histories, was concerned with detailing aspects of the history of learning, the arts, commerce and the manners, customs, dress and diets of the ancestors.[89] Henry did not produce illustrations to accompany his descriptions of the ancient Britons, but Strutt did, providing detailed images of the different regional types. Strutt was no doubt influenced by the publication of historical costume books around this time. An important and contemporary study in costume that may have influenced Strutt was Thomas Jefferys' *A Collection of the Dresses of Different Nations both Ancient and Modern* of 1757–72. Here Jefferys included the 'Habit of an Ancient Britain', in which a naked figure derived from Speed's stereotype is presented.[90] Strutt was also influenced by antiquarian studies of monuments, being aware of the illustrations resulting from work on the monuments of pre-Roman Britain, particularly that of William Camden and William Stukeley.[91]

In his introduction to *The Chronicle of England* Strutt seeks to account for the lack of interest in England's history before the Norman Conquest. The answer, according to him, lies in the belief that there was a lack of authentic materials available for reconstructing this early period: 'for few men of great abilities are possessed of patience equal to the task of turning over so many dry prolix records of barbarism and superstition as are absolutely necessary for the completing a history of the early ages'.[92] Strutt challenged this belief, making the case that information on the subject of manners, customs and habits could be 'collected from the most authentic materials'.[93] In addition to the classical authors, such authentic materials included detailed studies of armour and weaponry, manuscript illuminations, buildings, earth-works or the like and antiquarian studies on sites and monuments.[94] Strutt emphasized that he had reproduced details from these sources with the greatest exactness.[95]

In a chapter on the clothing, arts and habits of the Britons, Strutt presented a reconstruction drawing of five types of ancient Britons in a single landscape (figure 4.19). This picture synthesizes descriptions of the different tribes by Diodorus Siculus, Strabo, Caesar, Dio Cassius and

Figure 4.19. 'Figures of the ancient Britons, as described by Diodorus Siculus, Strabo, Julius Caesar, Dio Cassius, and Herodian.' Engraving by Joseph Strutt for his *The Chronicle of England . . .*, 1777–9, pl. V.

Heriodian. As de Bry had done with his ancient Britons, Strutt was at pains to specify all the details of the illustration in the text. The figure on the left, he informs us, represents a warrior from the south, who were known to wear tunics ornamented with flowers and garments called 'bracae' that covered the legs. Over this they wore a cloak of chequerwork and belts adorned with gold or silver, from which a sword hung by a chain of brass or iron. On their head they wore helmets made of brass with horns, and on their wrists and fingers, golden rings. The helmets are reminiscent of Cluverius' ancient Germans (figure 4.9) and Picardt's ancient Dutch (figure 4.6). The second figure on the left represents another type of southern Briton, who were known to wear long black tunics and a girdle around the waist. This is very similar to the 'alternative' ancient Briton depicted by Aylett Sammes (figure 4.5). The third figure represents an inland inhabitant, known to wear animal skins, and the fourth represents the northern tribes of the Maaeatae and Caledonians, who were described as naked warriors who wore large rings or chains around their necks and bellies. These were the warriors who painted themselves and used needles and the juice of herbs to make tattoo designs on their bodies. They were also the figures that inspired Le Moyne, White, de Bry and Speed to construct a generic type of ancient Briton. The female figure on the right wears the typical woman's dress consisting of a tunic with a girdle, buckles, chains of gold around the neck, bracelets on the arms and rings on the fingers. Unlike the other figures who represent generic types, she is a representation of a specific historical figure, Boudicca, who holds her spear ready for battle

Figure 4.20. 'Ancient Germans, as described by Tacitus. An ancient Saxon (the figure leaning on his spear) as represented by Sidonius, Apollinaris, Paulus Diaconus, &c.' Engraving by Joseph Strutt for his *The Chronicle of England . . .*, 1777–9, pl. XVIII.

with the Romans. As well as outlining the ancient dress of these ancestors, Strutt includes a section on armour in which descriptions of the weapons held by the figures are presented. Finally, in the background of the reconstruction are two stone monuments and a thatched circular hut, reflecting how Strutt combined both classical observations of ancient habitations and antiquarian descriptions of sites to provide a specific context for the figures.

Figure 4.20 shows Strutt's reconstruction of a group of ancient Germans, following the same formula as that created for the ancient Britons. Again, Strutt refers to the details of the image at length in the text. We learn, for instance, that the figure on the left has a particular type of head adornment, whereby the hair on the crown of the head has grown long and then been enclosed in a ring of copper. The two figures in the background wear the cloak known as 'sagum', which was fastened around the shoulders with a buckle or thorn. A similar cloak is worn by one of Cluverius' figures, where a thorn has been used as a fastener (figure 4.7). The second man on the right wears the the dress of a wealthier ancient German, which consisted of a close garment covering the whole body. The structures are also an important part of the illustration, deriving from classical descriptions of circular huts thatched on the top.

Both these images stand out from the other illustrations in the book, distinguished by their status as didactic pictures closely connected to the text. Moreover, they represent an important step in the establishment of conventions for the iconography of prehistory. Strutt's reconstructions are composite documents which assemble figures from different regions into a single landscape. With this innovation Strutt has created a fundamental pictorial device for conveying historical information. This device is paradoxical in character because, on the one hand, it is full of accurate details and thus seems authentic, but on the other, the way it is assembled is completely artificial. The standard or familiar method of presenting historical figures had been to present individuals, pairs, or groups from a particular region or period. Strutt changed the format in order to create a powerful didactic tool, and demonstrated how historical reconstructions could be used by the historian as an efficient mode of explanation.[96] This method of synthesizing knowledge of the past would become a primary means of representing prehistory in the next century. While Strutt had introduced an extremely effective means for shedding light on the past, he had also created an extremely problematic one. Although on one level the reconstructions had become more accurate, on another level they had become more abstract and unreal.

Pictorial histories and Samuel Rush Meyrick and Charles Hamilton Smith's ancient Britons

Illustrated histories with reconstructions of archaic peoples remained scarce in Europe in the early 1800s, reflecting how life in pre-Roman times was still not of great interest. However, around this time pictorial histories began to become more popular, as books were now consumed by a wider section of the public, and a great deal of interest had been generated by the costume book. A prominent example was G.L. Craik and Charles Macfarlane's *Pictorial History of England* of 1837, which contained numerous pictures of various episodes in British history. However, it lacked visual images of the remote period of British history, providing only a small picture of a Druid as part of a chapter heading.[97] Some books did however depict earlier history. Primary among these was Samuel Rush Meyrick and Charles Hamilton Smith's *The Costume of the Original Inhabitants of the British Islands* of 1815. This was a major work on the dress of the inhabitants of the British Isles from earliest times, with eleven figures from the pre-Roman period. Like Strutt, Meyrick and Smith aimed to ascertain more correctly than had yet been attempted the clothing, arms, decorations and appearance of historic characters in the earliest periods. Furthermore, they state that in studying savage life and the development of civilized society, investigations on the arts and manufactures, habits and customs, and religious and military characteristics of past societies were all 'intimately blended with COSTUME'.[98] This reflected increasing interest in describing habits and customs in national histories, a subject dependant on visual explanation. It was also associated with the increasing concern for historical accuracy in theatre costume around this time.[99] Interest in costume, which had been a major motivation for producing reconstructions of antiquity, was clearly becoming more closely associated with the writing of history. Perhaps it was an awareness of the importance of the visual that led the two authors to enlist the services of the well-known engraver and aquatint specialist Robert Havell, so as to ensure the production of quality images.[100]

Figure 4.21. 'A Briton of the Interior.' Aquatint by Robert Havell for S.R. Meyrick and C.H. Smith's *The Costume of the Original Inhabitants of the British Islands*, 1815, pl. 1.

While the focus of Havell's images of early British ancestors in Meyrick and Smith was ostensibly on dress and armour, the pictures also placed great importance on the accurate depiction of artefacts and sites. Meyrick was not only a specialist on armour, having produced a number of publications on the topic, but had also written on ancient British and Irish burials and monuments.[101] The images mark an important development from Strutt's in the sense that they demonstrate how archaeological evidence was starting to play a more important role in reconstructions of the past. More specifically they revealed how the antiquarian study of field monuments was gaining wider recognition among historians. In this context it is important to note the connection between this work and the art of ruins, associated with landscape painting.[102] Interest in ruins as an aesthetic subject grew out of the Renaissance love of classical remains and was later extended to include prehistoric monuments. Picturesque scenes with ruins became common in the late 1700s and were important in generating an interest in the past. John Brewer has considered the wider impact of such works, stating that 'Ancient British ruins not only provoked melancholic reflections on the transitory nature of life . . . but conjured up obscure and often frightening images of a barbarous and brutal past'.[103] By the early 1800s prehistoric ruins had become part of the national consciousness and, as Sam Smiles has shown, the prehistoric landscape, with its wild landscapes and megalithic ruins, becomes a distinct subcategory within the landscape painting of this period.[104]

What distinguished the work of Meyrick and Smith from that which had gone before was that their figures were more contextualized, the setting showing greater concern for a wider range of details.[105] The authenticity of the images is reinforced by the fact that specific artefacts and monuments are depicted, all of which are provenanced in the text. The extent to which material culture was becoming a primary source for understanding the past is reflected in the frontispiece to the book. Placed in front of a cromlech from Kilkenny, Ireland, is a cache of objects including an Irish harp, a golden crown, horns from the cabinet of the King of Denmark, a Miölner stone from the Pontoppidan Museum and a half-open kist-vaen containing a skeleton. Such materials are described as authorities in Meyrick and Smith's work, and attest to their knowledge of the monuments in other parts of Europe.

In a brief introductory section before the plates, Meyrick and Smith provide a general description of the Cimbrian savage of Britain and Ireland. In the same manner as Lucretius they dramatically describe the life of the original ancestor who, 'clad in the skin of the beasts he had slain, issued in search of his prey from a cave hollowed by nature, or a hut scarcely artificial, which the interwoven twigs and leaves presented in a wood'.[106] While some aspects of Havell's aquatints conform to this image, they hardly constitute a vision of the cave-dwelling savage. The inconsistency between the verbal description and the images, already noted in Cluverius, continued to characterize antiquarian iconography. Once again, the illustrations had recycled the Renaissance stereotype or icon of the Celtic warrior, naked and covered in body decoration.

The first image in Meyrick and Smith's series presents 'A Briton of the Interior' (figure 4.21). This ancestor is clothed and armed as Caesar described the Cassii and other inhabitants of the internal regions of Britain. In the accompanying text there is a detailed description of his weapons, particularly the British battle-axe hanging from his waist, which we are informed has a blade based on a specimen found in Britain.[107] Behind him is a fortification site, which serves to enhance his status as a warrior.[108] This image is clearly derived from the de Bry and Speed stereotype of the ancient Briton, with the distinctive long hair and moustache, and the spear. However, a notable omission is the decapitated head. More specifically, it looks like Strutt's representation of this regional type (figure 4.19). The third image in the series features 'A Maaeata and Caledonian', or representatives from the tribes who inhabited the plains and forests of North Britain (figure 4.22). These are naked warriors covered in tattoos who display their weapons. The detailed representation of tattoos, which include animals, geometric designs and suns, is reminiscent of the Renaissance portraits of White, but there is an emphasis on the method of pricking, rather than painted designs. They also have the torques and chains that were included in the earlier visions. The spears, swords and club-like weapon are based on classical sources and taken directly from engravings of such implements in scholarly works on armour. To the right is a monument known as a cromlech, which is based on a site found in Cornwall. In the distance is a mountain upon which a cairn is standing, based on a site recorded in Wales. Major characteristics of this image are the monuments included in the background and the more accurate provenancing of artefacts.

A scene featuring early British methods of fishing and tilling the land is the fifth image in the series (figure 4.23). The boats are based on classical sources, which refer to the use of skin-boats or coracles. They are also based on similar boats being used in Wales at the time.[109] The figures

Figure 4.22. 'A Maaeata and Caledonian.' Aquatint by Robert Havell for S.R. Meyrick and C.H. Smith's *The Costume of the Original Inhabitants of the British Islands*, 1815, pl. 3.

103

Figure 4.23. 'British fishing and husbandry.' Aquatint by Robert Havell for S.R. Meyrick and C.H. Smith's *The Costume of the Original Inhabitants of the British Islands*, 1815, pl. 5.

using the boats are naked and have long hair and sturdy frames. They stand in contrast to the figures tilling the ground with their wooden plough. These agricultural workers, who wear garments and have short hair, are thus by implication more civilized. We are informed that they are taken from a seventh-century illumination and are included to show that 'agriculture is of the earliest antediluvian antiquity'.[110] The two sets of figures, one ploughing and one fishing, appear completely incompatible. It is as if two distinct scenes have been placed together for didactic reasons. Meyrick and Smith appear to have wanted to illustrate how technologies were developed to exploit the resources of both land and sea, but the figures in the boats look like they are from an earlier stage in the evolution of subsistence strategies. Despite these problems, the significance of this image is that it attempts to reconstruct an ancient landscape. Where other images in the book portray landscapes, they are stylized and clearly function as a backdrop for the central figure and the monuments. In this image, however, the landscape is clearly an important component of the picture. However, the features of the landscape suggest that it is has been modelled on contemporary landscape painting rather than reality; as Smiles and Piggott have observed, it is an idyllic pastoral scene.[111] Despite this an attempt to evoke 'wildness' or a primitive quality is suggested by the mountains in the background.

The historical reconstructions of Meyrick and Smith build on the antiquarian images of their predecessors by including specific artefacts and emphasizing the presence of prehistoric monuments in the landscape. The importance they attribute to artefacts is evidenced by another visual convention they introduced, namely the vignettes of specimens at the bottom of each plate. Clearly, Meyrick and Smith were drawing on the increasing number of antiquarian studies that included illustrations of artefacts, sites and monuments. This is also suggested by their consistent references to findings reported in journals such as *Philosophical Transactions of the Royal Society* and *Archaeologica*, in which recently excavated sites were described.

Although the images produced by Meyrick and Smith, Strutt and others before them were distinguished by attention to detail, they were at the same time characterized by their visual simplicity. While presentation of details such as dress, weaponry, artefacts and sites appeared to be the main motivation for the production of a picture, another objective was to offer the image of an ancient ancestor for sheer visual impact. From an archaeological perspective it is exciting to see a sense of distinctive artefactual assemblages emerging in the pictures; however, it would be wrong to suggest that these images represented a comprehensive picture of the past. Sam Smiles has commented on the 'iconic simplicity' of Meyrick and Smith's illustrations which enabled them to 'crystallise concepts otherwise amorphously present in historical and antiquarian scholarship'.[112] This can be also applied to earlier images of ancient Celtic warriors, which, above all, made a statement about the status of our ancestors as savages. At the heart of these reconstructions was the general conception of less civilized peoples and the importance of the details lay in their contribution to creating a sense of this primitiveness.

The power and value of the images was that they embodied ideas not explicitly stated in scholarship. While the portraits look as if they were produced for their dramatic pictorial qualities, they reveal how people continued to rationalize the obscurely known past in terms of a singular digestible vision. The stereotype or icon of the ancient warrior was extremely useful as a means of knowing the unknowable. By assembling many small details into one picture the illustrators managed to convince their audience that they were dealing with a coherent whole, and above all, a historical reality. In the antiquarian illustrations we can see how ancestral images have moved from having a few core elements, often represented stylistically, to being full of detail, including costume, weaponry, monuments and artefacts. Despite the 'filling up' of the picture in this way, the basic iconography of primitiveness and of a lower stage of civilization was still at the heart of the image. We can also see how the engravers and authors picked up on visual elements from earlier pictures and just repeated them, suggesting that they were perceived to be true simply because they existed. As discussed in chapter 1, this was one of the most characteristic features of early scientific illustration, where it was common to repeat pictorial elements, often just small, seemingly innocent details. Such details were often included in new images simply for decorative purposes, their integrity as representations of historical fact not being questioned. By the act of repetition pictorial elements soon acquired an iconic status and pictures looked wrong if they not include them.

At a more general level any consideration of antiquarian images of national ancestors should take into account the seventeenth- and eighteenth-century debates concerning the concept of decline. During this time much philosophical discussion was devoted to the topic of the original state of humanity. Primitivist thinking, and the celebration of the simple lifestyle once had, is widely known through the work of Rousseau, but many scholars of the time were stimulated by the voyages of discovery to reflect upon a utopian past. While pictures of distant prehistoric ancestors were not constructed in the specific context of these debates, the pictures of national ancestors served to satisfy curiosity about a more universal prehistory. Furthermore, although the iconography of prehistory was developed in the context of interest in European national ancestries, it is here that we see the primitive become truly heroic.

CHAPTER 5

The Scientific Vision of Prehistory

The rise of the earth sciences in the eighteenth and nineteenth centuries had a profound impact on the perception of human origins. The discovery of a deep geological history and the subsequent dismantling of the biblical chronology fundamentally challenged all previous conceptions of the beginnings of humanity. Indeed, the story of how the age of the earth went from thousands to billions of years is one of the most important stories in the history of science. However, the biblical chronology was such a universal and powerful authority that it could not simply be replaced overnight, and the process by which it was dismantled reveals how scientists sought to harmonize newly discovered data into the traditionally accepted timescale. Integral to this harmonizing process was the contribution made by the new scientific visual languages of palaeontology and geology. As discussed in chapter 1, the new conventions for representing the natural world and its ancient inhabitants marked a significant departure in the history of scientific illustration. Whereas earlier illustrative genres were based on the observation of phenomena, this was based on the interpretation of phenomena in their reconstructed state. Thus it went beyond being a key aid in the description of phenomena to become central in the interpretation of findings. It was in association with the emergence of this visual language of palaeontology and geology that the first scientific images of ancient humans were produced. They were scientific images in the sense that they professed to be non-mythological, non-religious and non-historical, being based on the analysis of scientific phenomena such as fossils, ancient strata and artefacts in depositional contexts. The paradox about the supposedly 'new' scientific images was that they did not supplant previous images, but rather grew out of them.

The images of ancient humans produced from the mid-nineteenth century reveal the profound transformation that took place in the understanding of the earth's formation. However, they also tell us about resistance to the new scientific findings concerning human prehistory. While the concept of ancient beasts living in an incredibly deep past was accepted, the related theory that humans were also truly ancient was not. The palaeontological and geological reconstructions featuring humans had both a scientific and religious content, revealing how scientists were reluctant to disregard the established way of representing human creation. Thus, while the geological and palaeontological images were scientific in the sense that fossil species were represented, they were religious in the sense that our human ancestors were represented in them according to Genesis. The first truly scientific pictures of human antiquity did not appear until later in the nineteenth century when the coexistence of humans and extinct animals was finally accepted. These images were 'truly' scientific in the sense that they were based on discoveries of fossilized human skeletal remains together with animal ones; however, they retained many emblematic or iconographic elements from the surviving traditions of representation. In fact these iconographic elements, familiar to us from classical, early Christian, medieval, Renaissance and antiquarian imagery, continued to be used, either reinforcing strong resistance to the newly proposed theories about the antiquity of humanity, or endorsing them. Despite the persistence of pictorial motifs associated with primitiveness, there were some changes in the iconography of the images which revealed the gradual acceptance of human antiquity as more and more evidence was recovered from carefully excavated sites. However, this was by no means the end of the story.

A second major challenge to established thinking on human creation came when evolutionary theorists like Darwin argued that our species had evolved from ape-like ancestors. It is as a result of this development that we see images of early humans enlisting another illustrative traditions associated with the emergence of comparative anatomy and primatology. Ape iconography, or primate illustration, had existed since the seventeenth century, but until now had not really intersected with the imagery of human creation.[1] With the incorporation of visual elements from ape iconography, human ancestors were completely reconceptualized. The image of Adam and Eve in a woodland grove, which had shaped all western images of human ancestry from the first to the nineteenth century, was finally replaced with a vision of our ancestors as simian-like cave dwellers. The imaginative and often dramatic pictures of ape-like forebears were important because they played a major role in the success of the revolution concerning human origins. The contribution of imagery has been neglected in histories of this intellectual transformation, but it is crucial that we investigate how they facilitated the acceptance of new ideas. By presenting the theory of human descent from the apes in terms of long-established visual traditions of understanding, illustrators performed a vital task. Essentially what they did was make the unbelievable believable.

Important social and technological developments took place in the eighteenth and nineteenth centuries when these transformations in scientific thinking occurred. Of central importance was the rise in the production and consumption of literature. In his recent history of eighteenth-century English culture, John Brewer has documented the rise of a reading public, as evidenced by the establishment of circulating and subscription libraries.[2] He sums up this major change thus: 'books, print and readers were everywhere. Not everyone was a reader, but even those who could not read lived to an unprecedented degree in a culture of print, for the impact of the publishing revolution extended beyond the literature.'[3] Further developments occurred in the nineteenth century, not only in printing technology, but also in publishing practices and in the social, economic and educational contexts. The 1850s saw the decline in the use of the hand press and a rise in electrotyping, which promptly led to an marked increase in both the speed of production and the number of impressions that were made. Another important development was the massive growth in illustrated literature and illustrated magazines, which was connected to the Public Library Act of 1850 and the subsequent increase in working-class literacy. The opening of public libraries and working men's institutes meant that there was a greater market for books. Indeed, the Victorian age was characterized by the rise of literary and scientific societies, mechanics' institutes and museums. Changes in the state education system, such as the Education Act of 1870 and the Act for Compulsory Education of 1876, led to increased child literacy. The Great Exhibition of 1851 also had an impact on the public's desire for knowledge. Furthermore, new economic conditions meant that more people were able to afford books, and the completion of the rail network meant that the distribution of books was far more efficient.[4]

The increased production of illustrated books reflected the growing importance of the visual in education. As Simon Houfe has observed, the 1860s was a time when publishers marketed books on the strength of the pictures alone.[5] New production techniques made illustrations cheaper and more visually appealing. One of the most successful new categories of publication to take advantage of these developments was the popular science text. In chapter 1 the increase in scientific texts for the non-professional was related to developments in book illustration. Key to the success of the new books on geology, biology, anthropology and prehistory was the diverse range of visual aids that were employed to present data and communicate ideas.

Palaeontological illustration and Johann Jakob Scheuchzer's Bible

In the eighteenth century a growing interest in fossils and what they revealed about the earth's history led to some important changes in biblical illustration and the traditional depiction of Genesis. This development is most clearly seen in Johann Jakob Scheuchzer's *Physica Sacra* of 1731, which included scenes of biblical history relating to natural history. This massive work consisted of large folio engravings by the well-known engraver Johann Andreas Pfeffel. A physician from Zurich, Scheuchzer had a great interest in natural history and fossils. He believed that fossils were the result of the Deluge and claimed to have discovered the remains of a man who had witnessed the Flood.[6] For *Physica Sacra*, Scheuchzer instructed Pfeffel to illustrate specimens of extinct species both on their own and in the biblical scenes. Thus, while his series of engravings reflects the general artistic conventions for illustrating biblical scenes, it introduced another important element, which is the inclusion of fossils of extinct species. Detailed illustrations of fossils appear primarily in the highly elaborate border designs that frame the main picture, but they are also included in many of the biblical scenes themselves. In addition, a number of images are devoted solely to illustrating natural history specimens, which are laid out and presented as if in a scientific treatise.

In the engraving of the day of human creation we are presented with a fairly standard image of a naked Adam surrounded by plants and animals (figure 5.1). However, this picture is framed, and indeed almost dominated, by a unique border design, consisting of an array of foetal skeletons representing different stages of growth. There is a strange paradox here: Adam, who has appeared on the earth perfectly formed, contrasts with the sequence of foetal skeletons, which suggest evolution from earlier forms. While the skeletons are not actually fossils, they are rendered in the same style as the many other fossil images, suggesting by association that they are also ancient specimens. Furthermore, the skeletons are depicted in the same manner as anatomical illustrations of the time and, as historians of science have shown, it was common in such illustrations to endow human skeletons with symbolic gestures and stances.[7] The skeletons in Scheuchzer's engraving impart messages that were common to other representations of the time. For instance, the skeleton that is wiping its eye is very similar to the anatomical displays of Fredrik Ruysch, where a similar skeleton is using an injected omentum as a handkerchief.[8] The moral behind this image is embodied in Ruysch's use of the biblical text, that 'Man that is born of woman is of few days, and full of trouble'.[9]

Figure 5.1. 'Homo ex Humo.' Engraving by Johann Andreas Pfeffel for Johann Jakob Scheuchzer's *Physica Sacra*, 1731, pl. XXIII.

Following the day of creation is a picture of Adam and Eve after their expulsion, representing the episode in Genesis where God made coats of skin to clothe them (figure 5.2). Wearing their skins, Adam and Eve are situated in a strange environment with an array of strange creatures, including two hyena-like animals, a decapitated pig with its entrails hanging out and a long-necked animal with horns. Significant are the

Figure 5.2. 'Vestis Corporis Clypeus.' Engraving by Johann Andreas Pfeffel for Johann Jakob Scheuchzer's *Physica Sacra*, 1731, pl. XXXII.

smaller creatures at the feet of Adam and Eve, including the lizard, the armadillo and a tiny dog-like creature, as they add to the exotic menagerie. The skull on the ground is reminiscent of Picardt's illustrations (figure 4.16), and serves to emphasize the primitive almost animal-like existence of these ancestors. The depiction of bones and artefacts, in the form of knives, is also significant in the sense that it conveys an interest in artefacts and in what can be unearthed from the ground. Here, Adam and Eve have become completely transformed into Stone Age people who lead a primitive existence alongside primitive beasts.

Many other scenes in *Physica Sacra* are evocative of prehistory, including scenes of Adam and Eve at an altar, of people working in the fields and of people before the Deluge engaging in their pagan religious practices. A particularly important image is that of Esau the hairy man, who is featured standing alongside Nicolaas Tulp's orang-utang (figure 5.3). In the biblical story Esau, the brother of Jacob, did not get his father Isaac's blessing and was condemned to a life in the wilderness. A hunter who lived outdoors, he represented life without religion. The motivation behind the decision to feature him alongside an ape is hard to ascertain. Perhaps Scheuchzer instructed Pfeffel to portray these figures alongside each other by way of comparison. At this stage the notion that apes were linked to humans was not widely accepted, and certainly not by Scheuchzer, who maintained his commitment to the biblical explanation for the arrival of humans on earth. Perhaps the intention is simply to show that these two different species lived a similar kind of existence in the forest. Another possibility is that Scheuchzer had seen the Tulp image in a number of works and that he appropriated it as an interesting pictorial icon.[10] Finally, the tent-like structures in the background and the wooded landscape evoke a sense of primitive times.

Another important feature of the illustrations for this text is the incorporation of fossils and artefacts in the border designs. For example, pictures of grinding stones frame a scene of a man next to a pillar or altar, half unwrapped mummies surround a scene of a body being dissected, and a sequence of flint arrowheads decorate a picture of a child being circumcised.[11] Interestingly, there is a lack of consistency in the border decorations from the early section of Scheuchzer's Bible, in that fossils were not a feature of all the creation scenes. For instance, in an image preceding the day of human creation, representing the arrival of the quadrupeds, there are no fossils or skeletal illustrations in the main image or border decorations. However, in an image following the day of creation, representing the beginning of the Deluge, the border illustrations include a combination of fossils and an array of artefacts. However, whatever the precise meaning of all the border illustrations and their relation to the main images, their inclusion demonstrates how scientific findings on palaeontology were being incorporated into the iconography of the human past.

The influence of palaeontology in the perception of human antiquity can be seen in other biblical pictures produced early in the nineteenth century. This can be best seen in the work of the English painter and engraver, John Martin. Martin was well known for his dramatic visions

Figure 5.3. 'Esauus Villosus.'
Engraving by Johann Andreas
Pfeffel for Johann Jakob
Scheuchzer's *Physica Sacra*,
1731, pl. LXXXIV.

of vanished civilizations, in particular 'Belshazzar's Feast' of 1821, but is best remembered for his 1825–7 illustrations for Milton's *Paradise Lost* and the Bible, 1831–5. Indeed, this edition of *Paradise Lost* has been described by Gordon Ray as one of the great publishing enterprises of the nineteenth century.[12] While his favoured subjects were scenes from the Bible, Martin was also one of the few artists to work on illustrations of palaeontology and to include palaeontological findings in his works.

Figure 5.4. *Adam and Eve driven out of Paradise*. Mezzotint with etching and drypoint by John Martin, 1824/7.

His first picture of an antediluvian beast, the *Iguanadon*, which was produced for Dr G. Mantell's *Wonders of Geology* of 1834, has been defined as the first scientific illustration of a dinosaur. Illustrations such as this have led to Martin's pictures being seen as genuine attempts to represent the prehistoric world factually.[13] William Feaver states that Martin made prehistory credible with his images.[14] Furthermore, J. Wees argues that at this time to 'suggest a landscape peopled by monsters, in which man was alien, was not only heresy but quite unthinkable to the bulk of the community'.[15] Most significantly, Martin took the radical step of depicting ancient beasts in his painting of 'Adam and Eve driven out of Paradise' (figure 5.4). Martin's pictures of the prehistoric world may have been inspired by his contact with scientists exploring earth's antiquity. While other engravers of this time incorporated scientific knowledge in their work, Martin must be acknowledged for seriously addressing the question of deep time.

Martin also contributed to the iconography of prehistory by making landscape such a central and powerful element in the depiction of

Figure 5.5. *Adam hearing the voice of the Almighty*. Mezzotint with etching by John Martin, 1824/6.

human history. As Michael Campbell observes, Martin created a whole new style never seen before, a 'wild landscape style', characterized by Martin's depiction of caves, forests, mountains and large dramatic skies, all of which contributed to the creation of mood and atmosphere.[16] Unlike other history painters who made the figures the focus of the painting, Martin concentrated on the landscape, 'dwarfing' as William Feaver states, his figures in 'overwhelming schemes of things'.[17] This can be seen primarily in his series of twenty-four images for *Paradise Lost*. Martin's images of Adam and Eve in this series are very antediluvian in the sense that our original ancestors are featured amid caves, forests and rocks. Many other prehistoric elements can also be found. For instance, in 'Adam hearing the voice of Almighty' (figure 5.5), Adam stands in a dark and primeval forest, wearing his primitive garment of leaves; in 'Paradise – Adam and Eve – The Morning Hymn', Adam and Eve come out of a cave to greet the new world; in 'Approach of the Archangel Michael', Adam and Eve look out across a mountainous prehistoric landscape; and in 'Adam reproving Eve', the physical appearance of Adam is almost savage.

As history painters such as John Martin began to bring a distant past to life, scientists were making profound discoveries regarding the depth of that past. In parts of Europe fossils of humans were being found alongside bones of extinct animals. With these scientific discoveries of fossil beasts and fossil ancestors in the same geological context new visions of the past were again created.

Geological iconography and engravings for the texts of Franz Unger and Louis Figuier

The concept that the earth had undergone successive periods of geological change over millions and millions of years was the first major step in the recognition of a deep past. The belief that a succession of different types of extinct creatures had inhabited these periods was the second major step. While scientists accepted that the geological past could be represented in terms of a series of evolving epochs, and that the species of the animal world had evolved from earlier forms, they were hostile to the notion that humans may have lived in some of these ancient landscapes alongside extinct creatures. However, the palaeontological and geological images paved the way for the acceptance that humans were truly ancient by providing a 'real' prehistoric world in which we could envisage our ancestors living. The barren mountains of the monstrous races, the forests of Vitruvius, the idyllic woodland settings of Adam and Eve and the artificial landscapes of antiquarian imagery all lacked authenticity as prehistoric landscapes. Similarly, the animals were either domesticated or monstrous and did not relate to real prehistoric species. With the scientific images of ancient landscapes and extinct beasts, a truly prehistoric setting was created. Studies of rock formation, stratigraphy and the reconstruction of animal skeletons were incorporated into scenes, giving them a depth and providing a vivid sense of the distant prehistoric world.

Geological and palaeontological reconstructions of deep time rarely depicted ancient humans, and when they did include them, they were presented as fully modern Europeans who suddenly appeared at the very last stage of the earth's development. These first ancestors did not inhabit the world when different species of plants and animals existed, and the pictures clearly show that they are the most recent, and, indeed, final addition in the incredibly long history of the earth. An early example is Joseph Kussaweg's pictorial reconstruction in Franz Unger's book *Die Urwelt in ihren verschiedenen Bildungsperioden* (The Primitive World in its Different Periods of Formation) of 1851 (figure 5.6). Entitled 'The Period of the Present World', this picture is the last in a series of fourteen, each of which features a different geological epoch. To the left of the picture is the first 'family', including a male, two females and a child, in a clearing at

Figure 5.6. 'The Period of the Present World.' Illustration by Joseph Kuwasseg for Franz. Unger's *Die Urwelt in ihren verschiedenen Bildungsperioden*, 1851, pl. XIV.

the edge of a forest. In the background some horses are frolicking, signifying that this is the era of the modern world rather than that of the Jurassic. The family or group are surrounded by an array of tropical trees and plants, such as the banana and the palm, all meticulously rendered so as to reveal their distinctive features. Indeed, the emphasis in the picture is predominantly on plant life, reflecting Unger's professional status as a botanist. The landscape conveys a sense of prehistory through its symbolic woodland imagery and the inclusion of exotic plants that are not typical of modern Europe. However, while the figures are naked and lack knowledge of technology or the arts, they are completely modern in appearance. Kussaweg has clearly based his portrayal of the first humans on biblical imagery and the standard iconography of Adam and Eve. Indeed, the tree dominating the picture could be seen to represent the tree of life in the Garden of Eden. While this scene is 'scientific' in a geological sense, it is not based on scientific evidence regarding ancient humans, nor is it related to debates about the coexistence of humans with extinct beasts. As Unger states, 'no historian has yet attained a knowledge of the exact spot of man's origin; thus instead of copying faithfully the appearance of his paradise, we are obliged to invent it'.[18] This biblical vision is then described in emotional terms:

> The loveliest day of creation dawns at length. In a pure and cloudless sky appears the day star, shedding its beams on that earth, which, after so many shocks and revolutions, has reached at last a state of repose. . . . For many ages creative power had been exercised on the production of numerous forms of plants and animals, always

advancing from the simple to the complex, from masses roughly formed to nobler beings. Thousands of creatures were endued with life, all infinitely inferior to the work which was finally accomplished. Man appeared, the noblest creation of an omnipotent Master, whose will it was to vivify in him the thought of the universe. . . . In truth there was no necessity for the marvellous sowing of dragon's teeth to call him into being, for the germ of his life existed from the beginning of time, and awaited for its development only the coming of the appointed hour. Delighted, he contemplates himself as he rises from nature's slumber, and in gazing on the surrounding beauty, he understands the end of his existence.[19]

This biblical vision of human creation is enhanced by the portrayal of the first humans as perfectly formed, without need of weapons to defend themselves or structures to protect them. The primitive technology and rudimentary structures of the Vitruvian illustrations are absent. As Rudwick suggests, this picture presents the history of the earth as 'a long story of the gradual preparation of the world for the coming of humanity'.[20]

Despite the growing evidence of human existence in an era before this last stage of the earth's development, Unger can be forgiven for his depiction of the first humans as recent arrivals. All this was to change, however, when in 1859 incontrovertible evidence for the existence of humans far back in prehistory was finally accepted by the scientific community. Before 1859 there had been many excavations of cave deposits in which human bones had been found in association with the bones of extinct animals and pioneering individuals such as Boucher de Perthes, who worked on the Somme gravels in France, had sought to have the implications of such findings recognized.[21] His claim that humans were, like the extinct beasts, truly ancient was rejected. To overthrow established views on human creation would require a major controlled scientific excavation, overseen by a team of experts in the field. The excavations at Brixham Cave in Torquay, England, finally provided the clinching evidence required to dismantle the received wisdom on humanity's past. This was a time of great excitement in science, when society meetings and public lectures engendered much passion and popular interest. To argue that humans had appeared on the earth when it was in a primitive state and inhabited by primal beasts was, after all, suggesting that humans themselves were primal and less evolved beings. The contribution of visual images was central to this whole revolutionary episode in the history of science. Indeed, the images tell the story of how people resisted and then gradually accepted the most controversial theories regarding their species.

An image produced soon after the findings of 1859 reveals the initial resistance to the concept of human antiquity. In 1863 the science writer

Figure 5.7. 'Appearance of Man.' Illustration by Eduard Riou for Louis Figuier's *La terre avant le déluge*, 1863, fig. 310.

Louis Figuier published his highly successful *La terre avant le Déluge* (The Earth Before the Deluge), which had masterly engravings by Eduard Riou (figure 5.7).[22] The image of human origins is titled 'Appearance of Man' and, like Unger's, appeared at the end of a series of scenes depicting the evolving landscape of the earth. Here the first humans are featured as a naked couple in front of a cave or dark recess. The leafy garment covering the man is reminiscent of many of John Martin's pictures of Adam. The cows, sheep and other domesticated animals reveal that the world has reached its 'civilized' stage and, again like Unger's vision, this illustration clearly supported the theory of creation as opposed to that of human antiquity. As Stephen Jay Gould notes, Figuier 'fudged the contentious issue of human origins and opted for an Edenic scene of a Caucasian family carrying no weapons and surrounded by modern animals'.[23] The woodland setting, which in itself conveys a sense of antiquity, reflects how Riou drew on trends in landscape painting, where scenes of the wilderness and forest sanctuary were popular subjects for representation in garden art and the construction of the picturesque.[24] Aspects of the pastoral and rustic traditions of landscape painting, with their idealized natural settings and bucolic figures, can also be seen.[25] In general, these illustrations reflected the character of mid- to late nineteenth-century book illustrations, in which emphasis was placed on visionary imaginative landscapes.

Depictions such as those presented by Unger and Figuier represent the clash between the emerging science of prehistory and biblical chronology. Despite the growing evidence for human antiquity, palaeontological images with Adam and Eve as the original ancestors continued to be produced in the fast-growing body of popular science books on prehistory. There was a real paradox in the geological and palaeontological images in the sense that the authors referred to work being done on human prehistory but the pictures they used strongly denied its implications. On the one hand the images endorsed the concept of deep time and the general theory of evolution, but on the other they were constrained by the biblical framework. Despite the growing body of evidence proving human coexistence with extinct animals, the popular science texts did not endorse this view in their images. One example that stands out is the engraving by F. Besnier in Camille Flammarion's *Le monde avant la création de l'homme* (The World Before the Creation of Man) of 1886 (figure 5.8). Titled 'The Ascent of Life', this picture conveys the evolution of prehistoric animals through time, culminating in the glorious moment of human creation. It features a swirling sequence or chain of prehistoric animals beginning with sea creatures at the bottom and ending with two Adam and Eve-like figures at the top. This is a schematic rather than narrative image, which aims to show how animal species have evolved from earlier extinct forms. All the species are linked in the sense that they are in physical contact, but there is a space between the primates and the humans. There is thus some ambiguity as to whether the humans, like the other species, have evolved from the creatures below. In the previous chapter of the text the relations between humans and the orang, chimp and gorilla are discussed, but the reconstruction does not endorse a evolutionary link between the species. This picture is important from the perspective of examining the emergence of visual conventions for prehistoric iconography. As we saw with Strutt's historical reconstructions (figures 4.19, 4.20), the convention of artificially combining different types in one landscape was used for didactic purposes. Besnier's engraving developed this convention further by combining abstract or diagrammatic elements with naturalistic elements in order to convey how the creatures of the past looked and the process by which they related to the present.

The acceptance of human antiquity and Louis Figuier's sequence of human evolution

When the scientific community finally accepted the fact that humans were ancient and that our first ancestors had lived alongside extinct beasts, illustrators were faced with a great challenge.[26] How would they depict this fact? Images of ancient humans had been produced for many centuries, so what would be different about the new illustrations based on scientific evidence of human antiquity? Images of our ancestors

Figure 5.8. 'Ascent of Life.' Illustration by F. Besnier for Camille Flammarion's *Le monde avant la création de l'homme*, 1886, fig. 60.

would now have to convey the argument that the first humans lived in times when the environment and animals were very different from the present. Since the landscapes of distant geological times were reconstructed as harsh and wild, and the animals were envisaged as savage and bestial, the humans would have to be changed accordingly. A

Figure 5.9. 'Appearance of Man.' Illustration by Eduard Riou for Louis Figuier's *La terre avant le déluge*, 1867, pl. XXXII.

group of naked modern Europeans without technology or shelter would clearly not survive in such conditions. The newly discovered ancient humans would have to be equipped for this harsh and primitive world. Would Lucretius' vision be resurrected and our ancestors be represented as little different from the beasts they lived alongside? The ancestors would also have to have a different physical appearance. On subjects such as these the scientists themselves did not know very much; thus the illustrators they commissioned to represent their ideas were forced to turn to other sources. Predictably they turned to the images already fixed in their minds. The visual image of primeval cave life, which had enjoyed centuries of representation in book illustration and the visual arts, was consulted in order to fill in the gaps.

One of the first images to present the new theory of human antiquity appeared in a revised edition of Figuier's *The Earth Before the Deluge* (figure 5.9), which was published in 1867. Although the new picture marks a change in the iconography of human creation, it also has links with previous traditions of representing ancestors, other races and mythological figures. The new elements that have been used to convey the scientific vision of prehistory are largely symbolic. These include a crevasse, which serves to separate the humans from animals, wilder vegetation, which suggests we are witnessing another geological epoch, the extinct animals, which are in themselves a symbol of prehistory, the bones lying on the ground, which define our ancestors as hunters, and the depiction of a large social group rather than a nuclear family or couple, which suggests that prehistoric people needed to live in groups in order to survive. In addition there are the familiar emblems or icons of nakedness, cave home, animal skins and clubs. The prominence given to the cave reveals connections with geological imagery, where it had come to symbolize entry into the deep earth.[27] Together the emblematic components of the image comprise a synthetic statement on human antiquity. The only component that remains unchanged is the anatomy of the ancestors, which is still based on heroic or classical models; as Gould states, 'only so many conventions can be challenged at once'.[28] The geological reconstructions on which these are modelled are now changed in both composition and subject. First, our attention is no longer drawn to small figures on the side of the image, conveying how our original ancestors are dominated by the landscape and extinct creatures. Now the figures are full participants in the picture, sharing equal status with the plants and animals. Secondly, the calm serenity of the Edenic scenes has been replaced by a battle with monsters. This theme of combat would subsequently become one of the major subjects chosen for the representation of prehistory, implying that early life was a struggle; also confrontation with beasts was an appealing subject for graphic illustration. Emphasis on this theme saw the Golden Age vision of human origins finally replaced by the evolutionary idea.

Despite providing such a convincing reconstruction of Stone Age life, Figuier remained doubtful about it. On the one hand he diligently outlined the evidence relating to the question of human antiquity, summarizing the excavations of cave deposits in Europe, and recognizing the intellectual revolution confirmed by the work at Brixham Cave. For instance, he stated that from Brixham 'inferences of the greatest interest and significance' can be learned, which are that 'this country was, at one time, inhabited by animals which are now extinct, and of whose existence we have not even a tradition; that man, then ignorant of the use of metal, and little better than the brutes was the contemporary of the animals whose remains were found in the cave'.[29] On the other hand, Figuier remained loyal to the biblical story, discussing, for example, the Asiatic Deluge, where he talks of the opening up of the earth and the creation of human life on the banks of the Euphrates. It appears that in order to ensure the survival of the biblical version of human creation, Figuier still included his original Edenic image of the appearance of humanity (figure 5.7), which he used as the frontispiece of his book. That two such contrasting images could appear in the same book reveals how torn was the state of thought on human origins.

The new vision of prehistory provided by Figuier had many implications. Primary among these was that the imagery of human origins became tied in with other discourses or intellectual contexts. For example, images of ancestors began to reflect the nineteenth-century colonialist and imperialistic interest in other lands. They reveal

European ideas about empire and tie in with the appetite for exotic animals, peoples and landscapes, as seen in the World's Fairs and Expositions. Nineteenth-century ideas and attitudes about the colonies were reflected in the imagery of other races, and of the natural world and its history. This could be clearly seen in the imagery of dinosaurs engaged in combat and conflict. Nicolaas Rupke has summed this up nicely, stating that 'it was as though the geological reconstructions were journeys of discovery into a past as savage and unruly as the contemporary colonies. This picture of savagery enhanced the Victorians' self-image as civilising rulers'.[30] The same argument applies to the images of people fighting wild beasts in prehistoric times, in the sense that they provided a glimpse into times when the Europeans were as primitive as the blacks living in Africa were believed to be.

Once the reality of human antiquity had been accepted, the idea that prehistoric humans had, like prehistoric animals, lived through a series of different epochs was proposed. The conceptualization of human prehistory broken up into successive periods, including ages of stone, bronze and iron, was not new, having originally been proposed by the classical writers. What was different, however, was that prehistorians were now faced with the challenge of explaining how prehistoric life changed over time according to the evidence that was being found. The past, rather than being represented in geological reconstructions as one homogenous scene conveying all of human prehistory, was now portrayed in a sequence of scenes. Rudwick, in discussing the contribution of Figuier's series of images of geological time, has highlighted the significance of the creation of such series for the establishment of the reconstruction genre.[31]

One of the first scientifically based sequences of images suggesting chronological development in human prehistory was produced by Figuier, who had initially been so resistant to the idea of human antiquity. In 1870 he finally succumbed, using the genre he had been so central in creating to produce a comprehensive picture of human evolution in a book wholly devoted to the new subject. *L'homme Primitif* (Primitive Man) consisted of a sequence of thirty engravings depicting the history of human life from the Stone to the Iron Age. Figuier enlisted the services of the artist Emile Bayard, whose style was shaped by the romantic tendencies of historic painting at the time. Within the three main ages Figuier defined various stages, each representing an advance on the former. For instance, the Stone Age was divided up into the epoch of extinct animals (or the great bear and mammoth period), the epoch of migrating animals (or the reindeer period) and the epoch of domesticated animals (or the age of polished stone). It was in the first epoch (of extinct animals) that humans appeared on the earth. These ancestors are described by Figuier as being 'weak and helpless, in the midst of the inclement and wild nature'.[32] He emphasizes

Figure 5.10. 'The Production of Fire.' Illustration by Emile Bayard for Louis Figuier's *L'homme primitif*, 1870, fig. 7.

their miserable state, remarking that, 'however much our pride may suffer by the idea, we must confess that, at the earliest period of his existence, man could have been but little distinguished from the brute'.[33] Despite this our first ancestors are portrayed as fully modern Europeans, their primitiveness being indicated by their fur garments, cave homes and lack of sophisticated weapons. The ancestors of successive periods are equally modern in physical appearance, their status or position in the evolutionary scheme being signified by the type of material culture they use. Indeed, on first glance at Figuier's book one could be forgiven for thinking that the illustrations simply represent different activities undertaken by prehistoric peoples from the same period in the same region.

The first image in Figuier's series, which marks the first step in the march towards progress, shows a man in a shaggy fur making a fire (figure 5.10). Figuier informs us that fire was discovered by accident, clearly recycling the ancient authors' ideas. The next step in human progress was the making of implements, which enabled the prehistoric ancestor to 'repulse the attacks of the ferocious animals which prowled round his retreat and often assailed him'.[34] Thus, no sooner had they discovered fire than they had found themselves engaged in combat with cave bears (figure 5.11). Here primitive hairy men with clubs and hafted axes defend their cave home against a large bear. While archaeological details have been included in this scenario, it differs very little from the traditional iconography of 'man versus beast'. In essence the discoveries have little impact on the illustrations. Following the combat scene is an image of the first potter which is then followed by a scene of a funeral feast based on work done at cave sites by French

Figure 5.11. 'Man in the Great Bear and Mammoth Epoch.' Illustration by Emile Bayard for Louis Figuier's *L'homme primitif*, 1870, fig. 16.

Figure 5.12. 'Funeral Feast during the Great Bear and Mammoth Epoch.' Illustration by Emile Bayard for Louis Figuier's *L'homme primitif*, 1870, fig. 31.

prehistorians (figure 5.12). Figuier describes how this picture was inspired by the discovery of a hearth at the front of the cave at Aurignac – the remains underneath it were excavated by Edouard Lartet. He argues that these remains 'enable us to form some idea of the way in which funeral ceremonies took place among the men of the great bear epoch' and that the 'parents and friends of the defunct accompanied him to his last resting place, after which they assembled together to partake of a feast in front of the tomb soon to be closed on his remains'.[35] This image marks a departure from the traditional scenes of the past in the sense that it introduces a new theme clearly inspired by archaeological evidence. While hearths yielded burnt bones and shells, which were the remains of meals, the idea of a funeral taking place was probably added to give the scene a sense of drama.

The next epoch in the Stone Age, the reindeer period, is introduced with a portrait of a couple outside their cave home (figure 5.13). Their fur garments are not as shaggy as those of their antecedents and their implements have improved. The woman, who has her breast exposed in an erotic manner, is adorned with a bone necklace, suggesting that the people of this era have become concerned with their appearance. Her mate stands proud, equipped with a large bone weapon. Following this are scenes of a rock habitation, feasting, men hunting reindeer and then prehistoric artists, whose implements are clearly based on the studies of bone artefacts by Edouard Lartet and Henry Christy (figure 5.14). This scenario accords with Figuier's claim that the major advance of this epoch was that people 'manufactured somewhat remarkable implements in bone, ivory, and reindeers' horn'.[36] By the third and last epoch of the Stone Age, the age of domesticated animals or polished stone, humans had acquired the skill of polishing stone, as we can see in the first reconstruction of a man alongside a large grinding stone (figure 5.15). This was a great improvement on earlier epochs when stone implements simply consisted of flakes or fragments of stone. Other advances in this period included better fishing methods. Based on the recovery of fishing nets from the Lake of Robenhausen in Switzerland, Figuier's fishing scene shows that the 'art of fishing had arrived in the polished-stone epoch to a very advanced stage of improvement' (figure 5.16).[37] Manufacturing techniques also improved, as we can see in the representation of a workshop for shaping and polishing flints, which was based on work done at Pressigny in France (figure 5.17). Included in this scene is the actual polisher found at the site. Next is a scene of prehistoric breadmaking techniques, which is followed by an image of boat-making technology (figure 5.18). The latter is based on reports of boats found in lacustrine habitations in Ireland and Scotland. Figuier then addresses the theme of human conflict, giving 'a representation of the evidences which have been preserved even to our own days of the earliest means of attack and defence constituting regular war among nations' (figure 5.19).[38] The Stone Age ends with a picture of a tumulus, which was based on the discovery of fortified enclosures in Belgium.

Attention to detail and the link between the latest research findings and the images characterize this important sequence of scenes. Indeed, the editor, in his preface to the English edition, states that the reconstructions 'may seem somewhat fanciful, yet, setting aside the Raffaelesque idealism of their style, it will be found on examination that they are in the main justified by that soundest evidence, the actual discovery of the objects of which they represent the use'.[39] Figuier and Bayard skilfully appropriated traditional models as frameworks for

Figure 5.13. 'Man of the Reindeer Epoch.' Illustration by Emile Bayard for Louis Figuier's *L'homme primitif*, 1870, fig. 39.

Figure 5.14. 'Arts of Drawing and Sculpture during the Reindeer Epoch.' Illustration by Emile Bayard for Louis Figuier's *L'homme primitif*, 1870, fig. 68.

presenting the scientific data, adding current views of gender roles, by which women were stereotyped as nurturers and men as providers. The power of the images lay in their combination of detail, current research findings and dramatic quality. While great emphasis is placed on the site's artefacts that lay at the basis of the images, it was the composition, romantic style and subject matter of the engravings that made them so appealing. Indeed, they can be considered as works of art and situated within the realm of late nineteenth-century history painting. History paintings of the time often comprised natural cave-like settings in which great battles were fought between heroes and wild beasts.

Figure 5.15. 'Man of the Polished-stone Epoch.' Illustration by Emile Bayard for Louis Figuier's *L'homme primitif*, 1870, fig. 76.

Figure 5.16. 'Fishing during the Polished-stone Epoch.' Illustration by Emile Bayard for Louis Figuier's *L'homme primitif*, 1870, fig. 80.

Figure 5.17. 'The earliest Manufacture and Polishing of Flints.' Illustration by Emile Bayard for Louis Figuier's *L'homme primitif*, 1870, fig. 107.

Figure 5.18. 'The earliest Navigators.' Illustration by Emile Bayard for Louis Figuier's *L'homme primitif*, 1870, fig. 126.

Furthermore, Figuier's images not only reflected the Romantic movement, but imported elements from the iconography of chivalry.[40] The 'improvement' in artefacts and garments over time tells us how humans evolved from the simple to the more complex, but even in their simple state these ancient figures are noble and proud. This is most strongly exemplified in the frontispiece engraving, which conveys the romantic ideal of Stone Age life (figure 5.20). Again there is a tension between the message of the images and the arguments presented in the text. While there are many changes in the depiction of material culture, the figures are, from start to finish, fully modern beings. Similarly, while contemporary discoveries were being reflected in these images, they were conveyed in a very general way. The imagery reveals how difficult it was to absorb the full implications of the new discoveries. Despite this, with this series of images Figuier gave depth to the powerful stereotype of 'primitive man', adding new details to an already established canon of representation.

Finally, with *Primitive Man* Figuier secured his status as a leading synthesizer of prehistoric findings. In the first three months after its publication more than 5,000 copies of the book were sold, with an English translation being produced in the same year. Several features of the book may account for its success, including the fact that Figuier had an impartial tone for the time, not being overly religious like others.[41] He was still conservative, however, and while accepting human antiquity, vigorously sought to harmonize it with the biblical narrative. Thus he did display some polemics with his attacks against the 'monkey hypothesis' (see below). Perhaps the major reason that Figuier's book was more successful than those of his competitors was because of his

Figure 5.19. 'The earliest regular Conflicts between Men of the Stone Age; or, the Entrenched Camp of Furfooz.' Illustration by Emile Bayard for Louis Figuier's *L'homme primitif*, 1870, fig. 127.

effective use of a grand narrative of images. This is demonstrated by the fact that so many other science writers quickly adopted this format of explaining new findings in prehistory. Like de Bry's historical reconstructions, Figuier's images became a template for others wishing to illustrate their books on the newly discovered prehistoric past. One example is Henri du Cleuziou's *La création de l'homme et les premiers âges de humanité* (The Creation of Man and the first ages of humanity), published in 1887. Here we are presented with an array of scenes with figures in their cave homes, making tools, hunting animals and engaged in combat with wild beasts, all of which reinforce the narrative-like sequence of scenes.[42] Figure 5.21, which shows a group of naked men being chased and devoured by tigers, is a somewhat less romantic scene than those we have seen before. Rather than intending to summarize the findings from a particular site, or to convey a particular argument, this engraving aims to convey some of the excitement of life in these distant times. Figure 5.22, of a group of figures making stone tools, is less sombre, but is based on the interpretation of stone tool accumulations as workshops and conveys the idea of production in ancient times. A highlight of the series is the image of prehistoric man fighting a cave bear (figure 5.23). Here a man dripping in blood grapples with an enormous bear, competing for the cave behind them. On the ground human skulls have been added to the normal scatter of animal bones, suggesting that cave bears had been the victors in the past. Images such as these were designed to address the key questions of the age. As Camille Flammarion wrote in his introduction to Cleuziou's work, 'How did humanity begin? By what set of processes did primitive man, naked in mind and body, simple, without experience as without weapons, wild and barbarian in the middle of nature, arrive at this state?', and similarly, 'if man is a perfected monkey, by what miracle did this metamorphosis operate?'[43] Such questions revealed the fundamental and profound revolution that was taking place at the time, and the images placed in the text adjoining such questions were clearly an attempt to present some answers. With few data and an atmosphere where nothing seemed certain any more, the images provided enormous comfort. They constituted answers to the big unanswerable questions of the time because they took the few available data and presented them in a framework that made sense. The power of the images in preparing the mind and in paving the way for a real understanding of human antiquity must not be overlooked.

While dramatic images such as these gave life to new theories about the distant world, they clearly drew their inspiration from an established iconography which they married with current trends in the visual arts. The publication of numerous other sequences featuring the lives of Stone Age people did not really result in a major change to the standard

Figure 5.20. 'A Family of the Stone Age.' Illustration by Emile Bayard for Louis Figuier's *L'homme primitif*, 1870, frontispiece.

Figure 5.21. 'They risk their lives with ferocious beasts.' Illustration by E.A. Tilly for Henri du Cleuziou's *La Création de l'homme et les premiers âges de humanité*, 1887, p. 2.

images of the past. The problem seemed to be that while the concept of human antiquity was truly revolutionary, the data themselves lacked impact. As Stoczkowski has argued, the first archaeological remains were too fragmentary to bring about such changes, and thus they became 'props with which one embellished the old conceptions by giving them a semblance of science'.[44] In many ways Figuier had met the challenge of creating an identity or sense of remote prehistory.

Figure 5.22. 'Primitive man at work.' Illustration by E.A. Tilly for Henri du Cleuziou's *La Création de l'homme et les premiers âges de humanité*, 1887, p. 25.

Figure 5.23. 'Man the conqueror of the cave bear.' Illustration by Georges Devy for Henri du Cleuziou's *La Création de l'homme et les premiers âges de humanité*, 1887, p. 193.

However, an even greater challenge came with the realization that our original ancestors may have looked more like apes than the figures in classical Greek sculptures.

Ape-men, missing links, and the portraits of new fossil relatives

Images of human creation underwent a profound transformation when the theory that we evolved from apes was proposed. The idea that our ancient ancestors had not emerged in their final form, but rather had evolved from apes, constituted a dramatically different visualization from that suggested in previous images. When people such as Charles Darwin, Thomas Henry Huxley and Ernst Haeckel argued that humans should be classified in the same order as the apes, the response was one of horror and immediate rejection.[45] Not only was the theory ridiculed, but the scientists themselves became victims of degrading caricatures created by the media. Images, in the form of cartoons, played a vital role in denouncing human evolution, revealing how visual devices were used to address the controversial topic.[46] To accept and then assimilate the idea that humans were ancient was one thing, but to believe that there once existed different species of humans, which were also extinct like the mammoths, was another. Just as images had helped to introduce the idea of human antiquity in a digestible format, they played a similar role in presenting the idea of ape-like missing links.

After the evolutionary thinkers made the suggestion that there were missing links which represented an intermediary stage between human and apes, illustrators started to construct images of simian-like ancestors. Within the space of a decade, prehistoric scenes of our ancestors had gone from presenting images of Adam and Eve in idyllic settings to depicting modern humans living alongside ancient beasts and using prehistoric artefacts. Now they underwent another transformation. The suggestion that our first ancestors were not anatomically modern meant that illustrators had to create an image that blended characteristics of humans and apes. No longer would they restrict themselves to reconstructing ancient landscapes and living conditions; now they could turn to the reconstruction of the physical appearance of our first ancestors.

With the new statement of evolution in 1859 came an interest in the primates, and accordingly ape iconography came to play an important role in the construction of images of our ancestors. Although Greco-Roman writers described and sometimes depicted apes, Arabic philosophers were the first to make a genealogical connection and describe an evolutionary ancestor.[47] In medieval times interest in the question of human relations to the apes was restrained because of the belief that creatures were created in their final form.[48] However, apes and monkeys assumed a highly symbolic role, and in their depiction as sinners, fools and monsters we can see how they were considered aberrant humans rather than potential ancestors. It was in the seventeenth century that a scientific iconography of the apes emerged, revealing how studies in comparative anatomy led to the realization of our close relationship to apes.[49] Subsequent artistic renderings of monkeys in the seventeenth and eighteenth centuries anticipate Darwinian thinking regarding evolution, and the rich iconography of apes from around this time became a major source for prehistoric writers seeking to reconstruct ape-like ancestors.[50] The major new visual elements that were appropriated for prehistoric iconography were anatomical features such as a semi-erect posture, large lips, sloping forehead and hairiness.

Another major source of influence was ethnographic imagery, which as we have already seen played a critical role in the reconstruction of historical ancestors. While antiquarians had used pictures of Virginian Indians to add details to their reconstructions of the ancient Britons, the archaeological tradition treated them as a far more serious resource. Archaeologists used such images to provide information about the appearance of their ancestors and the activities in which they would have been engaged. As the 'customs and manners' of ethnographic peoples became the model according to which ancient human life was understood, illustrations of their lifestyles were transplanted into the Stone Age. In the late nineteenth century illustrators continued the tradition established with the reconstruction of ancient Picts and Britons based on North American Indians, turning also to the images of Africans and Australians in the vast body of illustrated travel accounts. Parallels were being drawn between prehistoric humans and the indigenous peoples thought to be at the bottom of the evolutionary ladder. A large literature on the growth of ethnographic illustration based on scientific voyages in Africa and the Pacific reveals the concern for scientific accuracy in the depiction of morphology.[51] Despite attempts to render facial and bodily features as true to life as possible, artists did not completely dispense with European artistic conventions. Despite this, evolutionists used the pictures of 'savages' in these accounts to imagine what life was like in the past. As with the ape imagery, the illustrators who were faced with the challenge of depicting truly ancient human ancestors appropriated several key elements from ethnographic illustration, including darker skin colour, body shape and emphasized facial features. The images of ancient humans that they produced must be seen in the context of European colonization. It is clear, for instance, that after African colonization prehistoric people were depicted as black or with darker skin.

Figure 5.24. 'Fossil Man.'
Illustration by Pierre Boitard
for his *Études Antédiluviennes.*
Paris avant les hommes, 1861,
cover.

The first scientific images of our ancestors as ape-like savages were used to discredit rather than support the new theory of human evolution. Figuier, who had led the field in illustrating prehistoric life, could not bring himself to accept that our species evolved from an ape-like ancestor. He vigorously rejected the views of those naturalists 'who represent man, at the beginning of the existence of his species, as a sort of ape, of hideous face, degraded mien, and covered with hair, inhabiting caves like the bears and lions, and participating in the brutal instincts of those savage animals'.[52] However, another French science writer and contemporary of Figuier took up the challenge. Pierre Boitard illustrated the theory that humans descended from apes with a gruesome vision of 'Fossil Man' (figure 5.24). Appearing in 1861 as the cover to his series *Études Antédiluviennes. Paris avant les hommes* (Antediluvian studies. Paris Before Men), this picture communicates Boitard's view that this intermediary ancestor was a 'horrible species' with a body that was 'stout, squat and thickly muscular'.[53] The portrait has a strong impact, featuring a hairy naked figure standing at the entrance to his cave holding a weapon. He is black, has ape-like feet and large protruding lips. The picture not only draws on ape and ethnographic iconography, it recycles the age-old imagery of the wildman, with the European appearance being replaced by an African model. Furthermore, the setting and the structure look like the ethnographic pictures of Africans or Australian Aboriginal people standing by their makeshift homes. Despite the fact that Boitard rejected the theory behind the image, he continued to use this picture on the cover of his booklets for the series. It would be reasonable to assume that he chose to retain the picture for the cover because it was so eye-catching and would draw the attention of prospective readers. The impact of the picture clearly lay in its shock value, being an extremely powerful statement on the primitive.

As well as producing his portrait of 'fossil man', Boitard attempted to reconstruct what life was like for these uncivilized ancestors (figure 5.25). His reconstruction of two ape-like figures on a rocky overhang is not successful as a dramatic image, but gains its power simply by being such a radical departure from Figuier's romanticized images. Boitard's new vision is an awkward compilation of motifs and traditional elements. The setting and landscape lack detail and depth, the most 'realistic' element of the picture being the extinct animal on the right, which was frequently depicted in palaeontological iconography.[54] Above all, the figures, which have been rendered in a simplistic, almost schematic style, are not convincing as ancestors. Boitard's illustrations were not of high quality, being characterized by an almost comic element. This can further be seen in the illustrations he did for his survey of 'primitive, semi-civilized and civilized' peoples, where pictures of modern hunters being attacked by wild animals are clearly designed to amuse the reader.[55]

With the link between humans and apes established, scientists now eagerly awaited the discovery of remains of the fossil species that were thought to represent an intermediary stage between humans and apes. The challenge of creating an authentic idea of the physical appearance of ape-like forebears was finally met when fossil evidence of missing links was recognized. Such remains had already been known for some time, but had not been reconstructed as such.[56] The first recognized fossil ancestor was the Neanderthal, whose remains were found in the Neander Valley, Germany in 1856.[57] Soon after, more Neanderthal fossils were found in Belgium.[58] In 1873 a pictorial reconstruction of the Neanderthal was published in *Harper's Weekly* in a brief report on the remains from the Neander Valley (figure 5.26). The image highlights the key features of the specimen, including the large eye ridges, the low

Figure 5.25. 'Anthropic Period; Last Palaeontological Age: Appearance of Man.' Illustration by Pierre Boitard for his *Études Antédiluviennes. Paris avant les hommes*, 1861, facing p. 239.

forehead and the elongated shape of the skull. The article describes how savage this newly discovered ancestor was:

> A more ferocious-looking, gorilla-like human being can hardly be imagined. The savage stands, almost in the attitude of an ape, before his den, where his female companion is seen slumbering, enveloped by shaggy furs. Always ready for attack or defence, he holds in his hand a hatchet of primitive character. . . . A bull's skull and other bones, one of them a split marrow-bone, attest the wild man's success as a hunter. Thus is supposed to have lived the contemporary of the mammoth![59]

Again we have the paradox of ancient humans as uncivilized ape-like creatures, yet powerful hunters. While our heroic ancestor has become recast as a savage brute, he retains his distinguishing attribute as a hunter. The type of life these prehistoric people led is a hard one, reflected in the expression on the male's face and the gesture of

Figure 5.26. 'The Neanderthal Man.' Illustration from *Harper's Weekly*, 1873, p. 617.

hopelessness in the female. Essentially, the vision of primitive life has taken on an edge of realism or hard primitivism.[60]

The depiction of missing links took a new turn when the remains of what was thought to be the first 'true' missing link were found in Java at the end of the century. The German evolutionist Ernst Haeckel had written a number of books in which he referred to a hypothetical missing link called *Pithecanthropus alalus*, or the speechless ape-man.[61] He even described the appearance of this ancestor in detail:

> The form of their skull was probably very long, with slanting teeth; their hair woolly; the colour of their skin dark, of a brownish tint. The hair covering the whole body was probably thicker than in any of the still living human species; their arms comparatively longer and stronger; their legs, on the other hand, knock-kneed, shorter and thinner, with entirely undeveloped calves.[62]

This description was brought to life in a striking engraving published in Henri du Cleuziou's *The Creation of Man and the first ages of humanity* of 1887 (figure 5.27). This image shows a tall male figure walking towards his cave home. He holds a large stick with a simple axe-head attached at the end. While he has a modern physical anatomy, this ancestor is characterized by ape-like features, such as his hairiness, ape-like feet and a woolly coat. These were primarily inspired by ape iconography, but the figure was also modelled on images of Africans, which accounts for the black skin colour and thick lips. This marks a significant departure from Figuier's white

Figure 5.27. 'Problematic reconstruction of *Pithecanthropus* according to Haeckel.' Illustration for Henri du Cleuziou's *La Création de l'homme et les premiers âges de humanité*, 1887, p. 89.

European ancestors, reflecting the extent to which ethnographic peoples came to be regarded as fossil representatives of the past.

Several years later another version of *Pithecanthropus alalus* was produced in connection with the discovery of skeletal remains thought to be those of a real 'missing link'. In 1891 the Dutch anatomist Eugène Dubois

Figure 5.28. *Family of the Ape People.* Painting by Gabriel von Max of 1894, reproduced in Ernst Haeckel's *Natürliche Schöpfungsgeschichte*, 1898, Table XXIX.

unearthed a skull cap, a femur and two teeth from the site of Trinil near Java. While Haeckel argued that the remains were too scanty to confer the status of missing link on the species, this did not prevent artists from reconstructing the ape-man from Java. In 1894 the painter Gabriel von Max brought Haeckel's 'missing link' to life in a painting which he gave to Haeckel on his birthday and which Haeckel reproduced in later editions of his major work *Natürliche Schöpfungsgeschichte* (The History of Creation) (figure 5.28). This dramatic picture features a docile couple with their infant. The male figure clings to a tree, suggesting he cannot stand up unassisted, and the female sits cross-legged on the ground feeding her baby. The male stares vacantly into space, perhaps contemplating his miserable situation, and the female gazes at the viewer, perhaps demanding sympathy for their plight. They both have many ape-like qualities, including the feet, the hairiness and the posture. Without garments, material culture or any form of structure, they appear very vulnerable. What remains interesting is that while Haeckel rejected the Trinil finds, he supported the authenticity of the reconstruction produced by Gabriel von Max. When first presenting the painting, Haeckel reported on the great deal of attention it attracted, and listed four examples of the interpretations made of it.[63] He emphasized Max's thorough knowledge of primate anatomy, stating that this and his extensive collection of skeletal remains enabled him to present a highly plausible interpretation.[64] Later, Haeckel referred to the genius of the artist in creating such an accurate representation.[65] The dramatic appeal of this painting, like Boitard's portrait, resulted in it being reproduced in many other texts on human evolution.[66]

The standard set of images

By the end of the nineteenth century research findings on prehistory were increasingly being translated into visual representations. Scientific images of prehistoric people had become a common feature of popular books on the earth and biological sciences and prehistory. Once illustrators and artists had represented the major theoretical breakthroughs concerning human creation, including human antiquity, the existence of different epochs and evolution from apes, they began to standardize the sequence of images. Figuier had presented the panorama of early prehistory according to a sequence of thirty images; however, this quickly became reduced to a basic set of about five or six images. Subjects were chosen not only because of their importance in the evolution of humanity, but because of their visual appeal and dramatic content. The standard sequence of scenes typically contained hunting, toolmaking, eating rituals, fire, combat with wild beasts and ultimately art. The next step was to associate certain species, such as *Pithecanthropus*, the Neanderthals and Crô-Magnons with these particular behaviours.

An example of a standard sequence of scenes is presented in H.N. Hutchinson's *Prehistoric Man and Beast* of 1896, which was illustrated by Cecil Aldin. Of the ten images in the sequence the first five are devoted to presenting life in the Stone Age. The first image presents combat, with a male defending his cave home from a cave bear, sabre-tooth tiger and hyena (figure 5.29). Following this is a scene of men hunting mammoth (figure 5.30), one of men hunting reindeer (figure 5.31), a feasting scene (figure 5.32) and then finally a gathering in a rock-shelter

Figure 5.29. 'An eviction scene at Wookey Hole, near Wells – Older Stone Age.' Illustration by Cecil Aldin for H.N. Hutchinson's *Prehistoric Man and Beast*, 1896, frontispiece.

Figure 5.30. 'Hunting the mammoth in southern France.' Illustration by Cecil Aldin for H.N. Hutchinson's *Prehistoric Man and Beast*, 1896, pl. II.

Figure 5.31. 'Hunting the reindeer in southern France.' Illustration by Cecil Aldin for H.N. Hutchinson's *Prehistoric Man and Beast*, 1896, pl. III.

(figure 5.33).[67] Like Figuier, Hutchinson draws on the evidence being recovered from cave deposits in Europe and links his images to particular sites that have been excavated. The image of 'Hunters feasting on horse-flesh in southern France' (figure 5.32) is significant because it reveals the extent to which ethnographic data were being used to infer the lifestyle of these Palaeolithic people. The tattoos, the body decoration, the tee-pees and the physical appearance of these ancestors are closely modelled on images of Native American Indians, which were

Figure 5.32. 'Hunters feasting on horse-flesh in southern France.' Illustration by Cecil Aldin for H.N. Hutchinson's *Prehistoric Man and Beast*, 1896, pl. IV.

Figure 5.33. 'Hunters in rock-shelter at night in southern France.' Illustration by Cecil Aldin for H.N. Hutchinson's *Prehistoric Man and Beast*, 1896, pl. V.

not only available in travel accounts, but also featured in the illustrated magazines and newspapers of the time.

Another example of a standard sequence of scenes is presented in Henry R. Knipe's *Nebula to Man* of 1905. After the frontispiece, which presents an Adam and Eve-like couple flanked by two primates, the first portrait presents *Pithecanthropus*, who stands ready for attack outside his cave home (figure 5.34).[68] Next are the Neanderthals who are featured making tools and knawing on bones, based on discoveries in southern Europe and descriptions of the Neanderthals in Huxley's *Man's Place in Nature* (figure 5.35).[69] The third image in the series features a hunting scene which demonstrates evolution in fighting methods (figure 5.36). Finally, representing the ultimate development in our evolution is an image of the Crô-Magnons creating art (figure 5.37). Knipe follows his predecessors in emphasizing the scientific content of his images and thus reinforcing their authenticity, but this was not enough to provide a convincing vision of prehistory.[70] The problem with this series was the variable quality of the illustrations themselves; like Boitard's, they had an almost comic element. The quality of the images in such texts was extremely important and their success, to a large degree, depended on whether the picture worked artistically.

By the late nineteenth century it was common to find pictures of fossil humans in books on the Stone Age. There is no doubt that these were critical in informing readers of the latest findings concerning the evolution of humanity; however, they did not represent a radical departure from that which had gone before. The pictures produced before and after scientific evidence was found maintained a continuity and, as we saw with the antiquarian imagery, the images essentially represented an accumulation of more accurately sourced details. The basic composition of the scenes remained the same, but one could identify more and more artefacts and other scientific elements in the picture. The pictures show how writers and illustrators coped with the revolutionary concepts of human antiquity and human descent from apes by slotting scientific data into visual images. Above all, however, they provided access to an unknowable past.

As with all approaches to depicting the past, there was an underlying social agenda to the images. The recognition of the prehistoric past was taking place at a time when ethnographic peoples were attracting academic interest. The displays of indigenous peoples at world fairs and

Figure 5.34. 'Pithecanthropus.' Illustration by Lancelot Speed for Henry Knipe's *Nebula to Man*, 1905, facing p.165.

Figure 5.35. 'Early Palaeolithic Men.' Illustration by Ernest Bucknall for Henry Knipe's *Nebula to Man*, 1905, facing p. 190.

Figure 5.36. 'Mammoth Hunt.' Illustration by Joseph Smith for Henry Knipe's *Nebula to Man*, 1905, facing p. 195.

Figure 5.37. 'Cave Men (Hunter-Artists).' Illustration by Ernest Bucknall for Henry Knipe's *Nebula to Man*, 1905, facing p. 200.

in exhibitions provided an immediate context for making sense of the past. Such displays revealed how audiences rationalized other continents and peoples through visual means. Colonial representations of other cultures were not explicitly described as views of the prehistoric past, but nevertheless a fundamental connection existed.[71] As with the classical images of foreign peoples, nineteenth-century artists used pictorial conventions to convey physical distance and also to imply historical separation. Thus, the imagery reinforced the belief that white European culture was superior and that people with darker skin were not only less civilized but that they represented an earlier stage of existence.

CHAPTER 6

Popular Presentations

The recognition of a prehistoric past in the mid- to late nineteenth century provided the visual arts, the media and museums with an exciting new subject that had vast scope for graphic representation. The success of the new scientific iconography of human antiquity, as evidenced in the popularity of books such as Figuier's *Primitive Man*, inspired leading artists to add prehistory to their repertoire of subjects. In the late nineteenth century a number of works of art in which human prehistory was the main theme were exhibited at the Salons of Paris. This theme corresponded with a wider interest in portraying national history, where a number of major painters produced scenes of their Gallic heritage.[1] Around the same time the print media began to take an interest in the Stone Age. Seeing reconstructions of earliest times published in a number of popular texts, the editors of illustrated newspapers and magazines recognized the value of such images as a primary means for reporting on archaeological discoveries. An important leader in this area was the *Illustrated London News*, which used reconstructions to convey general information about the prehistoric past, and to introduce new fossil ancestors as their remains were unearthed in various sites around the world. Another group involved in manufacturing images to explain the story of human evolution were the museum and educational publishers. Inspired by the didactic potential of these illustrations, museums began to produce large murals to accompany their exhibits on prehistory and human evolution. A leader in this area was the American Museum of Natural History in New York. Such increased interest in producing images of the past in the various communicative and educational media led to the emergence of a specialist reconstruction industry. Since the 1940s especially, several key individuals have made major contributions to the representation of human evolution and Palaeolithic life. Notable are Maurice Wilson, Zdeněk Burian, Jay Matternes and John Gurche, whose illustrations continue to be recycled in texts and museum exhibits.

The proliferation of images of human evolution reflects the rapid growth of Palaeolithic archaeology as a sub-discipline of archaeology. Over the past century there have been numerous discoveries of great significance, all of which have provided insights into the way in which humans evolved from the apes in Africa and then spread around the world.[2] Many of the major discoveries of fossil hominids have taken place in Africa, by Louis, Mary and Richard Leakey at Olduvai Gorge, Don Johanson at Lake Turkana, and Raymond Dart, Robert Broom and Robert Brain in South Africa. In China the site of Zhoukoudian yielded masses of material relating to the life of *Homo erectus*, and in Europe the systematic excavation of numerous Palaeolithic sites has enabled the reconstruction of what life may have been like for the ancestors of the middle and late Stone Age periods. In addition to the analysis of ancient assemblages of artefacts and animal bones, many new hominids have been identified: the various species of australopithecines, *Homo erectus*, *Homo habilis*, the Neanderthals and archaic modern humans have been added to the family tree. Pictorial reconstructions have charted this escalation and growth in the database, playing a key role in assimilating the new findings into established frameworks of understanding.

The massive increase in the production of illustrations must also be viewed in the context of the growth in publication of educational texts from the 1920s. In England, for example, publishers like Batsford inaugurated series focusing on different periods of the past. *Prehistoric Peeps* and *Everyday Life in . . .* by Marjorie and C.H.B. Quennell were particularly successful, both being characterized by the wealth of scenes of daily life in the past. Such texts were an important addition to educational material in schools, not only because they introduced a new subject to the curriculum, but because they provided an alternative to the predominantly religious literature given to children. Leading reconstruction artists such as Amadée Forestier became involved in producing illustrations for such texts, and numerous other illustrators were similarly commissioned.[3]

Some of the important changes in pictorial reconstructions over the last century have already been documented.[4] However, the work of professional reconstruction artists this century demands a detailed study in its own right, which would shed much light on how we have come to understand human origins. This study will concentrate on some of the key figures involved in creating a flourishing reconstruction industry as an important practical limitation is imposed on any discussion of twentieth-century images by the fact that the artworks produced from 1920 are still in copyright, and thus reproduction of them is an extremely costly venture.[5] Nevertheless, a brief analysis of twentieth-century images demonstrates that the iconic dimension of ancestral imagery has retained its grip on perceptions of the past.

Prehistory painting in the Paris Salons

The emergence of a distinct genre of prehistory painting in France in the 1880s must be seen in the context of rising interest in history painting in Europe from the eighteenth century. An important trend in history painting in the late nineteenth century was that artists began to pay far more attention to archaeological detail in their works. Some artists were even known to conduct research on museum collections for their paintings, so as to ensure the accuracy of the archaeological details they represented.[6] As Graham Reynolds has observed, it was around this time that the 'attempt at archaeological correctness becomes even more pronounced' and that the realization that life in these 'legendary days was of quite a different order from that in the nineteenth century becomes more complete'.[7] History painting of the late nineteenth century also relates to interest in the Orient as an artistic theme, which resulted in paintings of the North African deserts, of the Egyptian pyramids and of the nomads of Algeria being exhibited. Although portraying contemporary times these paintings conveyed a sense of history and appealed to people as glimpses into an ancient way of life. As Hugh Honour has commented, these Orientalist paintings kept 'alive the myth of an unchanging Orient as the antithesis of the dynamically progressive Occident'.[8] Living displays of North African communities at World's Fairs reinforced this interest in foreign exotica as a representation of the past.

Before the discovery of human antiquity, history painters of the nineteenth century tended to present the evolution of human culture in classical terms. While the evolutionary view of Lucretius was rarely favoured above the Hesiodian view of the Golden Age, there were some important exceptions. Notable is James Barry's cycle of six murals on the rise of culture, produced for the Great Room of the Society of Arts in London in 1784. In depicting the progressive stages of human culture Barry aimed to show that happiness depends upon the cultivation of the human faculties. He commented:

> We begin with man in a savage state, full of inconvenience, imperfection and misery; as we follow him through several gradations of culture and happiness, which, after our probationary state here, are finally attended with beatitude or misery.[9]

The first painting in Barry's cycle thus features humans in a state of barbarism. Entitled *Orpheus*, this painting shows savage ancestors on the verge of their transition to a more civilized state (figure 6.1). At the centre is Orpheus, the founder of Grecian theology, who has come to introduce religion, law, philosophy and the arts to the primitive

Figure 6.1. *Orpheus.* Engraving by James Barry, 1791, based on original painting of 1784. Royal Society of Arts, London. The inscription under the etching reads 'Orpheus Instructing a Savage People in Theology and the Arts of Social Life. Sylvestres homine sacer – The Wood-born Race of Men when Orpheus tam'd, From Acorns and from mutual Blood reclaim'd'.

ancestors. On either side of him are people dressed in skins with wild hair and rude implements. Barry describes these listeners as being in a 'state of nature, a state far short of the golden age and happiness some have wisely imagined'.[10] He also explains that he has placed Orpheus in a 'wild and savage country, surrounded by people as savage as their soil . . . most of them armed with clubs, and clad in the spoils of wild beasts, with courage and strength to subdue lions and tigers, but without wisdom and skill to prevent frequent retaliation on themselves and their more feeble offspring'.[11] Clearly, Barry has based his illustration of these ancestral humans on the work of Lucretius, reinforcing the evolutionary vision of a primitive race who lived in caves and woods. More specifically the painting imports prehistoric elements developed in antiquarian imagery. For instance, the male figure on the left with the lion's helmet looks like one of Cluverius' ancient Germans.

149

Figure 6.2. *Cain*. Painting by Fernand Cormon, 1880. Musée d'Orsay, Paris.

By the late nineteenth century, when human antiquity was accepted and the findings of scientists were more widely known, history painters began to provide more detailed views of the evolutionary model. The major artists who exhibited scenes of prehistory included Fernand Cormon, Paul Jamin and Leon-Maxime Faivre.[12] Fernand Cormon was a well-known history painter whose paintings of prehistory were reproduced in many texts on the past. His painting *Cain*, of 1880, constituted a protoype for the genre. Although a representation of a biblical scene, it was clearly informed by work on the Stone Age (figure 6.2). Here Cain is shown wandering in the wilderness as punishment for killing his brother Abel. His desperate expression conveys the difficulties of life in the desolate regions of the earth. Behind him a female figure rides on her litter with the carcasses of bloody beasts. The scene is distinguished by the depiction of people armed with their Stone Age weapons and wearing fur garments. The classic stereotype of the primitive warrior is embodied in the figure on the left, who has a large spear and an animal carcass hanging over his shoulder. Bruce Bernard has commented on the symbolic importance of the axe, stating that it 'indicates that we are in the Stone Age'.[13] This is significant because it demonstrates how items of material culture were used as markers or signifiers; their very presence informs the viewer of the period of prehistory they are witnessing. Cormon created another powerful vision of prehistory in *Le retour e la chasse à l'ours a l'age de la pierre polie* (Return from a bear hunt in the age of polished stone) of

1883 (plate 9). Here a proud warrior lays down his trophy in front of a senior member of the tribe. This old man sits with his stone axe leaning up against his legs. While the axe signifies that we are looking at the Stone Age it also indicates that these people were hunters. The group of onlookers includes women and children, all dressed in skins, with primitive artefacts and tools. They appear to be living in a built-up cave or shelter. Of special importance is the stone polishing block on the right, which is a specific detail taken from prehistoric texts. We have already seen how these polishing blocks became an icon in the engravings for Figuier's *Primitive Man* (figure 5.15). While details such as this gave the scene a mark of authenticity, the impact of the picture is achieved by capturing a dramatic moment in time.

Paul Jamin was another major historical artist who exhibited paintings of prehistory. As well as painting scenes of Gallic warriors, he took a great interest in life in the most distant of times.[14] Jamin was known to have collected artefacts and made models which he used in his reconstructions.[15] While he was respected for his attention to detail, one of the main criticisms of his work was the fantastical element of his scenes.[16] One of Jamin's most successfully exhibited works was *Un Rapt* (The abduction), shown at the Paris Salon in 1888 (figure 6.3). This painting features a naked woman being attacked by a primitive-looking dark-skinned man while another fair-skinned man tries to rescue her. The difference in skin colour between the men is used to distinguish the different races or 'types' living in Europe, with the darker-skinned man appearing more wild and primitive than the more civilized and European-looking one.[17] While the woman's assailant is covered by a fur garment and wears a necklace made from bone, the rescuer has a bone ornament in his hair and a bag hanging from his shoulder. These details help to make the painting appear convincing as a representation of prehistory, but again, it is the drama of the scene which brings this remote era alive. Other paintings by Jamin that were exhibited at the Salon included *Le Mammoth*, shown in 1885, *Un drame à l'âge de la pierre*, shown in 1887, and *Un peintre décorateur à l'âge de la pierre. Le portrait de l'aurochs* shown in 1903.[18] All are characterized by the way in which they capture dramatic moments in the lives of our prehistoric ancestors, with an emphasis on the struggle for survival against the beasts. Also notable is the decorative aspect of the figures, who are adorned with bone necklaces, hair ornaments and fur hats.

A third artist to contribute to the genre of prehistory painting was Leon-Maxime Faivre, who exhibited *Deux Mères* (Two Mothers) at the Salon in 1888 (figure 6.4). Here a young mother shields her children from a cave bear, which, now barely visible, stands inside the cave with her own young. Covered in a fur garment and decorated with bone ornaments, the prehistoric woman fiercely grips her axe, creating a very

Figure 6.3. *Un Rapt à l'âge de la pierre*. Painting by Paul Jamin, 1888. Musée de Beaux Art, Reims.

tense atmosphere. Again, the axe is a critical icon serving to locate the event in time. The bone ornaments were included not only because they added a decorative dimension to the picture, but because bone implements were being found in sites in France and illustrations of them were being published in prehistory texts. While Faivre has used a stock theme from the imagery of prehistory, that of animal–human combat, he has managed to create a greater sense of drama than is

Figure 6.4. *Deux mères*. Painting by Leon-Maxime Faivre, 1888. Musée d'Orsay, Paris.

typically achieved. He accomplishes this not only by capturing the specific or climatic moment of the encounter between the two mothers, but by replacing the stereotype of a man and spear with a mother defending her children.

In these paintings the archaeological details were not as important as the way in which the lives of prehistoric people were sympathetically evoked by the artists. The significance of the representation of prehistory in the visual arts was that the wide popular appeal of such paintings ensured that they, in turn, fed back into the illustrations from which they derived. Furthermore, their influence on the popular media's further development of representations of the prehistoric past was considerable.

The Illustrated London News *and the work of Amadée Forestier*

The print media made a fundamental contribution to the reconstruction enterprise by employing specialist artists to produce reconstructions. This development corresponded with the rise of the illustrated newspapers and magazines in the late nineteenth century. The advent of pictorial journalism in Europe was marked by the first edition of the *Illustrated London News*, a weekly paper, in May 1842.[19] Emphasis was placed on the presentation of accurate visual reports, which was achieved by hiring specialist artists who were sent on location to capture the stories as they occurred.[20] Because the images were central to the success of the paper, illustrators, artists and wood-engravers of experience and high standing were employed.[21] The engaging and dramatic quality of the illustrations meant they were reproduced in many other newspapers and journals of the time. The dominance of the *Illustrated London News* was challenged in the early 1900s when photography started to replace drawings; the half-tone photo-engraving became a feature of popular daily picture-papers such as the *Daily Graphic* and the *Daily Mail*, with which the *Illustrated London News* could not compete.[22] In response to these developments the *Illustrated London News* sought to distinguish itself from the daily picture-papers by producing art-quality engravings and paintings of special events, particularly royal family and historical events. The paper also established a reputation for its interest in scientific developments, particularly archaeological discoveries. The subject of archaeology provided great opportunities for pictorial journalism; foreign lands, treasures and moments of discovery were visually appealing topics. Throughout the late 1800s and early 1900s the *Illustrated London News* played a leading role in introducing the subject of archaeology to the wider public and quickly became recognized as a major international forum for reporting archaeological news from home and abroad.[23] Indeed, there were specialist writers for the archaeology stories, and leading archaeologists of the day regularly wrote for the magazine.[24]

While other illustrated magazines, such as the *Sphere* occasionally featured stories on archaeology, it was the *Illustrated London News* that made a commitment towards reporting the rapid growth in all fields of the discipline of archaeology.[25] While the *Illustrated London News* primarily gained a reputation for reporting discoveries of the archaeology of ancient civilizations, it was also very consistent in its coverage of prehistoric discoveries. In addition to introducing the subject of Assyrian archaeology and reporting on discoveries in Greece, Egypt and South America, the paper also covered important finds relating to the beginnings of prehistoric archaeology. For instance, from

Figure 6.5. 'Modern Man, the Mammoth-slayer: The Briton of 170,000 years ago.' Drawing by Amadée Forestier, *Illustrated London News*, 1911, March, p. 305.

as early as 1861 the readers were informed of the discovery of flint implements and bones of extinct animals by Boucher de Perthes in France. Following this, discoveries of prehistoric remains in Europe were presented on a regular basis.[26] Most stories on archaeology were accompanied by vivid images of objects and excavations in progress, and the *Illustrated London News* also commissioned artists to produce dramatic reconstructions of life in ancient times. The favoured topic for such reconstructions was human evolution. This stemmed not only from the fact that the actual artefacts and structures of this period of prehistory were perceived as visually unappealing, but also from the great curiosity about the appearance of the ancestors being discovered in Africa, Asia and Europe. Vivid portraits of our ancestors soon occupied a prime position in the paper, often on the front cover itself.

A number of illustrators were employed by the *Illustrated London News* to produce reconstruction drawings, but the major figure specializing in this area was the artist Amadée Forestier.[27] Born in Belgium, Forestier came to work for the *Illustrated London News* in 1882 and until 1899 was the special artist who illustrated royal occasions and ceremonial functions. After this he devoted himself entirely to the illustration of archaeology, producing reconstructions of prehistory, pre-classical and classical civilizations, and the Saxon and Medieval periods.[28] Of all of these areas he was most interested in early prehistory and the lives of the fossil ancestors.[29] Indeed, Forestier made a major contribution to the iconography of prehistory with his images of missing links. An analysis of all the reconstructions produced by Forestier warrants a separate study in itself, but a brief discussion of one of his early pictures reveals the impact of his images in presenting the subject of human evolution.

In 1911, as part of its quest to find the oldest European ancestor in Britain and thus establish Britain's central place in the heritage of humankind, the *Illustrated London News* had Forestier present the first British Man (figure 6.5). This image reflected how, after *Pithecanthropus* and the Neanderthals had been introduced as missing links from Asia and France, attention turned to ancestors found in Britain. Based on the discovery of skeletal remains at Galley Hill in an ancient terrace of the Thames at Upminster in Essex, 'The Briton of 170,000 years ago' was portrayed by Forestier as an ancient hunter with a spear in one hand and axe in the other, preparing to kill a mammoth.[30] His hair is tied up, he wears a fur garment and his posture is heroic. We are told that this original Englishman is characterized by his thick neck, elongated skull, a narrow and protruding chest, and legs 'slightly more bent than are those of the Englishman of to-day'.[31] Forestier appears to have been influenced by the romantic images of Gallic warriors and the work of Figuier. Numerous other reconstructions of the early ancestors were produced by Forestier over the next decades, all of which played a key role in presenting new discoveries to an international readership.[32]

The American Museum of Natural History and the work of Charles Knight

Besides the popular press, museums also became involved in manufacturing pictures of prehistory. There was one particular artist who contributed to developing the reconstruction genre within the museum context and that was Charles Knight who worked for Henry Fairfield Osborn at the American Museum of Natural History early this century. His appointment as a specialist in reconstructing extinct species was an important landmark in the history of prehistoric reconstruction and must be considered in the context of the trend towards providing educational displays in American museums at the time.[33]

For Henry Fairfield Osborn, the curator of Vertebrate Palaeontology at the American Museum of Natural History, public education was a priority and in the 1890s he started to use paintings to portray prehistoric animal life.[34] He enlisted the anatomical illustrator Charles Knight to produce pictures of dinosaurs for his publications and as displays in the museum. Knight's paintings played an enormous role in shaping the public conception of dinosaurs.[35] Soon after, he began to produce images of human ancestors, which became equally important in defining the public's understanding of prehistoric life.[36] Indeed, as Charlotte Porter has argued, 'more Americans derived their notions about prehistoric man from the joint efforts of Osborn, Knight, and McGregor than from any other single source'.[37]

It was in association with the discoveries of Palaeolithic rock art in the caves of southern France, Boule's work on the Neanderthals and the Piltdown discoveries that Osborn became interested in palaeoanthropology.[38] After visiting some of the cave sites in France and Spain, Osborn wrote *Men of the Old Stone Age* in 1915, which was to become an enormously influential and popular text on human evolution. The book presents Osborn's argument that modern humans are distinct from the people of the Palaeolithic.[39] His views on human evolution have been shown to reflect his involvement in the eugenics movement and his concern to preserve nature from the contamination of modernization.[40] These political views were translated into two reconstructions of early humans that Knight produced for the book, one being of the Neanderthals and the other of modern humans or Crô-Magnons.[41] The effectiveness of these images, Knight's talent as an illustrator and Osborn's concern for education then led him to commission Knight to produce a series of three murals for the 'Hall of the Age of Man' at the American Museum of Natural History. This display constituted a even greater contribution to the popularization of prehistory than did *Men of the Old Stone Age*. Begun in 1915 and opened in 1924, Knight's murals were the central feature of an exhibition on human evolution, being designed to depict prehistoric humans in association with the ecological features of the Pleistocene period.[42] This pioneering scientific exhibit was, like Osborn's other work, motivated by his political ideas and, as Porter has shown, it tied in with his interest in racial hygiene.[43] However, the exhibition was important for a number of other reasons. Not only was it one of the first major exhibits

Figure 6.6. *The Neanderthal Flint Workers*. Mural painting by Charles R. Knight, 1924, for the American Museum of Natural History, New York.

devoted to human evolution, but, more significantly, it revealed how visual reconstructions had become the primary means of communicating the topic of human evolution to the public. The importance attached to this genre of representation is indicated by the enormous financial investment made to produce the murals. Knight was paid a total of $43,000 for 18,600 squ. ft of panel, much of which Osborn himself paid. To put this in perspective, of the $10,000 budget assigned to the Department of Vertebrate Palaeontology for 1924, $7,000 was earmarked for Knight's murals.[44] Osborn and Knight did research before producing the murals and wrote to many authorities, including Abbé Henri Breuil, in order to obtain their opinions on how the ancestors should be depicted. However, not of all this advice was taken. For instance, Sylvia Czerkas and Donald Glut report how questions arose over the clothing worn by early humans beings; while Knight would have preferred to follow Breuil's suggestion that they remain unclad, he 'acceded to Osborn's request, if for no other reason than modesty, that the cavemen be inoffensively draped in animal skins'.[45]

Osborn and Knight's set of murals showed three stages of human evolution, including the Neanderthals, the Crô-Magnons and the Neolithic period.[46] The first mural, entitled 'The Neanderthal Flint Workers', represents a family group consisting of a grandfather, mother and baby, father with his spear and their two sons, whose daily activities have been interrupted by the appearance of woolly rhinoceroses in the valley below (figure 6.6). All are busy working at the entrance to their home, which is the cave of Le Moustier in southern France. The grandfather is busy working flint, the father stands prepared for action with his flint-tipped spear and one of his two sons is bringing flint up

Figure 6.7. *Crô-Magnon artists.* Mural painting by Charles R. Knight, 1924, for the American Museum of Natural History, New York.

from the lowlands. Knight followed Osborn's instructions that 'each man must be in a pose natural to wild men, without chairs, who are accustomed to damp or stony ground, and therefore squat, or kneel on a rough piece of skin'.[47] Furthermore, the image was produced in line with Osborn's request that the picture contain no evidence of any building structure or features that could suggest an advanced stage of cultural evolution.[48] These ancestors not only lack traits of culture but they look incredibly primitive and clearly promote Osborn's view that Neanderthals were savage brutes with no connection to modern humans. Indeed, Knight claimed that these 'hardy little people led no easy life, yet the tribes lived perhaps for hundreds of years in just such gloomy and inhospitable surroundings'.[49] The argument that they were a side branch in human evolution is primarily communicated by their anatomy and facial features. As Porter notes, their faces have been drawn in profile in order to emphasize their prominent eye ridges and sloping chins.[50]

In the second mural, featuring the Crô-Magnons, a male artist is seen adding the final touches to his depiction of a great beast on the cave wall (figure 6.7). This reconstruction represents ancient life at the cave of Font-de-Gaume at Les Eyzies-de-Tayac, France, reflecting Osborn's view that the cave paintings of southern France represented the birth of modern art. The figure holding a staff appears to be a person of status, perhaps instructing the young artist and passing on cultural traditions. While the anatomy of these artists is distinctly modern compared to that of the Neanderthals, and while these ancestors have more 'superior' material culture, it is the practice of producing art that symbolizes the great distance between the two species. The symbolic meaning of art as an ancient cultural practice is enhanced by Knight's atmospheric setting, which conveys a sense of ritual and mystery.[51] Significant is the omission of women, which was an explicit instruction that Osborn gave to Knight.[52] This omission adds another dimension to the sexual division of labour in reconstructions, introducing the notion that women were not involved in areas of cultural achievement such as the production of art.

The success and impact of Knight's murals is reflected in the fact that the museum was deluged with requests to reproduce the pictures. It was not simply Knight's graphic abilities that led to this success, but the effectiveness by which he communicated messages or ideas about the past. It was at this point that the role of reconstructions as vehicles through which theories could be advanced was fully realized, and there is no doubt that it was this feature that led to the emergence of a whole new generation of specialist reconstruction artists.

The work of Maurice Wilson and Zdeněk Burian

While Forestier and Knight dominated the scene up until the 1930s and '40s, two new artists began to launch their careers in the reconstruction industry. Maurice Wilson and Zdeněk Burian became key figures in publishing illustrations of human evolution. Many other individuals made important contributions to the field, but these two artists were distinguished by their close involvement in prehistory.[53] Not only did they work closely with scientists and acquaint themselves with the relevant discoveries and data, but they also sought to apply anatomical principles to their reconstructions.

Maurice Wilson was an illustrator of natural history who was regularly commissioned to produce work for books and institutions, such as the British Museum of Natural History, from the 1940s until he died in 1982.[54] During this time he produced an enormous number of images of fossil animals and humans, many of which were used in texts on human evolution and continue to be recycled in the texts of today. Much of the appeal of his work lay in his distinctive style, which consisted of using dark outlines with watercolour. Many of his paintings of human ancestors have been assembled in a recent publication entitled *Man's place in evolution* by Peter Andrews and Chris Stringer and an example of his work is presented here in figure 6.8, of the life of *Homo erectus* at the site of Zhoukoudian in China. The picture is based on excavations at this site near Beijing from the 1920s till the 1940s during which hominid skulls, jaws and teeth, bones of deer and rhino,

Figure 6.8. *The Life of Homo erectus at Zhoukoudian, China.* Painting by Maurice Wilson, 1950, British Museum of Natural History, London.

burnt animal bone, stone tools and ash from hearths were all found. The skulls are thought to be the remains of the hunting community who camped in the cave where the meat was also cooked. The animal bones were thought to be the result of ancient butchering practices and to represent the remains of meals. The skull in the foreground may signify that these people were cannibals. It is a classic scene of cave life, where activity centred around the fire and the making of tools is the focus. Like many earlier images, this picture emphasizes the importance of fire in human evolution. The fire in this case was where people gathered to cook and then share their food. The familiar icons of cave, skins, fire and tools have all been used to make sense of an enormous body of empirical data. The composition of the image, with the cave encompassing the activities, provides an atmosphere of homeliness and situates it within our own realm of experience. These ancestors are primitive but they are on the way to becoming like us. In the caption the authors state that it is 'not clear to what extent *Homo erectus* actually cooked in the cave or whether the damaged human skulls found there indicate the practice of cannibalism'.[55]

Zdeněk Burian was a Czech artist who worked closely with Palaeolithic archaeologists to produce illustrations of prehistory from the 1940s until his death in 1981.[56] In terms of style, Burian appears to have been influenced by Knight's illustrations with their wild and decidedly unromantic quality. He is best known for his series of fifty-two illustrations in the enormously popular text, *Prehistoric Man*, which was published in 1960. The introductory section for this text was written by the Professor of Palaeontology, Josef Augusta, who directed Burian's illustrative work, making sure that the archaeological details were correct and that the scenes reflected current interpretations of the major sites discussed. This book is reminiscent of the old nineteenth-century geology books pioneered by Unger, where the panorama of prehistory was explained via images of the changing epochs of time. The series of pictures for this book starts with the ape-like australopithecines, who are situated in a desolate landscape with bones in their hands, and ends with the very European-looking modern humans who are busy tilling the fields. As one turns the pages of the book the long journey from humanity's primitive origins to its civilized state unfolds before us. A comparison between this book and Figuier's *Primitive Man*, produced ninety years earlier, shows how far the discipline of prehistory has come in terms of accumulating such vast amounts of new data. However, there remain strong parallels with the romantic narrative of images created by the French science writer. For instance, interspersed with images of recently discovered ancestors are the familiar images of mammoth-hunting, confrontations with cave bears, stone tool-making, cave life and making art. On the one hand Burian's work differs enormously from Bayard's engravings for Figuier, particularly in the way that he made the early ancestors appear very ape-like. However, on the other hand, it seems that Figuier's book had provided the template for Burian. *Prehistoric Man* was particularly important because it brought many of the European discoveries, which had often been overshadowed by the African ones, to light. Twenty years after this key text was published Burian illustrated another similar book written by Vratislav Mazák, which included many new pictures.[57]

Figure 6.9 presents one of Burian's most famous pictures. Entitled 'The Neanderthal encampment', it has been widely reproduced in texts on human evolution. The picture features a classic Neanderthal family at their 'home' in Europe. While the male figures, equipped with clubs and stone tools, prepare to hunt the animals below, the female figures tend to the fire in their cave shelter. In the left foreground is a selection of stone tools, including a hand-axe, scrapers and points, all of which have been precisely rendered so as to indicate the range of different implements used by the Neanderthals. The large animal skull, which is held by the child, is not only used to inform us that these ancestors were hunters, but is in itself an icon of the Stone Age. The suggestion of communication between members of the group, indicated by a pointing gesture and eye contact, is especially important as it implies that a crucial step has been made in the advance of the hominids. Indeed, it may be this feature that accounts for the claim in the caption that these are the 'first true human beings to appear on the earth'. In the caption we are also told that these ancestors were robustly built, strong, that

Figure 6.9. *The Neanderthal encampment*. Painting by Zdeněk Burian for Josef Augusta and Burian's *Prehistoric Man*, 1960, pl. 8.

their legs were short and bent, that they walked with a shuffle, that they sat on their haunches and that because the upper half of their body leaned forward their balance was maintained by bending their knees. Furthermore, the caption refers to a natural division of labour, where males did the hunting and butchering and women treated the skins, gathered fruit and roots and maintained the fire. While all these aspects are communicated in the image, additional things are also suggested or implied. This brings us to one of the major characteristics of scientific illustrations and, more generally, the power of the image, namely that they can imply things not explicitly stated in the text. For instance, why is the club included when there was no such evidence found at the site? Clearly Burian has simply adopted a core motif in the artistic representation of primitiveness. Furthermore, the figure in the foreground, with its hunched and hairy back, looks like an animal. This depiction suggests the bestiality of this species and in many ways contradicts the claim in the text that these were the first 'true human beings'. There is a paradox within the picture: these are meant to be efficient hunters and tool-makers and thus, by implication, are fit to be our ancestors, yet their slouching posture and docile expressions suggest that they really were a dead end branch of the human lineage. Thus, despite the archaeological details, the crucial ingredients are all still there, including the skins, the large club, the cave and the fire. This image, and others in the book, contributed to the characterization of the Neanderthals as hunch-backed, thick-necked brutes. Although Burian tried to capture the complexity of this species it was impossible for him to escape the stereotype that had already been created and which lay at the heart of his own images.

One feature of both Wilson's and Burian's reconstructions is the way in which their work continues to be recycled to this day. This brings us to the point raised in chapter 1, that images effectively disproved by new information were still used by authors and publishers. While some authors refer to the problems of the interpretations presented in the images, such as the queries raised about cannibalism in Wilson's image, others reprint the old images as if they are still valid. For instance, many of Burian's paintings are reproduced in John Pfeiffer's *The Emergence of Man* of 1978 with captions that simply state they are artistic impressions.[58] The Neanderthal image discussed above is reproduced with a caption explaining that this is a home base in a limestone shelter at the beginning of a rhinoceros hunt.[59] No attempt is made to locate them in time or in relation to their own particular historical context. Burian's images are so powerful and dramatic that they will continue to be used, but they have now become historical documents in themselves and should really be presented as such.

The work of Jay H. Matternes and John Gurche

Following in the footsteps of Knight, Wilson and Burian, two new North American illustrators became the leaders in the field. Jay H. Matternes and John Gurche are two of the more recent professionals who have specialized in reconstructions. The major development evident in their work is that they made a concerted effort to distinguish the genre from art and to define it as a particular class of scientific illustration. Furthermore, these artists produced reconstructions not only to present new evidence and theories as they came to light, but also to show how certain interpretations regarding the behaviour and lifestyle of species had changed.

In the 1960s the American illustrator Jay H. Matternes began to dominate the reconstruction scene. Early examples of his work appeared in the highly successful Time Life series on human evolution, particularly in the volume by F. Clark Howell entitled *Early man*, which was published in 1965. Here Matternes produced illustrations of life as it may have been at the site of Olduvai Gorge in East Africa, creating a particularly striking image of two different species confronting each other.[60] Other illustrations in the book reflect current scientific debates regarding the significance of hunting in human evolution. For example, images of the australopithecines as meat-eaters and as vegetarians are presented alongside each other. Following this Matternes started to produce work for *National Geographic* and for palaeoanthropologists seeking to illustrate their books.[61] One of his most famous paintings for *National Geographic* is of a 'family' of *Australopithecus afarensis* walking across the ash-covered plains of Laetoli.[62] In terms of his work for palaeoanthropologists, the reconstructions he did of 'Lucy' for Don Johanson are particularly important because they made the species so well known.[63] Matternes' work is distinguished by the premium placed on accurate anatomical detail. Like Knight before him, he sculpted models of the hominid species before he produced his paintings and he became well known as an anatomical illustrator who used forensic techniques and set the standard for well-researched representations of hominid anatomy.

A recent set of reconstructions of hominid ancestors was done by Matternes for *National Geographic*.[64] Of key importance is the image of a group of Neanderthals processing the carcass of an ibex and making stone tools.[65] The picture is explained in a detailed caption which informs us that the Neanderthals are preparing their kill at a summer camp in southern France. Immediately noticeable are the different roles accorded to the sexes. Significantly it is a female figure who stands at the centre of the picture with a stone tool in her hand, and another woman stands next to her making some kind of sign language. This is clearly a revised view of Burian's Neanderthal encampment, with females replacing the males as the dominant figures. In the background is a group of males, as opposed to females sitting in the cave. The fire has also been taken from inside the cave and placed outside in the open, making it seem less 'homey'. What is significant about this image is that it conveys some of the new views of human ancestors promoted in the 1980s. Not only was the illustrator concerned to show females as more active participants in the past, he also took pains to show greater interaction between males and the young and to present children as having a role. This was a reaction to some of the inherent biases in reconstructions, which typically depicted women feeding infants or skinning hides and men clubbing mammoths or planning their next hunt. Matternes' paintings of *Australopithecus afarensis* and *Australopithecus africanus*, appearing in the same series of pictures, also convey new or revised ideas about these species. Both images avoid presenting the earliest ancestors living in caves, wielding clubs, fighting cave bears, or sitting around hearths waiting for the hunters to come home.[66] These are important changes that should be acknowledged because they seek to provide alternative visions of the past. The fact that new conceptions of the very beginnings of humankind were being translated into reconstructions reveals how some artists sought to replace entrenched stereotypes. Unfortunately, however, these were in a minority and publishers continued to recycle the familiar and stereotypical images.

John Gurche is an anatomical illustrator who has worked for major magazines and museums since the 1970s. Like Matternes, Gurche has acquired considerable knowledge on anatomy which he brings to his reconstructions, as recently demonstrated in a series of photographs in *National Geographic* showing how he modelled the head of the Ice Man, whose remains were discovered on the border between Austria and Italy in 1991.[67] An early example of his work appears in Johanson and Edey's book *Lucy*, where he presents a reconstruction of an australopithecine being devoured by a leopard in a tree. This is a very important image because it presents the theory that our ancestors were victims of leopards.[68] Like Matternes, Gurche became involved in re-representing species according to new findings and new interpretations of the data.

Plate 10 shows one of Gurche's reconstructions which appeared in Roger Lewin's book, *In the age of mankind*, in 1988. This image of *Australopithecus africanus* challenges stereotypical images of the first ancestors as hunch-back brutes, presenting them with a distinctively human-like glance.[69] The way in which these ancestors are shown confronting the viewer with their gaze has the effect of bringing us right into the picture. Similar challenges are made by placing the female figure in the foreground with the male behind her. They are not in a cave or hunting; it is as if we have come across them by chance strolling across the savannah. This brings us to another critical feature of the reconstruction – its photographic style. The photo-realistic nature of the image enhances the believability of the scenario put before our eyes. Essentially, it makes us feel that we have stepped back into very scene we observe. Despite these changes, some important continuities with the older images remain. For instance, what is the significance of the bone implement being clenched in the male's hand? It is clearly an icon inherited from the past which provides a fundamental connection between past and present images. Again there is a paradox in the image – it is scientific in its inspiration but artistic in its representation. The constant tension between aesthetic and scientific concerns has already been raised in relation to reconstructions, yet one comment is worth making in relation to this figure.[70] Referring to the image, Lewin states that the 'detail and expression around the eyes are the province of the artist, not science . . . yet this final nonscientific touch is necessary to make the connection with the distant past complete'.[71] This point is critical because its acknowledges the fact that pictorial conventions play a fundamental role in the communication of scientific ideas. Thus, while the anatomical details are founded on sound scientific principles and extensive research, it is the way that the eyes are artistically rendered that is the most powerful feature of the image.

The nature of the interaction between Matternes or Gurche and the professional palaeoanthropologists is important because it reveals how the mechanics of producing reconstructions have changed. It is noticeable that the authors of palaeoanthropological works began to verify and authenticate the illustrations, firmly integrating them in their discussions and almost denying their status as artistic work. For instance, in discussing Matternes' work Howell stated that 'to enhance the realism of his charcoal drawings, he first sculpted busts of the figures, adding muscles and skin in clay, combining the latest scientific evidence with a measure of his own intelligent artistic speculation'.[72] Johanson and Edey note that 'Matternes has specialised in this work for twenty years and brings to it a highly refined knowledge of anatomy'.[73] More recently his painstaking and scientifically based methods have been outlined by Boyce Rensberger.[74] The well-researched and intricate nature of John Gurche's work has been similarly emphasized. For instance, Lewin states that he has 'spent years learning the complex facial anatomy of apes and humans by careful dissection'.[75] Like Matternes, Gurche has been photographed in his workshop looking at skulls as if a scientist in a lab.[76] The significance of this is that authors have made a concerted effort to disengage these images from their artistic heritage. Indeed, there is confusion about whether these professional illustrators are scientists or artists. On the one hand they are described as anatomists and on the other as artists.[77]

Through the work of these two professionals new visions of the past have been presented. The early species have been given new roles, no longer so centred on violence and aggression. The earliest ancestors have been recast as scavengers and foragers who lived part of their lives in the trees, as opposed to being hunters with clubs living in caves. In many senses the work of recent professionals such as Matternes and Gurche can be seen as providing revolutionary images, but in many ways it can also seem incredibly familiar. In summary, it is fair to say that the recent imagery has played a fundamental role in introducing new ideas about human evolution, that artists have become ever more precise in their rendering of anatomy and the archaeological details and that the images have become technically more refined and their artistic influences have diminished. Despite this the images are still very formulaic in the way that they assemble and incorporate the age-old iconic elements. The continued use of icons reflects our reliance on visual cues in order to bridge the gap between past and present.

Conclusion

The aim of this study has been to look at the origins of the visual tradition we have developed for understanding the creation of our species. In looking at the iconographic dimension of the imagery and in tracing the genealogy of this iconography, it becomes clear that the question of human origins has been accompanied by a rich iconography with a long heritage. Furthermore, the visual language of human origins has inherited pictorial attributes from a vast range of different visual traditions. Many of these attributes can be described as icons that served symbolic functions relevant to the historical contexts of the time. In essence, however, the function of these icons is to convey primitiveness and the lesser stages of cultural advance. The meaning of these frequently repeated icons thus appears to have been changed very little despite the different historical and intellectual contexts in which they have been used. This trend or characteristic reveals that there is a basic visual vocabulary for explaining human beginnings which has been in existence for thousands of years.

In this book we have seen how artists and illustrators were constructing pictures of human and human-like creatures living a primeval life long before scientific research on human prehistory was conducted. Such scenes resulted not only from an interest in the topic of human creation, but also from a concern with understanding our status as human beings, our identity as different nations and our current situation in the world. Up until the mid-nineteenth century, all these images had been produced without the aid of scientific evidence systematically excavated from archaeological sites. However, the fact that these pre-scientific images were largely hypothetical did little to detract from their effectiveness and impact in explaining human origins. When classical vase painters, medieval illuminators, Renaissance painters and book illustrators, and antiquarians portrayed ancient human life, they were unaware of the vast knowledge of human prehistory that would soon come to light. Yet all the iconographic traditions they created were imbued with ideas about prehistory and human origins, and because these were expressed in such a visually compelling way the scientists of the late nineteenth century did not abandon them. Although new visions of early prehistory were created when the evidence for human antiquity was finally accepted, these visions fitted comfortably within the already established pictorial frameworks.

As stated in the introduction, this study has not been about the history of thinking and research on human origins, but rather it has dealt with the visualization of our creation and early beginnings. The aim has been to demonstrate how the imagery of the past has made its own contribution to defining ancient humanity and that this has not simply been an inconsequential by-product of research. In the classical period we saw how ideas about the past were communicated in the representation of particular mythological figures and other races. Such figures were defined by distinctive visual attributes that were developed as their meaning or status was established. This process involved the selection of a limited number of details or characteristic features which served to symbolize the essence of the figure. It was thus, at this early stage, that key icons for signifying the distant past were established, including the club, the animal skin, nakedness, hairiness and dark skin colour. These attributes effectively became visual symbols that played a critical role in communicating primitiveness and in separating non-Greeks and non-Romans. They signified an outsider or barbarian status and summed up the qualities of a non-civilized existence.

With early Christian and medieval imagery we saw how ideas regarding human origins were visually expressed in biblical iconography and in illustrations of the monstrous races, the wildman of the woods and the classical theories about the past. In biblical iconography we can see how the set of basic icons for communicating a wild and primitive existence were used for presenting particular scenes and figures. Within the secular imagery of the middle ages images of hybrid creatures utilized many of the same icons in order to symbolize their outsider status. While the monstrous races and the wildman of the woods were predominantly imaginary creatures, they were also seen as representations of the prehistoric condition of humanity. While they inherited motifs from classical iconography, some took on a more powerful meaning relating to the past. For example, greater emphasis was placed on hairiness as a symbol of primitiveness, and landscape imagery, particularly that of the forest, became an important signifier of primeval beginnings. In the Renaissance we saw how in the illustrations of classical texts and in paintings visual themes were introduced to communicate the distant past, such as the control of fire and building of huts. In a general sense the visual icons developed in early Christian, medieval and Renaissance times functioned as part of a wider dialogue on how non-Christians were to be defined. This dialogue was inherently visual and relied on symbolic ways of conveying the primitiveness of a pagan existence.

The antiquarian images of ancestors produced from the sixteenth to the early nineteenth century saw the iconography of human origins take on an explicitly historical dimension. In addition to maintaining the classical, early Christian, medieval and Renaissance icons that were used to convey primitiveness, illustrators and artists were inspired by the decorative images in costume books and the imagery of peoples encountered in the New World. The visual stereotype of the naked warrior covered in body decoration became in itself an icon used to evoke a sense of earliest times. The symbolism that was established with this stereotype functioned as part of a wider interest in understanding national origins and, in particular, in defining a pre-Roman barbarian existence.

In the mid- to late nineteenth-century scientific images of human prehistory new scientific facts were communicated using the now well-established icons and artistic conventions. The imagery of prehistory built on this established repertoire of icons by incorporating aspects from ape iconography and ethnographic illustration. While scientists were initially uncomfortable with using the new type of illustration known as the reconstruction drawing, they soon realized its value in understanding their subject. Thus, after first being presented as 'artistic' impressions, reconstructions soon became redefined as 'scientific' illustrations, and were enlisted by professionals as part of a standard repertoire for reporting new findings and presenting their theories. Subsequently, the artistic dimension of the reconstruction was denied and its scientific veracity asserted. Furthermore, ancestors were attributed with different 'grades' of material culture, each of which signified the stage of human evolution they had attained. These often dramatic images of ancient ancestors related to the imperialist context in which they were manufactured, revealing how the characterization of a wild, untamed and primitive past functioned as part of the colonialist and imperialist agenda.

Finally, with the popular presentations of the late nineteenth century and this century, which have featured in paintings, the print media and popular science texts, we see how ever-increasing levels of detail have been added to the images of the past. On one level the incorporation of findings from large-scale research projects on human evolution has resulted in some important changes to the standard iconography. However, on another level, the images have retained an inherent quality of 'sameness'. For instance, while some new themes in the story of the past have been outlined, and while attempts have been made to address biases in the imagery, the familiar icons of cave, fire, simple tools, animal skins, hairiness and dark skin have retained their grip on the imagination. The fact that the more recent images have not appeared to differ from images produced before scientific data were available suggests that we have continued to view the distant past in terms of basic visual concepts inherited from classical times. This reflects how the images have functioned to assist in making the most distant and unimaginable of times accessible to the scientific mind.

It is now time to return to the themes raised in chapter 1, where we looked at three aspects of scientific illustrations and how they functioned within the disciplines they served. First was the role of the images in the practice of science, second was the characteristics and conventions of the images and third was the problematic nature or complexity of their status.

With regard to the role of the imagery in the practice of science, there are four features worth highlighting. First, the images have played a role in creating theories about how humans have evolved. My argument here is that the power of the images lies not in the way that they reflect or represent ideas, but more in the way that they construct those very ideas. They have done this by defining key stages or more precisely by suggesting that humans evolved by acquiring particular behaviours. For instance, a major convention of the images is that they depict frequently repeated themes, such as the discovery of fire, combat with wild beasts, hunting, making stone tools, communal feasting, erecting shelter, burying the dead and creating art. The impact of these themes is reinforced by their constant repetition and the fact that they appear in chronological order, with art, as the pinnacle of human cultural achievement, at the end. A second feature concerning the images' role in scientific practice is the way in which they embody ideas that are not mentioned in the texts they serve to illustrate. For instance, they imply that human evolution has moved in the direction of western civilization while non-westerners maintain primitive traditions from the past. Thirdly, such images are very persuasive, managing to convince us of the plausibility of the scenario being presented. By using familiar settings and projecting elements of our own existence back into the past, these images seem inherently reasonable as interpretations of that past. The fact that they satisfy a basic need for narrative and shared experience is critical to their success, reflecting how the primary function of the imagery is to reassure us of our relationship or connection to the distant past. Related to this is the fourth and final point, which is to note that the images play a harmonizing role by slotting new scientific evidence into familiar frames of reference. As we saw with traditions of zoological and anatomical imagery, the archaeological imagery did not simply replace older images when new data were found, but rather incorporated new into the old pictures.

If we now turn to the characteristics and conventions of the imagery, there are two major points worth highlighting. First is that the practice of importing pictorial motifs from the visual arts often shaped the meaning of the images. The way in which artists have represented the past is as meaningful as the discoveries or ideas they seek to represent. For instance, the way the figures are portrayed tends to shape the meaning of the image more strongly than the illustration of particular artefacts or sites. The use of landscape imagery, although apparently in the background, created an atmosphere and helped to evoke a vivid sense of deep time. Secondly, it is important to recognize the way in which key images were recycled in different contexts. The resistance to update and replace such images reveals the appeal and power they had as visions of the past. The fact that they had been superseded by other images did not appear to concern publishers and writers, who clearly chose to recycle familiar images which comforted the viewer and made him or her feel close to rather than alienated by the past.

The problematic or complex nature of illustrating the past is reflected in the characteristic features of the images. First, they have underlying social and political agendas. For instance, images of earliest times can reflect mythological and religious ideas, concepts of cultural difference, perceptions of national history and notions of empire. The way in which the images have conflated geographical distance with depth in time reflects how foreigners were perceived to be living a lower stage of cultural existence. Furthermore, the visual conventions developed for scenes of human origins reveal how explanations of who we are and where we came from depend on an iconography of negation. This refers to the way in which imagery has been used to define an outsider status or 'otherness'. The visual language of distant time thus continues an age-old tradition of constructing ancestors, non-western peoples, non-Christians and animals in terms of their opposition to *us*. This brings us to the way early life has generally been characterized, and to the underlying duality of primitivism and anti-primitivism in the imagery of human ancestry. The image of the first ancestors living free from the corruption of civilization, or as savages struggling to survive, has remained a persistent theme throughout the ages. While the scientific vision of human beginnings as harsh and troubled has dominated the more recent imagery, the idea that we have regressed from an idyllic state of being was a popular visual theme for centuries. A convention of reconstructions relating to this point is that they gain their meaning by being part of a sequence. Each image is presented as a stage in the narrative of evolution, its position being indicated by the degree of primitiveness conveyed.

Related to such agendas is the issue of accuracy. One of the major conventions of pictorial reconstruction is the way in which different species, events or moments have been combined into a single scene. While the tendency to place many species from different epochs in a single landscape was inherited from palaeontological scenes, it also derived from the earlier antiquarian images in which different peoples were placed in a single scene.

Finally, reconstructions are charaterized by the way in which they utilize a set of icons or attributes to convey ideas about the past. Throughout this book we have seen how the imagery of human origins has relied on icons to simplify, and thus make comprehensible, the representation of distant times. These icons serve to communicate the essence of what it meant to be primitive and, by implication, prehistoric. Included among these icons were the cave, the skin, the club, nakedness, hairiness, dark skin and the rocky or wooded landscape. The cave, a pictorial motif used in the visual arts for centuries, signified beginnings, birth, remoteness, wilderness and an animal existence. In ancestral images the cave can be seen as signifying an early home, but beyond that, it also suggested savagery, as caves were also the home of the wild animals. The skin garment symbolized closeness to nature and, again, the life of animals. It also indicated an absence of cultural skills such as sewing and weaving. Dress has always been used as an indicator of status in art, and in ancestral imagery it was explicitly used to communicate time depth. The club was a rude weapon denoting lack of evolution, wildness, male virility and brutality. Male figures who used clubs were ignorant of chivalric weapons and the military customs of civilized westerners. This primitive weapon communicated a will to survive and defined the figures who used it as hunters. In scientifically inspired reconstructions the club became the hafted tool, the flint-tipped spear and the Stone Age axe. Nakedness symbolized closeness to nature and the lack of knowledge to protect oneself. It was used to signify bestiality and a lower stage of cultural advance. Similarly, hairiness represented an affiliation with the animal world, differentiating humans from the ape-like missing links. In terms of landscape, forests, woods and mountains all took on an iconic status, in order to communicate wilderness and the nature of life outside cities. Beyond these major icons there were other notable emblematic elements of ancestral imagery, such as extinct animals, bones strewn on the cave floor, animal carcasses, artefacts and body decoration.

Of all these characteristics, it is the iconographic dimension of pictorial reconstructions that is the most important. This brings us to the final point concerning the dependence on symbolically recognized icons. It is here that we can see the fundamental paradox of pictorial reconstructions. Images appear to be creative and free of constraint, yet at the same time they serve to confirm and reinforce established ideas. Since the medium of the reconstruction is 'artistic' and the images employ a limited number of iconic elements, it is difficult to formulate alternative viewpoints. It is clear that once we had imagined the past and translated this into imagery, it effectively became what we pictured it to be. Despite this problem, because our images of the most distant forebears satisfy such a fundamental human desire, they will continue to play a major part in our understanding of who we are and where we came from.

Notes

Foreword

1 Unstead 1955.
2 Stoczkowski 1992, 1994.
3 Pagden 1986, 45.
4 Pagden 1986, 44.
5 Clark 1946, 18.
6 Gamble 1993, 16–28.
7 Spencer 1990.
8 Larsson 1992.
9 Unstead 1955, 4.
10 Berger, Welply and Strejan 1987.
11 Frere's letter was dated 22 June 1797.
12 Evans 1897, 527.
13 Evans 1897, 574.
14 *Palaeo* – old, and *lithic* – stone.
15 Max's painting was described by the great authority on *Pithecanthropus*, G.H.R. von Koenigswald as follows: 'It is a very remarkable picture: under a tree a woman with long, lank hair sits cross-legged suckling a child. Beside her stands her husband, fat-bellied and low-browed, his back thickly covered with hair. He looks at the spectator good-naturedly and unintelligently, with the suspicious expression of an inveterate toper. It must have been a very happy marriage: his wife could not contradict him, for neither of them could speak' (1956, 27–8).
16 Hemming 1995; Moser 1993a, 80.
17 Moser and Gamble 1997, 204–5.
18 Moser 1993a.
19 Gifford-Gonzalez 1993.
20 Hurcombe 1995.
21 Hemming 1995.
22 Gifford-Gonzalez 1993, 34.
23 Gifford-Gonzalez 1993, fig. 10.
24 Gifford-Gonzalez 1993, 34.
25 Moser 1992.
26 Stringer and Gamble 1993.
27 H.G. Wells, *The Grisly Folk* (1921); William Golding, *The Inheritors* (1955). But see also how each generation reworks the story: Jean Auel, *The Clan of the Cave Bear* (1980); Isaac Asimov, *The Ugly Little Boy* (1958); and the earliest fictional account of Neanderthals, J.H.Rosny-Aîné, *La Guerre du Feu* (Quest for fire) (1911). These are all discussed by Stringer and Gamble (1993, 31–3).
28 Ward and Stringer 1997. These results show there was probably half a million years of independent evolution of the lines which led to Neanderthals and to modern people. They cannot be the ancestors of modern Europeans.

29   Boule 1911, 1912, 1913.

30   See Hammond 1982 for a full treatment.

31   By one of those curious coincidences that probably mean little but are nonetheless worth a footnote, the two key works of cubism, Picasso's *Demoiselles d'Avignon* (1906–7) and Braque's *Nude* (1907–8), appeared at the same time as the La Chapelle-aux-Saints Neanderthal. Oh, if only *they* had been asked to represent him instead of the two artists steeped in the historical iconography of their craft!

323 Daniel 1962, 57.

Introduction

1   For example, in their recent book on hominid fossil remains, Johanson and Edgar (1996, 21) acknowledge how reconstructions of our ancestors commonly feature on covers of magazines which become the best-selling issues of the year. However, while Don Johanson and other palaeoanthropologists such as Richard Leakey and Roger Lewin have been involved in producing many reconstructions of early hominids, they have been reluctant to discuss the implications of these images for explaining the past. See Leakey 1981; Leakey and Lewin 1977; Lewin 1988. A recent exception to this can be found in Tattersall 1992.

2   Recently some scholars have started to look at the archaeological reconstruction drawing, and they too have challenged the common tendency to ignore and devalue the significance of this type of illustration. For example, in his analysis of reconstructions produced for Dutch schools, Bakker (1990, 31) states, 'It will be seen that preparing a prehistoric or historical school picture involved a great deal more than might be suggested by the patronising smile reserved for children and the simple-minded, which is all that some can spare for this subject.' Also, in his discussion of the process of creating reconstructions, James (1997, 24) refers to the 'iconophobia' among academics, whereby reconstructions are seen as unscholarly pictures that are good for kids but which 'imperil one's academic credibility'.

3   See Moser 1992, 1993a, 1996.

4   Moser and Gamble 1997.

5   Stoczkowski 1994.

6   Stoczkowski 1997, 253.

7   A brief history of museum displays in the form of dioramas has been presented in Moser 1998.

8   Mathews 1993, 11.

9   This argument was originally presented in Moser and Gamble 1997, where images produced since the mid-nineteenth century are the focus of discussion.

10   Stoczkowski 1997, 253.

Chapter 1

1   Notable scholars in the area include James Ackerman (e.g. 1985a, b), Samuel Edgerton (e.g. 1975, 1985, 1991), William Ashworth (e.g. 1984, 1985, 1987) and Martin Kemp (e.g. 1981, 1992). Important edited volumes on art and science in the Renaissance include Shirley and Hoeniger 1985, Ellenius 1985 and Kerseth 1991. Useful articles on the subject include those by De Santillana 1959, Crombie 1980, Topper 1990 and Ellenius and Geus in Mazzolini 1993.

2   On the discovery of linear perspective see Edgerton 1975. On the contribution of leading artists to science see Kemp 1981 on Leonardo da Vinci, and Panofsky 1955 on Albrecht Dürer.

3   Herdeg 1973, 8.

4   General works on the history of scientific illustration include Herdeg 1973, Ford 1992 and Robin 1993.

5   Smith 1992, 39.

6   The authoritative works on the history and impact of printing are Eisenstein 1979, 1983 and Ivins 1969. More recent perspectives on the emergence of printing in Europe are presented in Tyson and Wagonheim's 1986 and Landau and Parshall's 1994 volumes.

7   See Bland's (1958, 1962) comprehensive studies on the history of the illustrated book. See also Febvre and Martin

1976. For late eighteenth- and nineteenth-century developments see Wakeman 1973, Ray 1976, 1982, Daniels 1988 and Houfe 1992.

8   The *Nuremburg Chronicle* by Hartmann Schedel was printed in Germany by Anton Koberger. 645 blocks were repeated to result in a total of 1,809 pictures.

9   For the history of biblical illustration see Strachan 1957 and Berkowitz 1968.

10   Eisenstein (1979) and Ivins (1969) have discussed the poor quality of early engravings and the way in which they were incorrectly inserted in the text and recycled in inappropriate contexts. Eisenstein (1979, 258) states that the early woodcuts in Bibles and scientific books fell short of faithfully duplicating the work of medieval scribes.

11   This was particularly the case with the classics, which were not illustrated until the 1500s because of the humanists' disdain for illustrated books. See Febvre and Martin 1976, 98.

12   Febvre and Martin 1976, 96.

13   Bland 1958, 108.

14   The history of an 'accurate' artistic recording of the New World is presented in Sturtevant 1976. See also Alexander 1976, Cummings *et al* 1976 and Honour 1976, which document the imagery produced in association with the expeditions.

15   See Hulton 1977, 1978, 1984, 1985; Hulton and Quinn 1964.

16   Cited in Ackerman 1985b, 113–15.

17   On early zoological illustration see Lloyd 1971, Knight 1977 and Ashworth 1985.

18   See Kemp 1993, 1996, Schultz 1985.

19   Sawday 1995, 101.

20   A comprehensive selection of these and other early anatomical illustrations is presented in Roberts and Tomlinson 1992.

21   As Robin (1993, 40) notes, artists and illustrators displayed great skill in 'counteracting the gruesomeness of flayed, dissected corpses by setting figures in quasi-normal postures against pleasant landscapes'. Also, Sawday (1995, 103) observes that the flayed and dissected figures were situated in pastoral landscapes of richly furnished chambers 'as though oblivious to the violent reduction to which they had been subjected'.

22   See Winkler and van Helden 1992.

23   See for example Hall 1996, and also Ashworth 1987.

24   This point has been made for zoological imagery by Ashworth (1985), for ethnological imagery by Hulton (1984) and for anatomical imagery by Sawday (1995).

25   Important studies on the imagery in travel accounts from this period include Stafford 1984 and Jacobs 1995.

26   See Rudwick 1972 on the illustration of fossils; and Piggott 1965, 1978, Michell 1982, and Smiles 1994 on the illustration of ancient monuments.

27   The trend of painting the picturesque in nature was especially influential. On the picturesque see Hunt 1976, 1992, Wiebenson 1978, Andrews 1989 and Copley and Garside 1994.

28   For example, Roberts and Tomlinson (1992, 326) note how anatomists reacted to the backgrounds of the illustrations in Albinus' treatise of 1747.

29   On biological illustration see Myers 1990. For a history of palaeontological and geological illustration see Rudwick 1976; on the iconography of geography see Cosgrove and Daniels 1989.

30   These developments are discussed more fully in chapter 5.

31   See Rudwick 1976, 1992, Rupke 1993 and Gould 1989, 1993.

32   Discussions on the role of visual representation in science include Latour 1986, Bastide 1990 and contributions in Lynch and Woolgar 1990, Mazzolini 1993 and Baigrie 1996.

33   Edgerton 1985, 168.

34   Edgerton 1985, 168.

35   See Baigrie 1996, xviii.

36   Studies of the iconography of particular disciplines include Miller 1984 and Ashworth 1987 on physics; Rudwick 1992, Rupke 1993 and Gould 1993 on geology and palaeontology; Knight 1993, 1996 on chemistry; Piggott 1965, 1978, Adkins and Adkins 1989 and Moser 1992 on archaeology.

37   Kemp 1996, 42.

38   Ackerman 1985, 11.

39   Gould 1993, 12.

40   Myers 1990, 235. I have omitted a misplaced 'the' from the original quote.
41   Rupke 1993, 513.
42   Gesner 1551.
43   Tulp 1641. Wittkower (1942, 191) argues that Tulp's inclusion of this image reflects how scientists harmonized new evidence with old ideas.
44   Cited in Roberts and Tomlinson 1992, 326.
45   Many examples of images that have acquired such an iconic status occur in zoological illustration. See Ashworth's 1985 paper on the recycling of key zoological images.
46   See Ackerman 1985b, 120.
47   See Campbell 1988, 209.
48   See for example Theodore de Bry's engravings representing the experiences of Hans Staden among the cannibals of Brazil, which are reproduced in Alexander (1976, 90–121).
49   Sawday 1995, 105.
50   Topper (1996, 266) makes this point in relation to Dürer's illustration of a rhinoceros, which was based on a sketch made in Portugal.
51   Ackerman 1985b, 113.
52   Herdeg 1973, 113.
53   This is a distinctive convention of palaeontological imagery and is discussed by Rudwick 1992 and Gould 1993.
54   This convention of ethnological imagery is noted by Sturtevant (1976, 418).

Chapter 2

1   See Dodds 1973, Sparkes 1989 and Schnapp 1996, 70.
2   Pausanias, *Description of Greece*, I. 35.5–8, II. 10.2, III. 22.9, VIII. 32.5. In II. 10.2 Pausanias refers to a huge bone in Corinth which he claims to be that of a sea-monster.
3   Hesiod, *Works and Days*, 106–201.
4   In the introduction to his translation of Hesiod's *Works and Days* West (1978, 177) argues that this origin myth was Mesopotamian in origin.
5   For instance, in *Protagoras* Plato (320–3) describes how the first mortals were naked, unshod, unbedded and unarmed until they received the gifts of the arts and fire from Prometheus. With the arts humans then discovered speech, built houses, made shoes and clothes and bedding.
6   *Metamorphoses*, I. Ovid simplified the Five Races down to four ages, including the Golden Age, the Silver Age, the Bronze Age and the Iron Age. He describes the first as being one where there was no fear of punishment, no war, no need for laws and where people led a peaceful life gathering berries and acorns.
7   *Georgics*, I, 128–9, 150–4. In his book on agriculture Virgil describes how in the Golden Age no tillers subdued the land and that Ceres was the first to teach men to turn the earth with iron after berries and acorns could no longer feed them.
8   Lucretius, *De rerum natura*, V, 922–33 (Esolen 1995, 185).
9   Ibid., 934–49 (Esolen 1995, 185).
10   Ibid., 950–62 (Esolen 1995, 185–6).
11   Ibid., 963–84 (Esolen 1995, 186).
12   Ibid., 1411–13 (Esolen 1995, 198). Also, as Lovejoy and Boas (1935, 229 note 9) point out, Lucretius does not expand on how the art of making fire came about, which is a primary theme in the other Greek accounts of human evolution. Lucretius does, however, state that lightning brought fire to earth, where it spread to the trees and woods, and that one or the other gave early humans fire.
13   Diodorus Siculus, *Bibliotheca historica*, I, 1.
14   Vitruvius, *De architectura*, II, 2 (Morgan 1960, 38).
15   A comprehensive account of the primitivist and anti-primitivist lines of thought in classical thinking is presented in Lovejoy and Boas 1935.
16   Pausanias, *Description of Greece*, Book VIII, 1, 2.
17   Schama 1995, 26–7.

18 Schnapp 1996, 70. He also notes, 'And just as history remained the art of story-telling, in which critique, and above all the establishment of the sources, was of secondary importance, so, in the case of prehistory, the quality and ingenuity of the reconstruction was the prime objective' (1996, 71–2).

19 Volkommer 1988, 93.

20 Cohen 1994, 697.

21 Arias 1962, 380. He notes how this scene may have been inspired by gigantomachy on the inside of the shield of Athena Parthenos.

22 Henle 1974, 52.

23 Carpenter 1991, 75. He shows how in early scenes giants are simply warriors with no distinguishing characteristics, but then they acquire animal skins and their identity as barbarians is secured.

24 Borgeaud 1988, 178. He has also discussed the symbolism of the cave in relation to Pan (1988, 50).

25 DuBois 1982, 30.

26 Tyrrell 1984, 46.

27 Tyrrell 1984, 55.

28 Stewart 1997, 189.

29 Both Carpenter (1991, 75) and Cohen (1994, 703) discuss how the distinguishing attributes were slow to develop.

30 Romm 1992, 47. I am grateful to John Creighton for recommending this important study to me.

31 A concise account of the classical conceptions of the monstrous races is provided by Wittkower (1942, 159ff).

32 Pliny describes these races in detail in Book 7 of his *Historiae Naturalis*.

33 Sparkes 1997. See also Vercoutter *et al.* 1976.

34 Sparkes (1997, 144) and Vercoutter *et al.* (1976, 152) discuss this image more fully.

35 Sparkes (1997, 149) and Vercoutter *et al.* (1976, 144–5) discuss this image more fully.

36 There is a large literature on this subject in classical studies, e.g. Hall 1989.

Chapter 3

1 Boas 1948. He begins with the second century AD and the work of Theophilus, continuing through the sixth century AD and the work of St Isidore of Seville, and ending with the twelfth-century discussion of the topic as a result of the rediscovery of the classics.

2 Gould 1993, 14.

3 Grabar 1967, 67.

4 A review of iconographic studies in this area can be found in Erffa (1989–95, 482–7). See also Prests' 1981 survey of Garden of Eden imagery and Strachan 1957 and Berkowitz 1968 for surveys of early biblical illustration.

5 Ferrua 1990, 80. For discussion of the clothing of Adam and Eve see references listed by Erffa (1989–95, 491).

6 Ferrua 1990, 159.

7 For example, in the Pantheon Bible of 1125–30 Adam and Eve are featured wearing shaggy furs (Vatican Library, Rome. MS Vat. lat. 12958, folio 4 verso). Another example is in the St Albans Psalter of 1120–35 (St Godehard, Hildesheim, p. 18). Yet another example appears in the Palatine Chapel in Palermo from the late twelfth century.

8 Camille 1995, 250. The image is reproduced on p. 248. Camille's focus in this analysis is on how the labouring imagery conveys aspects of medieval agricultural practice.

9 Examples of St John the Baptist wearing his camel-skin garment include the mosaic of the Baptism scene in the Arian Bapistry, Ravenna, dated to the first half of the sixth century; Domenico Ghirlandaio's *Adoration of the Magi* of 1488 in Spedale degli Innocenti, Florence; Botticelli's *The Virgin and Child* of 1485 in the Staatliche Museen, Berlin; Domenico Veneziano's *St John the Baptist and St Francis* of *c.* 1460 in the Museo dell'Opera, Sta Croce, Florence; Joachim Patenier's *Baptism of Christ, c.* 1500, in the Kunsthistorisches Museum, Vienna; and Piero della Francesca's *Baptism of Christ* of the late fourteenth century in the National Gallery in London. An early example of Elijah wearing a hairy mantle appears in the Via Latina Catacombs.

10 I am grateful to Frances Flatman for pointing out the ambiguous status of both cities and wilderness in the Christian tradition.

11 An example of Esau depicted as a hairy man is Giotto's painting of Isaac blessing Jacob in the Upper Church of St Francis, Assisi, *c.* early fourteenth century. Another image of Esau is discussed in chapter 5, figure 5.3.

12 Three copies of this manuscript are in existence, including one from around 1000 in the British Library (Cotton Ms. Vitellius A.xv), one from the eleventh century in the British Library (Cotton Ms. Tiberius B.v, vol.i) and one from the twelfth century in the Bodleian Library (Ms. Bodley 614). The images in the second copy are by far the best in quality and thus the following discussion is based on the Cotton Tiberius Ms.

13 James (1929, vii) believes the Tiberius Ms to have an ancient and royal pedigree. He has attempted to locate the sources of the text, referring to a ninth-century letter by Fermes to the Emperor Hadrian, which appears to be a version of a Greek original. Fermes was a traveller who spoke of capturing specimens of animals and men to send to Rome. While his letter constitutes a great part of the *Marvels* text, it does not contain all of it. The manuscript is thus not a homogenous book, but rather, as James states (1929, 11), 'a compilation, of which the principal ingredient is a text of Fermes'. In addition to Fermes the other sources for the *Marvels* include the Pentinence of James and Mambres, Isidore and folk tales.

14 Dodwell 1993, 112.

15 Wittkower (1942, 176) presents a range of evidence to make this case, particularly the maps of the world.

16 Husband 1980, 40.

17 Campbell 1988, 72. She cites, for example, the visual representations of dogs' heads which remained constant throughout centuries of stylistic change because the bare minimum of features necessary for definition were used. Once these features had been sketched the image of the dog head was evoked to the limits of its usable significance.

18 Wittkower 1942; Friedman 1981. See also Campbell 1988 who in chapter 2 examines the place of the monstrous races in medieval theological discourse.

19 See Wittkower 1977 for a discussion of the imagery in the Marco Polo manuscripts and *Mandeville's Travels*.

20 Friedman 1981, 207.

21 Also, as James (1929, 25) has noted, one of the major characteristics of the literature and imagery of the *Marvels* is that 'one writer certifieth another', and that from the *Odyssey* through to medieval writings a mass of literary borrowing took place.

22 Campbell 1988, 140.

23 Wittkower 1942, 159, 192.

24 Husband (1980, 2) notes that the 'universal attribute of the wild man is a large club, or occasionally an uprooted tree'.

25 Berheimer 1970, 10.

26 Husband 1980, 44.

27 Friedman 1981, 31.

28 Friedman 1981, 33. Paradoxically, wildmen were a common feature of heraldic devices such as shields.

29 Ring 1949, 241.

30 There is also a connection between the wildman and Christian hermits, who lived apart from the corrupting influences of society.

31 Berkowitz 1968, xviii.

32 Bland 1962, 17.

33 Ferguson 1993.

34 Illustrated editions of *Metamorphoses* appeared as early as 1497. See Bland 1958 for reference to some of these editions.

35 Million and Lampugnani 1994, 75.

36 Thomas 1975, 172–3.

37 For example, such a structure appears in De Bry's image of Adam and Eve on the title page of his *America*.

38 For instance, they appear in ethnographic imagery and anatomical illustration. An example of the former is Andre Thevet's illustrations of Brazilian Indians, referred to in the next chapter. An example of the latter is Juan de Valverde's anatomical treatise *Historia de la composición del cuerpo humano* of 1556.

39 As Schnapp (1996, 68) states, illustrations for this text 'provided the occasion for an iconography of the discovery of the arts which threw off medieval traditions'.

40 Gombrich 1972.

41 Friedländer and Rosenberg 1978, 121.

42 Panofsky 1962.

43 Fermor 1993, 63. She argues that the different phases of evolution are not as clearly distinguished in the series as one might expect in a cycle on the progress of civilization.

44 Boas (1948, 59) notes how these primitive garments were called 'campestria', which was derived from the custom of youths, who used to exercise naked in the athletic field, to cover their genitals.

45 *The Battle of San Romano* is in the National Gallery, London. Uccello presented similar figures in shortening in his painting of *The Flood and the Retreat of the Waters*, *c.* 1447, in Santa Maria Novella, Chiostro verde, Florence.

46 *Christo Scorto* is in Brera, Milan. Since this painting was found in Mantegna's studio after his death in 1506, it may not have been known by Piero.

47 *c.*1515–20. The John and Mable Ringling Museum of Art, Sarasoto.

48 Pollaiuolo's engraving can be seen in the British Museum, London.

49 Fermor (1993, 74) has also referred to the correlation between Lucretius' scheme and the details of this painting.

50 See Lloyd (1971), who documents the representation of African animals in the art of this period.

51 Ritterbush 1985, 156.

52 The giraffe was drawn after one came in a shipment of rare animals that the Egyptian Sultan sent to Lorenzo de' Medici of Florence in 1487. Lloyd (1971, 49) shows how this giraffe was painted by several artists.

53 Fermor 1993, 78. Rykwert (1981, 113) also says that fire is a prominent feature of the paintings.

54 Panofsky 1962, 58. Bernheimer (1970, 118) also stated that di Cosimo treated primitive life as a reality.

55 For example, Panofsky (1962, 67) states, 'primitive life is not transfigured in a spirit of Utopian sentimentality, as is the case with the poetic and pictorial evocations of 'Arcadia', it is re-enacted with the utmost realism and concreteness'. In addition, Fermor (1993, 74) states that the representation of early human life in the first two paintings 'is rendered with almost scientific interest and precision'.

56 Ritterbush 1985, 156.

Chapter 4

1 Piggott 1975, 1976, 1989; Smiles 1994.

2 Hulton 1977, 1978, 1984, 1985; and Hulton and Quinn 1964.

3 For a fuller discussion of the climate of thought regarding British antiquities in the sixteenth and seventeenth centuries, see Piggott's work, Kendrick 1950, Mendyk 1989.

4 Haskell 1993.

5 Eisenstein 1979, 257–8.

6 The history of 'scientific' or accurate images produced in association with voyages to the New World has been outlined by Sturtevant 1976.

7 For biographical information on de Heere see Cust 1894 and Yates 1959.

8 Heere 1577.

9 Strong 1984. See also Hollander 1993, who has looked at how costume was used in Renaissance pageants to indicate past time.

10 Strong 1984, 106. Another example was the 'Fontainebleau' festival of 1564, where figures in boats were dressed in Turkish costume and the defenders of the island were dressed as North Americans.

11 For a reproduction of this tapestry see Yates 1959 pl. 2.

12 Yates 1959, 13.

13 Morgan 1997. In another study of the representation of Ireland in the visual arts, Cullen (1997, 8–9) has reproduced early woodcuts of the 'Wilde Irish' by John Derricke, which were based on earlier woodcuts by Hans Holbein the Younger.

14 Morgan 1997, 20.

15 See McClintock 1950 for a history of the imagery of the Irish and Scottish in the 1500s and 1600s.

16 Heere 1573–5. A reproduction of the painting is in Chotzen and Draak's 1937 study, chapter 6, pl. LIII.

17 While some have assumed that De Heere's illustrations reflect the influence of ethnological images, I agree with Piggott (1989, 75) that De Heere's pictures show no such influence, and that all the details, including the body paint, the shields and the swords come from classical sources.

18 Alexander 1976, 8. As Hulton (1985, 20) has already shown, Le Moyne did not display the same amount of

scientific accuracy as White in his drawings. However, this can be explained by the fact that the colony established by his expedition came to a violent end and that he therefore had to complete his field sketches when back in England.

19 Hulton (1977, 10) states that there was an exchange of ideas between the two artists. He then suggests that because White had access to Le Moyne's work it is probable that he used it or copied it (1977, 80). In another publication Hulton (1978, 214) states that there was a degree of mutual indebtedness between the two artists.

20 Morgan 1997, 20.

21 This consisted of eighteen watercolours, which were finished in England based on original field sketches made in 1584, 1585–6, 1587.

22 These pictures are reproduced in Hulton 1984, pls 63 and 64. White probably sailed with Frobisher in the 1570s.

23 Hulton 1984, 20.

24 Hulton 1985, 23.

25 A representation of this costume appears in the Valois Tapestry known as 'Fontainebleau'. See Yates 1959, pl. 1 for a reproduction.

26 This is evidenced by the title page of Speed's *Historie of Great Britain*, as noted by Piggott 1989, 82.

27 For an example of such an Indian, see Hulton 1984, pl. 48.

28 Hulton and Quinn 1964, 148.

29 This picture has been reproduced in Hulton 1984, 78.

30 Piggott (1989, 76) asserts that the old English chronicle was actually Scottish because of the focus on Picts and the Scottish origin of the archaeological details.

31 Hulton and Quinn 1964, 10. They then go on to discuss the many sources of inspiration upon which White drew when free of the restrictions of recording from the life.

32 Hulton 1985, 23–4.

33 Hulton (1977, 15) describes De Bry as a 'reliable interpreter of this new kind of ethnic and natural historical material'.

34 Hulton and Quinn 1964, 10.

35 The Virginian expedition had already been published in 1588 by Thomas Hariot under the title *A briefe and true report of the New Found Land of Virginia*. The first part of de Bry's *America* series, also known as *The Grand Voyages*, was published in 1590 in French, English, German and Latin. Part II was based on the French expedition to Florida and was published in 1591 in German and Latin.

36 Alexander (1976, 9) states that Hakluyt sought vindication for the discredited English colony in Virginia.

37 Alexander 1976, 10.

38 I am grateful to Stephanie Pratt for making this important observation.

39 Stafford 1984, 503. The title page of de Bry's *America* has Adam and Eve standing next to the tree of knowledge.

40 While Le Moyne had included a background to his painting, White had not. The complete set of engravings with their original captions has been reproduced in Hulton 1984. The set of engravings featuring ancient Picts and Britons has been reproduced in Piggott 1989 and Smiles 1994.

41 Modernized spelling has been used here as de Bry did not have a good command of English and the caption is difficult to interpret. For the original text see the reproduced caption in Hulton 1984, 131.

42 See Pratt (1989, 18), who outlines how de Bry constructed an iconic type: 'something was present in the manner in which de Bry had devised his subjects and in their containment in a packaged design which helped to encase the idea of the Indian within a familiar and Eurocentric viewpoint'. She argues that it was his synthesis of disparate material into a coherent whole that resulted in the creation of a unified vision of American Indian culture.

43 Pratt 1989, 24.

44 Piggott 1989, 76, 85.

45 Kendrick 1950, 123.

46 Pratt 1989 documents the recycling of this iconic type in illustrations and the visual arts.

47 See Smiles 1994, who traces how the visual arts constructed an image of the ancient Britons over the eighteenth and nineteenth centuries. See also Champion 1997, who looks at images of Gallic warriors from the mid- to late nineteenth century. The image of the ancient warrior is a legacy in Iron Age studies which archaeological evidence has helped challenge.

48 There were images prior to de Bry's that claimed to have such accuracy but these were not primary field sketches. Sturtevant (1976, 420) lists the illustrations before de Bry which demonstrated some elements of accuracy. Pratt (1989, 15–16) emphasizes how de Bry's publication had an authenticity other publications did not have because it was based on original sketches.

49 See Ashworth 1985, who shows how a number of key zoological icons were repeatedly reproduced.

50 Smiles 1994, 129.

51 These appear in chapter VII, which is entitled 'The Portraitures of the Ancient Britaines, of their nakedness, painting and figuring their bodies'. The figures are on pp.180–1 (2nd edition, 1623).

52 Speed 1623, 179.

53 Speed 1623, 179.

54 A recent reproduction of this image appears in the illustration section at the beginning of Mendyk 1989.

55 Sammes 1676, 113.

56 Sammes 1676, 111.

57 Sammes 1676, 116.

58 Sammes 1676, 117.

59 Sammes 1676, 118

60 The reconstruction appears on p. 101 and is discussed more fully by Smiles (1994) in his comprehensive treatment of Bardic and Druidic imagery.

61 Daniel 1612, 5.

62 As Piggott (1989, 74) notes, what is important is that the paintings of White were seen and commented on by Camden.

63 In the title page to the 1607 edition of Camden's *Britannia*, two naked Britons are featured; however, these do not have the Indian elements seen in Speed's illustrations. For a reproduction of Camden's title page see Mendyk 1989, frontispiece.

64 Lafitau 1724, Pt 3, tom. 2, 4.

65 Sturtevant (1976, 417–18) lists twelve distorting elements in ethnological illustrations. He notes that it was common to use European details when American ones were not known, and that de Bry did this when he included French or Belgian hoes and pack baskets in his pictures of the Florida Indians.

66 The production of artistic representations that were scientific was a very slow-developing practice. Hulton (1985, 31) emphasizes how slow scientific realism was in asserting itself in the face of tradition. Sturtevant (1976, 419) states that the human form was not depicted realistically until the seventeenth century, the first example being of Brazilian Indians in 1641–3 by Albert Eckhout. Also, Grafton (1992, 126) discusses the slow process of overthrowing classical authority.

67 Grafton 1992, 157.

68 See Partsch 1891 for a review of his career and publications.

69 Tacitus' ideas were central to the search for a national German identity because he had highlighted the virtues of their primitive existence, contrasting them to the evil and corrupt life in Rome.

70 The problems with this theory are subsequently outlined by Paartsch (1891), who argues that Cluverius' selection of sources is bad.

71 Tacitus, *Germania* 16, 114.

72 Tacitus, *Germania*, 16.

73 Tacitus, *Germania*, 20.

74 Schama 1995, 98.

75 This can be most clearly seen in the portrait of Paracoussi King of the Rio de la Plata, which is reproduced in Sturtevant 1976, fig. 26.

76 See map of Brazil from 1555 reproduced in Sturtevant 1976, fig. 17.

77 See Boorsch 1976 on the display of American Indians in festival presentations in Europe around this time. See also Hodgson 1964, chapter IV and Foreman 1943 on live displays of American Indians in Europe.

78 Schama (1995, 101) suggests that the images undercut Cluverius' criticism by playing up the austere dignity of warriors and primitive families.

79 See Ferguson 1993 on Renaissance use of anti-primitivist models to make sense of national origins.

80 Bakker 1990, 39.

81 I am grateful to Sandra Langereis for this biographical information on Picardt.

82 Kircher 1665, 56.

83 See Cohn (1996, 44–6), who refers to the impact of Kircher's work in the scientific world. For another perspective see Stafford (1984, 15), who refers to Kircher as an unorthodox scholar who investigated strange and exotic cultures.

84 For a reproduction of this illustration see Piggott (1978, 14–15).

85 Michell 1982, 43.

86 The illustrations from these voyages has been reproduced in Alexander 1976. See especially pp.180–1, for figures similar to Picardt's. Among the many illustrations of machinery, geological formations, crystals and maps in this book, Kircher presents a selection of giants based on the discovery of large bones of prehistoric animals.

87 One important example is Du Choul's *Discours sur la castramentation* . . . of 1557, which used images as a major source for outlining aspects of Roman history. In addition to illustrations of medallions and individual figures, it presented scenes of Roman warriors and workers.

88 Haskell 1993, 292–5.

89 Henry (1771, vi) challenges the ideas that these topics are unworthy of a place in history. He also notes that the subjects of manners, customs, dress and diets have been completely neglected in historical accounts (1771, ix). Strutt's chapter outline is very similar to Henry's, with sections on civil and military history, religion and government being followed by a dissertation on manners and customs. An earlier model for this structure was Sammes *Britannia antiqua illustrata* of 1676, in which a chapter is devoted to the 'Customs and manners of the Britains: their laws and government'.

90 The dress of an ancient Briton appears on p. 177. Jefferys was a geographer who had produced maps for the voyages to America. His illustrations of costume represent an extensive collection of different cultural traditions, totalling 240 illustrations in the first and second volumes alone. For a comprehensive account of Camden and Stukeley's topographical studies see Piggott 1976, chapter III, 1985, 1989.

91 For a comprehensive account of Camden and Stukeley's topographical studies see Piggott 1976, chapter 3, 1985, 1989. For a more recent discussion of antiquarian research in the 1600s see Parry 1995.

92 Strutt 1777–9, iii.

93 Strutt 1777–9, iv.

94 Daniels (1988, 15) reports that Strutt used the manuscripts in the British Museum to produce his book. With reference to archaeological sites, Strutt refers to Stukeley's study of Stonehenge and Borlass's study on Cornwall, p. 257. He also refers to unpublished works on sites such as the plans made of Silchester, pp. 301–2.

95 Strutt's grandson, William, emphasized the huge amount of labour involved in researching the book and stated that 'his illustrations are faithful copies (not cooked-up reproductions) from the original illuminated manuscripts, for which, in every case, he gives the authority' (1896, 23).

96 As Haskell (1993, 295) states, the 'resulting mixture of authentic crudity and contemporary artistic fashion . . . was to become very widely adopted and seems to have won credibility as an effective means of throwing light on the past'.

97 Craik and Macfarlane 1837, 3. This picture accompanies the introductory section entitled 'View of the original population and primitive history of the British Islands'.

98 Meyrick and Smith 1815, 1 (original emphasis).

99 In discussing this trend, Anne Hollander (1993, 291) has argued that 'Historical accuracy in visual terms is a compelling idea; and the public, once convinced it was possible, never ceased to love thinking it was being given a glimpse of the past brought to life'. See also Newton 1975 on the increasing interest in historical dress in theatre.

100 Robert Havell came from a family of artists and was well known for his aquatint engraving.

101 Meyrick's expertise on the history of armour is attested to by his 3-volume work *A critical inquiry into ancient armour* . . . of 1824.

102 The literature on the art of ruins is vast and is often discussed in relation to garden history, the interest in the picturesque in landscape painting, and the travel imagery of eighteenth- and nineteenth-century scientific expeditions. Key references include Hunt 1976,1992; Wiebenson 1978; Stafford 1984; Bermingham 1986; Andrews 1989; and Copley and Garside 1994.

103 Brewer 1997, 582. For a more detailed account of the impact of ruins on cultural thought see Janowitz 1990.

104 Smiles 1994, 22. See also Evans (1994), who shows how some artists went on to specialize in depicting

prehistoric themes. Evans goes on to demonstrate that such paintings played an important role in raising awareness about monuments, and that before prehistory became a discipline, prehistoric monuments were appreciated through artistic representations.

105 As Smiles (1994, 32) has argued, this work was an early example whereby a fuller context for the Britons was provided.
106 Meyrick and Smith 1815, 1–2.
107 Champion (1997, 216) comments that these are an accurate Late Bronze Age shield and socketed axe.
108 Tim Champion has informed me that this is a very schematic and totally unrealistic representation of two hillforts, presumably of Iron Age date, in Scotland. These monuments are now known as the Brown and White Cathertuns.
109 A photograph of these Welsh boats appears in Piggott 1989, 64. This reconstruction is copied in Craik and Macfarlane's history (1837, 56).
110 Meyrick and Smith 1815, 22.
111 Piggott 1989, caption for fig. 13; Smiles 1994, 133.
112 Smiles 1994, 44.

Chapter 5

1 One exception where ape iconography and the imagery of human creation intersected was in Pfeffel's engraving of the biblical figure Esau alongside Tulp's representation of an orang-utang as shown in figure 5.3.
2 See Brewer 1997, chapter 4.
3 Brewer 1997, 187. See also Stafford 1994 on the rise of visual education during this period.
4 For details of these developments see Goldman 1994, chapter 3.
5 Houfe 1992, 138.
6 Cohn (1996, 90–1) outlines how Scheuchzer came to this conclusion.
7 Roberts and Tomlinson 1992.
8 The omentum is the lining attached to the stomach and linking it with other abdominal organs. Anatomists would inject such organs with dye in order to see the internal vascular structure.
9 Roberts and Tomlinson (1992, 294) discuss the scientific and moral messages of Ruysch's exhibits.
10 For example, it appeared in Olfert Dapper's *Beschrijving van Africa* of 1668 and Edward Tyson's *Orang-Outang, sive Homo sylvestris: or the anatomy of a Pygmie compared with that of a monkey, an ape, and a man* of 1699.
11 Scheuchzer 1731, pls LXXXVII, CXIV, CXX.
12 Ray 1976, 44.
13 Wees 1944, 68.
14 Feaver 1975, 146–8.
15 Wees 1944, 65.
16 Campbell 1992, 1.
17 Feaver 1975, 24.
18 Unger 1851 (English translation 1863), opposite pl. xiv.
19 Unger 1851 (English translation 1863), opposite pl. xiv.
20 Rudwick 1992, 130.
21 Detailed historical accounts of the various excavations and the individuals who carried them out can be found in Grayson 1983 and Van Riper 1993.
22 The success of this book is indicated by the fact that it was translated into English in 1865 and that new editions in this language were published in 1867, 1872 and 1891.
23 Gould 1993, 17. Also, Rudwick (1992, 206) sees it as surprising that Figuier had the figures portrayed in a way that made no reference to current debates about human antiquity.
24 See Hunt 1992, Wiebenson 1978, Andrews 1989 and Copley and Garside 1994.
25 The rustic landscapes of Gainsborough and Constable, for instance, provided an atmospheric setting in which to situate the biblical visions of human ancestry. On this see Bermingham 1986, Cafritz *et al.* 1988 and Daniels 1994.
26 The story of how human antiquity came to be accepted is told by others, notably Laming-Emperaire 1964, Gruber 1965, Grayson 1983, Bowler 1986 and van Riper 1993.

27 The importance of the underground or caves in geology and the nature of early geological discourse as one centred around the metaphor of penetration of the earth is discussed by Shortland 1994.

28 Gould 1993, 17.

29 Figuier 1863 (English translation 1872), 474.

30 Rupke 1993, 528.

31 Rudwick 1992, chapter 6.

32 Figuier 1870 (English edition), 39.

33 Figuier 1870 (English edition), 39.

34 Figuier 1870 (English edition), 52.

35 Figuier 1870 (English edition), 68.

36 Figuier 1870 (English edition), 86.

37 Figuier 1870 (English edition), 137.

38 Figuier 1870 (English edition), 178.

39 Edward Burnet Tylor, in Figuier 1870 (English edition), vi.

40 Girouard 1981.

41 See Blanckaert 1993, 31.

42 The majority of these scenes appear in the long introductory section by Camille Flammarion who was a well-known popular science writer at the time.

43 Flammarion, in Cleuziou (1887, 2).

44 Stoczkowski 1997, 261.

45 Huxley 1863, Haeckel 1876 and Darwin 1871.

46 Examples of the simianizing of evolutionary theorists in cartoons are discussed by Curtis in his study of Victorian comic imagery of the Irish (1997, 193, notes 216–17).

47 The Greeks noted the resemblance of apes to humans. Herodotus, for instance, wrote of creatures from western Libya in his *Historia*, which are possibly apes, and Ctesias, in his book on India, describes similar creatures. Also Aristotle in *Historia Animalium* described the primates, as did Claudius Galen in *Anatomical procedures*. The Roman encyclopaedists also reported sightings of animals thought to be primates. Pliny, for instance, talks of a race of wild creatures called *silvestres* in his *Historiae Naturalis*, which fits in with descriptions of monkeys. Later, Solinus, in the third century, and Martianus Capella, in the fifth century, elaborated on these descriptions of apes. It is the Arabic writer, Nizâmî al-'Arûdî, who in the twelfth century made a connection between humans and apes when he talked of *Nasnâs* in his work *Chahâr magâla*, which was a kind of ape that lived in the plains of Turkestan. For discussion on the descriptions and imagery of apes see McDermott 1938, Janson 1952, O'Malley and Magoun 1962, Morris and Morris 1966 and contributions in Corbey and Theunissen 1995.

48 Thus their role in evolution was not really addressed, except by Boccaccio who in *De Genealogia Deorum* suggested that apes were involved in evolution, with his story of Vulcan among the apes. Another notable exception was Albertus Magnus (1206–80), who in *De animalibus* looked at the connection between humans and apes and the animal kingdom.

49 Edward Tyson, the English anatomist, is well known for his ideas about the close relationship of apes to humans, resulting from his dissection of a chimpanzee. See Montagu 1943.

50 Levy and Levy (1986) have shown how paintings of the seventeenth century reveal links between monkeys and humans, in particular those of Jan Brueghel II. They state that 'Brueghel observed animal features and gestures so keenly that the painting could serve as a visual primer for Leibniz's Great Chain of Being' (1986, 96). Furthermore, the 'anthropomorphism exhibited in monkey paintings by Brueghel, Teniers, and Chardin is at odds with observations of monkeys in their natural environment and yet encourages fruitful scientific analogies between man and beast' (1986, 105). While Buffon, in 1753, raised the idea that humans and apes have a common origin, he was forced to withdraw this by the Church. Significantly, artists were not censored, and thus in a metaphorical sense they gave life to an idea that was later confirmed in nineteenth century. Later in the eighteenth century ideas about evolutionary connections between apes and humans were raised by the Scottish judge, Lord Monboddo.

51 See for example, Bernard Smith (1985, 1992), who has documented the role of images in the history of these explorations.

52 Figuier 1863 (English translation 1870), 470. Figuier (1870, 26) also stated 'are we compelled to admit that man by insensible transformations, and gradual improvements and developments is derived from some other animal species and particularly that of the ape? . . . We strongly repudiate any doctrine of this kind'.

53   Cited in Rudwick 1992, 168.

54   For example, this species features on the cover of Flammarion 1886 (Italian translation 1893).

55   Boitard 1865. See particularly p. 421, where a hunter is being strangled by a monkey.

56   For a historical overview of these discoveries see Grayson 1983 and Spencer 1990.

57   The first Neanderthal remains had actually been unearthed in 1829 in Engis, Belgium by Schmerling. See Stringer and Gamble 1993, 13.

58   See Table 1 in Foreword.

59   Anonymous 1873, 618.

60   Trinkhaus and Shipman (1993, 399–400) have commented on the way in which this image acts as a metaphor for the Victorian view of gender roles.

61   In his *Generelle Morphologie* of 1866 Haeckel made his first attempt to reconstruct the human lineage. This was developed in his *Natürliche Schöpfungsgeschichte* of 1868.

62   Haeckel 1876, 282.

63   The first describes the painting as a parody of the theory of human descent from apes, the second as an act of blasphemy, the third as a failed attempt to demonstrate the translation from ape to man, and the fourth as a serious and successful attempt to present the missing link (1898, lvii–lviii).

64   Ludwig (1981–3, 125) reports how Max had a substantial collection of prehistoric and ethnographic materials, and how he was interested in primates and their evolutionary relationship to humans.

65   Haeckel 1911, 716.

66   Clodd, for instance, used the picture as a frontispiece to his book *Primitive Man* of 1909.

67   The significance of the first illustration in terms of the development of an archaeological perspective on the prehistoric past is discussed more fully in Moser 1993b.

68   Knipe (1905, vii–viii) acknowledges that there was still some controversy as to the position of this creature among the primates, but states that 'many good authorities regard him as the "missing link"'.

69   Knipe 1905, 241.

70   For example Knipe (1905, 241) cites findings reported in W. Boyd Dawkin's *Cave Hunting. Researches on the evidence of caves respecting the early inhabitants of Europe*, 1874, and *Early Man in Britain and his place in the Tertiary period*, 1880.

71   There is a large literature on colonial representations of other races in visual media. Such studies have been produced within the context of art history, museum studies, history of anthropology, African studies and the history of world's fairs.

Chapter 6

1   Notable among these painters were Jean Lecomte de Nouy and Evariste Luminais. One of de Nouy's major works was *Les Gardes – côtes gaulois*, in the Musée du Louvre. Luminais is known for paintings such as *Les Eclaireurs gaulois* in the Musée des Beaux-Arts, Bordeaux and *La Fuite d'un prisonnier* in the Musée des Beaux-Arts, Mulhouse.

2   A general history of the discovery of new ancestors can be found in Reader 1981.

3   See below for a discussion of Forestier's work. For examples of such reconstructions see Baikie 1928.

4   On the way that gender roles have been represented see Moser 1993a and Gifford-Gonzalez 1993; on the changing representation of the australopithecines see Moser 1996.

5   Because the cost of reproduction rights for works still in copyright is so high only a very select sample of images by twentieth-century artists is presented.

6   For example, the French painter Penguill undertook such research when painting his *Roman City after the conquest of the Gauls*. See House 1995, 110.

7   Reynolds 1966, 117.

8   Honour 1989, 123.

9   Cited in Pressly 1981, 90.

10   Cited in Pressly 1981, 92.

11   Barry 1783, 2.

12   For biographical information see Ritzenhaler 1987 and Cavanna 1991.

13   Bernard 1988, 277.

14 For a review of his paintings of prehistory see Capitan 1903. He was particularly well known for his painting *Le Brenn et sa part de butin* of 1893, which featured a classic Gallic warrior returning from battle. (Now in the Musée des Beaux Arts de la Rochelle.)

15 For example, for his painting *Le Mammoth* of 1889, he made copies of real artefacts and a model of a mammoth based on a skeleton from a museum.

16 Ritzenhaler 1987, 218.

17 See Capitan 1903, 312. Jamin wanted to show a fight between the Neolithic invaders and the descendants of the Magdalenians and, above all, the fights between men for the possession of women.

18 These three paintings are reproduced in Capitan 1903, pls II, III, V.

19 See for example, Vries 1967, 1974.

20 This was mainly the case with wars. Bishop (1992, 33) states how the paper became known for sending its own artists to cover stories in war zones.

21 Jackson (1885, 295) comments that the first illustrations were of inferior character, but by the second year of production the paper employed better artists to ensure the quality of the images.

22 The *Daily Graphic* started in 1890, and the *Daily Mail* in 1896.

23 As Bacon (1976, 11) notes, from the 1920s the paper became known as one of the few general periodicals that consistently reported archaeological discoveries and 'not solely when some spectacular discovery momentarily has rivalled a Royal wedding, a revolution, or a war in their claims for popular attention and journalistic newsworthiness'. At one stage there was a regular column, 'Archaeology of the Month'.

24 With regard to prehistory the major writers included W.P. Pycraft, assistant to Ray Lancaster, who was an osteologist from the Department of Zoology at the British Museum of Natural History. See Spencer (1990, xxiv) who describes Lancaster as being one of Arthur Smith Woodward's main museum consultants on the Piltdown remains. Other writers included Grafton Elliott Smith, Arthur Keith, Reid Moir, Louis Leakey and Raymond Dart.

25 See Bacon (1976) who assembles the major articles on archaeological discoveries. While the focus is on the archaeology of civilization, a number of articles on prehistory are included.

26 There were on average two major articles on prehistory every year. In addition to this, brief notes on discoveries would regularly appear in the section devoted to science news.

27 The other major artist working for the paper around this time was Alice Woodward, but she tended to do portraits rather than scenes, and focused more on prehistoric animals.

28 Many of his original drawings on non-archaeological subjects for the *Illustrated London News* are held by the Department of Prints, Drawings and Paintings, Victoria and Albert Museum. His original illustrations of prehistory were all lost in the fire that destroyed the *Illustrated London News* archives during the Second World War.

29 This is evidenced by the work he did outside the *Illustrated London News*. For instance, Forestier was commissioned to do reconstructions of prehistory for popular texts of the time, such as Baikie 1928. His reconstructions were also reproduced in prehistoric texts such as Burkitt 1933.

30 Galley Hill is now known to be a recent age skull.

31 *Illustrated London News* 4 March 1911, p. 305.

32 Some important examples include Ipswich Man, *Illustrated London News* 23 March 1912, p. 447; Piltdown Man, *Illustrated London News* Supplement 28 December 1912, pp. iv–v; Broken Hill Man, *Illustrated London News* 19 November 1921, pp. 684–5; and the Taungs child, *Illustrated London News* 14 February 1925, p. 239. See also fig. iv.

33 A brief account of the history of museum displays of prehistory in North America can be found in Moser 1998.

34 Rainger (1991, 88) documents Osborn's concern for education.

35 Rainger 1991, 99. Also Czerkas and Glut (1982, 19) state that 'Having seen his illustrations in the popular press people flocked to the palaeontology halls of the AMNH to see the newly acquired skeletons mounted in exciting, realistic poses and the life restorations by Knight'. Knight is described by Czerkas and Glut (1982, 1) as the first and greatest artist to reconstruct prehistory with scientific accuracy.

36 For published examples of his illustrations of human ancestors see Knight 1935, 1942, 1949.

37 Porter 1983, 31. McGregor was the physical anthropologist on staff at the American Museum of Natural History who reconstructed models of fossil skulls.

38 The birthplace of humankind also became of interest to Osborn in the sense that he supported his student R.C. Andrews' expeditions to Asia to find the 'missing link' (Rainger 1991, 100).

39   *Men of the Old Stone Age* was more a synthesis of findings in prehistoric archaeology than an original piece of research. Rainger (1991, 145) notes the claim that the book was largely written by N.C. Nelson, the principal archaeologist at the American Museum of Natural History.

40   See Rainger 1991 and Porter 1983.

41   The reconstruction of the Neanderthals appears as the frontispiece and that of the Crô-Magnons appears on the page facing p. 358. The former appears in the foreword (fig. v). These were reproduced in the *National Geographic* the following year (1916, 29 (2), 124).

42   Rainger 1991, 169.

43   Porter 1983.

44   Porter 1983, 29.

45   Czerkas and Glut 1982, 28.

46   The third mural, which represents the Neolithic, is not discussed here.

47   Memo from Osborn to Knight, in Porter 1983, 29.

48   Rainger 1991, 174.

49   Knight 1935, 112.

50   Porter 1983, 30.

51   Indeed, it is this atmospheric setting which has led to the continued recycling of this image. A recent example is Tattersall (1993, 174), where the caption reads, 'Although it reflects a rather archaic understanding of the Crô-Magnons themselves, it nonetheless evokes the strange and wonderful atmosphere of these remarkable places'.

52   Porter 1983, 29.

53   For example, I do not discuss the work of the notable reconstruction artist Arthur Sorrell because he did not illustrate scenes of human evolution.

54   For a brief account of Wilson's career see the introduction by Alan Charig in Andrews and Stringer (1989, 7).

55   Andrews and Stringer 1989, 38.

56   For a biographical account of Burian see Lagardère 1990.

57   Mazak and Burian 1980.

58   These appear in Pfeiffer 1978, 60, 86, 88, 152, 154, 196–7.

59   Pfeiffer 1978, 152.

60   The clash of ancestors at Olduvai Gorge uses icons to demonstrate the difference between the species. This painting is discussed more fully in Moser 1996, 207.

61   An important example of his work for *National Geographic* was the reconstruction of *Homo habilis* published in 1973 (143(6), 824).

62   *National Geographic* 1979, 155(2), 446.

63   Johanson and Edey 1981, 354–7.

64   Weaver 1985. Unfortunately Matternes has refused permission to reproduce any of his images, since he feels that there would be a conflict of interest relative to his own plans for their publication (Matternes, pers. comm.)

65   Weaver 1985, 615.

66   Weaver 1985, 594, 598. These two images are discussed by Moser (1996, 212).

67   *National Geographic* 1993, 183(6), 48–9.

68   Johanson and Edey 1981, 67. This image is discussed more fully in Moser (1996, 208–11).

69   Lewin 1988, 77. This image is discussed more fully in Moser (1996, 212). For a more recent representation of the australopithecines by Gurche, which conveys how the species *Australopithecus afarensis* is now thought to have lived in a range of environments, and the latest ideas on their body form, see *National Geographic* 1996, 189(3), pp. 104–6.

70   For a discussion of the difficult marriage between artistic and scientific considerations see Moser 1998.

71   Lewin 1988, 67.

72   Howell 1965, 63.

73   Johanson and Edey 1981, 354.

74   Rensberger 1981.

75   Lewin 1988, 66–7.

76   See for example photographs in Lewin (1988, 66–7) and in *National Geographic* 1993, 183(6), 139. For photographs of Matternes see Rensberger 1981.

77   For example, Lewin 1988, 181.

Picture Credits

The author would like to thank the following libraries, art galleries, museums and individuals for supplying photographs and for permission to reproduce the following figures:

American Museum of Natural History, New York: figs 6.6, 6.7.

Ashmolean Museum, Oxford: pl. 2.

British Library, London: figs 3.2, 3.3, 3.4, 3.5, 3.6, 3.9, 3.10, 3.11, 3.13, 3.14, 3.15, 3.16, 4.3, 4.4, 4.5, 4.21, 4.22, 4.23, 5.1, 5.2, 5.3, 5.8, 5.21, 5.22, 5.23, 5.24, 5.25, 5.27.

British Museum, London: figs 2.10, 4.2, 5.4, 5.5, pl. 7, pl. 8.

British Museum of Natural History, London: fig. 6.8.

Department of History of Art Library, University of Oxford: fig. 3.12.

École National Superieure des Beaux-Arts, Paris: 3.8.

Eirik Aranqvist: fig. ii

Hirmer Verlag, Munich: fig. 2.8.

Illustrated London News Picture Library, London: fig. 6.5.

John Gurche: pl. 10.

Metropolitan Museum of Art, New York: figs 2.6 (Fletcher Fund 1931), 2.7 (Rogers Fund 1912), pl. 3 (Gift of Robert Gordon. Photo © 1981 MMA), 3.18.

Musée de Antiquités Nationale, St Germain-en-Laye: pl. 9 (Photo © Réunion des Musées Nationaux by J.G. Berizzi).

Musée de Beaux-Arts, Reims: fig. 6.3.

Musée d'Orsay, Paris: figs 6.2, 6.4. (Photos © Réunion de Musées Nationaux.)

Musées Royaux d'Art et d'Histoire, Brussels: fig. 2.5.

Museo Archaeologico Nazionale, Naples: fig. 2.2.

Museo Nazionale di Villa Giulia, Rome: fig. 2.4.

Museum für Kunst und Gewerbe, Hamburg: fig. 2.9.

Museum of Fine Arts, Boston: fig 2.3 (Henry Lillie Pierce Fund).

Nasjonalgalleriet, Oslo: fig. 3.17. (Photo © Nasjonalgalleriet by J. Lathion.)

Nationale Bibliothèque, Paris: fig. 3.7.

National Gallery of Canada, Ottawa: pl. 5.

National Gallery, London: pl. 2.

National Museum, Athens: fig. 2.1.

Pierpont Morgan Library, New York: pl. 1.

Royal Society of Arts, London: fig. 6.1.

Society of Antiquaries, London: figs 4.6, 4.7, 4.8, 4.9, 4.10, 4.11, 4.12, 4.13, 4.14, 4.15, 4.16, 4.17, 4.18.

University Library of Ghent, Ghent: fig. 4.1.

Wadsworth Atheneum, Hartford: fig 3.19 (The Ella Gallup Summer and Mary Catlin Summer Collection Fund).

Yale Centre for British Art, New Haven: pl. 6.

References

Ackerman, J.S. 1985a. Early Renaissance 'Naturalism' and scientific illustration. In A. Ellenius (ed.) 1985, pp. 1–17.

—— 1985b. The involvement of artists in Renaissance science. In J.W. Shirley and F.D. Hoeniger (eds) 1985, pp. 94–129.

Adkins, L and R.A. Adkins. 1989. *Archaeological Illustration*. Cambridge: Cambridge University Press.

Alexander, M. 1976. (ed.) *Discovering the New World. Based on the works of Theodore de Bry*. London: London Editions.

Andrews, M. 1989. *The Search for the Picturesque: Landscape aesthetics and tourism in Britain, 1760–1800*. Aldershot: Scolar.

Andrews, P and C. Stringer. 1989. *Human Evolution*. London: British Museum of Natural History.

Anon. 1873. The Neanderthal Man, *Harper's Weekly* 17(864), 617–18.

Arias, P.E. 1962. *A History of Greek Vase Painting*. London: Thames and Hudson.

Ashworth, W.B. 1984. Marcus Gheeraerts and the aesopic connection in seventeenth-century scientific illustration, *Art Journal* 44, 132–8.

—— 1985. The persistent beast: recurring images in early zoological illustration. In A. Ellenius (ed.) 1985, pp. 46–66.

—— 1987. Iconography of a new physics, *History and Technology* 4, 267–97.

Augusta, J. and Z. Burian. 1960. *Prehistoric Man*. Translated by Margaret Schierl. London: Hamlyn.

Bacon, E. 1976. *The Great Archaeologists*. London: Book Club Associates.

Baigrie, B (ed.) 1996. *Picturing Knowledge: Historical and philosophical problems concerning the use of art in science*. Toronto: University of Toronto Press.

Baikie, J. 1928. *Men of the Old Stone Age*. London: A. and C. Black.

Bakker, J.A. 1990. Prehistory visualised: hunebedden in Dutch school pictures as reflections of contemporary research, *Berichten can de Rijksdienst voor het Oudheidkundig Bodemonderzoek* 40, 29–71.

Barry, J. 1783. *An Account of a Series of Pictures, in the Great Room of the Society of Arts*. London: Printed for author by William Adland, sold by T. Cadell and J. Walter.

Bastide, F. 1990. The iconography of scientific texts: principles of analysis. In M. Lynch and S. Woolgar (eds) 1990, pp. 187–229.

Berger, M., M. Welply and J. Strejan. 1987. *Early Humans: A prehistoric world*. Los Angeles: Child's Play International.

Berkowitz, D.S. 1968. *In Remembrance of Creation. Evolution and art and scholarship in the medieval and Renaissance Bible*. Waltham, MA.: Branders University Press.

Bermingham, A. 1986. *Landscape and Ideology: The English rustic traditions, 1740–1860*. Berkeley: University of California Press.

Bernard, B. 1983. *The Bible and its Painters*. London: Orbis.

Bernheimer, R. 1970. *Wild Men in the Middle Ages. A study in art, sentiment and demonology*. Cambridge, MA.: Harvard University Press.

Bishop, J. 1992. The story of the *Illustrated London News*, *Illustrated London News*, Anniversary edition, 29–34.

Blanckaert, C. 1993. Les bases de la civilisation. Lectures de L'homme primitif de Louis Figuier (1870), *Bulletin de la Société Préhistorique Française* 90(1–2), 31–49.

Bland, D. 1958. *A History of Book Illustration. The illuminated manuscript and the printed book*. London: Faber and Faber.

—— 1962. *The Illustration of Books*. London: Faber and Faber.

Boas, G. 1948. *Essays on Primitivism and Related Ideas in the Middle Ages*. Baltimore: John Hopkins University Press.

Boitard, P. 1861. *Études Antédiluviennes. Paris avant les hommes*. Paris: Passard.

—— 1865. *Les Mille et une Singularités des Moeurs et Coutumés des Peuples sauvages, demi-civilisés et civilisés des Deux Mondes*. Paris: Passard.

Boorsch, S. 1976. America in festival presentations. In F. Chiapelli (ed.) *First Images of America*, pp. 503–15. Berkeley: University of California Press.

Borgeaud, P. 1988. *The Cult of Pan in Ancient Greece*. Chicago: University of Chicago Press.

Boule, M. 1911. L'homme fossile de la Chapelle-aux-Saints, *Annales de Paléontologie* 6, 1–64.

—— 1912. L'homme fossile de la Chapelle-aux-Saints, *Annales de Paléontologie*, 7, 65–208.

—— 1913. L'homme fossile de la Chapelle-aux-Saints, *Annales de Paléontologie*, 8, 209–79.

Bowler, P.J. 1986 *Theories of Human Evolution: A century of debate, 1844–1944*. Oxford: Basil Blackwell.

Brewer, J. 1997. *The Pleasures of the Imagination. English culture in the eighteenth century*. London: HarperCollins.

Burkitt, M. 1933. *The Old Stone Age*. Cambridge: Cambridge University Press.

Bry, T. de 1590. *America. Part 1. A briefe and true report of the new found land of Virginia*. Frankfurt: T. de Bry.

Cafritz, R.C., L. Gowing and D. Rosand. 1988. *Places of Delight: The pastoral landscape*. New York: Clarkson N. Potter.

Camille, M. 1995. 'When Adam delved': laboring on the land in English medieval art. In D. Sweeney (ed.) *Agriculture and the Middle Ages*. pp. 247–76. Philadelphia: University of Pennsylvania Press.

Campbell, M. 1988. *The Witness and the Other World: Exotic European travel writing, 400–1600*. Ithaca, NY.: Cornell University Press.

Campbell, M.J. 1992. *John Martin. Visionary printmaker*. York: Campbell Fine Art.

Capitan, L. 1903. Le peintre préhistorien Jamin, son oeuvre, *Revue de l'ecole d'anthropologie* XIII, 311–16.

Carpenter, T. 1991. *Art and Myth in Ancient Greece*. London: Thames and Hudson.

Cavanna, F. 1991. *Nos Ancêtres les Gaulois*. Paris: Albin Michel.

Champion, T. 1997. The power of the picture. The image of the ancient Gaul. In B. Molyneaux (ed.). 1997, pp. 213–29.

Chotzen, T.M. and A.M.E. Draak. 1937. *Beschrijving der Britsche eilanden door Lucas de Heere*. Antwerp: De Sevev Sinjoren.

Clark, J.G.D. 1946. *From Savagery to Civilization*. London: Cobbetts Press.

Cleuziou, H. du 1887. *La Création de l'Homme et les Premiers Ages de Humanité*. Paris: C. Marpon and E. Flammarion.

Clodd, E. 1909. *Primitive Man*. London: George Newnes.

Cluverius, P. 1616. *Germaniae Antiquae*. Lugduni Batavorum: Apud Ludovicum Elzevirium.

Cohen, B. 1994. From bowman to clubman: Herakles and Olympia, *Art Bulletin* LXXVI(4), 695–715.

Cohn, N. 1996. *Noah's Flood. The genesis story in western thought*. New Haven, CT.: Yale University Press.

Copley, S. and P. Garside (eds) 1994. *The Politics of the Picturesque: Literature, landscape and aesthetics since 1770*. Cambridge: Cambridge University Press.

Corbey, R. and B. Theunissen (eds) 1995. *Ape, Man, Apeman: Changing views since 1600*. Leiden: Department of Prehistory, Leiden University.

Cosgrove, D. and S. Daniels (ed.) 1989. *The Iconography of Landscape*. Cambridge: Cambridge University Press.

Craik, G.L. and C. Macfarlane. 1837–41. *The Pictorial History of England*. 4 vols. London: Charles Knight.

Crombie, A.C. 1980. Science and the arts in the Renaissance, *History of Science* 18, 233–46.

Cullen, F. 1997. *Visual Politics. The representation of Ireland 1750–1930*. Cork: University of Cork Press.

Cumming, W.P, R.A. Skelton and D.B. Quinn. 1971. *The Discovery of North America*. Toronto: McClelland and Stewart.

Curtis, L.P. 1997. *Apes and Angels. The Irishman in Victorian caricature*. Washington DC: Smithsonian Institution Press.

Cust, L. 1894. Notice of the life and works of Lucas D'Heere, poet and painter of Ghent, *Archaeologica* LIV, 59–80.

Czerkas, S. and D.F. Glut. 1982. *Dinosaurs, Mammoths and Cavemen. The art of Charles R. Knight*. New York: Dutton.

Daniel, G. 1962. *The Idea of Prehistory*. Harmondsworth: Penguin Books.

Daniel, S. 1612. *The First Part of the Historie of England*. London: Nicholas Okes.

Daniels, M. 1988. *Victorian Book Illustration*. London: British Library.

Daniels, S. 1993. *Fields of Vision: Landscape imagery and national identity in England and the United States*. Cambridge: Polity Press.

Darwin, C. 1871. *The Descent of Man*. London: Murray.

De Santilla, G. 1959. The role of art in the scientific Renaissance. In M. Clagett (ed.) *Critical Problems in the History of Science*, pp. 33–65. Madison: University of Wisconsin Press.

Diodorus Siculus. *Bibliotheca Historica*. Translated by E. Murphy, 1985. London: McFarland.

Dodds E.R. 1973. *The Ancient Concept of Progress*. Oxford: Clarendon Press.

Dodwell, C.R. 1993. *The Pictorial Arts of the West 800–1200*. New Haven, CT.: Yale University Press.

DuBois, P. 1982. *Centaurs and Amazons: Women and the prehistory of the great chain of being*. Ann Arbor, MI.: University of Michigan Press.

Du Choul, G. 1557. *Discours sur la Castramétation et Discipline Militaire des Romaines*. Lyon.

Edgerton, S.Y. 1975. *The Renaissance Discovery of Linear Perspective*. New York: Basic Books.

—— 1985. The Renaissance development of the scientific illustration. In J.W. Shirley and F.D. Hoeniger (eds) 1985, pp. 168–97.

—— 1991. *The Heritage of Giotto's Geometry: Art and science on the eve of the scientific revolution*. Ithaca, NY.: Cornell University Press.

Eisenstein, E.L. 1979. *The Printing Press as an Agent of Change: Communications and cultural transformations in early modern Europe*. 2 vols. Cambridge: Cambridge University Press.

—— 1983. *The Printing Revolution in Early Modern Europe*. Cambridge: Cambridge University Press.

Ellenius, A (ed.). 1985. *The Natural Sciences and the Arts: Aspects of interaction from the Renaissance to the twentieth century*. Stockholm: Almqvist and Wiksell International.

Erffa, H.M. von. 1989–95. *Ikonologie der Genesis*. 2 vols. München: Deutsher Kunstverlag.

Evans, C. 1994. Natural wonders and national monuments: a meditation upon the fate of the Tolmen, *Antiquity* 68, 200–8.

Evans, J. 1897. *Ancient Stone Implements of Great Britain*. 2nd edition (1st edition 1872). London: Longmans.

Feaver, W. 1975. *The Art of John Martin*. Oxford: Clarendon Press.

Febvre, L. and H.J. Martin. 1976. *The Coming of the Book: The impact of printing 1450–1800*. Translated from French by D. Gerard. London: NLB.

Ferguson, A. 1993. *Utter Antiquity: Perceptions of prehistory in Renaissance England*. Durham, NC.: Duke University Press.

Fermor, S. 1993. *Piero di Cosimo. Fiction, invention and fantasia*. London: Reaktion Books.

Ferrua, A. 1990. *The Unknown Catacomb*. Translated by Iain Inglis. New Lanark: Geddes and Grosset.

Figuier, G. L. 1863. *La Terre avant le Déluge: Ouvrage contenant 25 vues idéals de paysages de l'ancien monde*. Paris: Hachette et Cie. English translation, 1872, by W.S.O. London: D. Appleton.

—— 1870. *L'Homme Primitif*. Paris: Hachette et Cie. English translation, 1870, edited by Edward Burnet Taylor. London: Chapman and Hall.

Flammarion, N.C. 1886. *Le Monde avant la Création de l'Homme*. Italian translation, 1893. Milan: Edoardo Sonzogno.

Ford, B.J. 1992. *Images of Science: A history of scientific illustration*. London: British Library.

Foreman, C.T. 1943. *Indians Abroad 1493–1938*. Norman: University of Oklahoma Press.

Friedländer, M.J. and J. Rosenberg. 1978. *The Paintings of Lucas Cranach*. London: Sotheby Parke Bernet.

Friedman, J.B. 1981. *The Monstrous Races in Medieval Art and Thought*. Cambridge, MA.: Harvard University Press.

Gamble, C.S. 1993. *Timewalkers: The prehistory of global colonization*. Stroud: Alan Sutton.

Gesner, C. 1551. *Historiae Animalium*. Zurich.

Gifford-Gonzalez, D. 1993. You can hide, but you can't run: representations of women's work in illustrations of Palaeolithic life, *Visual Anthropology Review* 9(1), 23–41.

Girouard, M. 1981. *The Return to Camelot. Chivalry and the English gentleman*. New Haven: Yale University Press.

Goldman, P. 1994. *Victorian Illustrated Books 1850–1870*. London: British Museum Press.

Gombrich, E.H. 1972. *Symbolic Images. Studies in the art of the Renaissance*. New York: Phaidon.

Gould, S.J. 1989. *Wonderful Life: The Burgess Shale and the nature of history*. London: Penguin.

—— 1993. Preface. Reconstructing (and deconstructing) the past. In S.J. Gould (ed.) *The Book of Life*, pp. 6–21. New York: W.W. Norton.

Grabar, A. 1967. *The Beginnings of Christian Art 200–395*. London: Thames and Hudson.

Grafton, A. (with A. Shelford and N. Siraisi). 1992. *New Worlds, Ancient Texts*. Cambridge, MA.: Belknapp Press of Harvard University Press.

Grayson, D.K. 1983. *The Establishment of Human Antiquity*. New York: Academic Press.

Gruber, J.W. 1965. Brixham cave and the antiquity of man. In M.E. Spiro (ed.) *Context and Meaning in Cultural Anthropology, in honor of A.I. Hallowell*, pp. 373–402. New York: Free Press.

Haeckel, E.H. 1876. *The History of Creation*. London: Murray.

—— 1898. *Natürliche Schöpfungsgeschichte*. Berlin: Druck and Verlag von Georg Reimer.

—— 1911. *Natürliche Schöpfungsgeschichte*. Berlin: Druck and Verlag von Georg Reimer.

Hall, B.S. 1996. The didactic and the elegant: some thought on scientific and technological illustrations in the Middle Ages and the Renaissance. In B. Baigrie (ed.) 1996, pp. 3–39.

Hall, E. 1989. *Inventing the Barbarian. Greek self-definition through tragedy*. Oxford: Clarendon Press.

Hammond, M. 1982. The expulsion of the Neanderthals from human ancestry: Marcellin Boule and the social context of scientific research, *Social Studies of Science* 12, 1–36.

Haskell, F. 1993. *History and its Images. Art and the interpretation of the past*. New Haven: Yale University Press.

Heere, L. De 1573–5. Corte beschryvinghe van England, Scotlande, ende Ireland. Ms. Additional 28, 330, British Library, London.

—— 1577. Theatre de tous les peuples et nations de la terre, avec leurs habits et ornemens divers tant anciens que modernes diligemment depeints au naturel par Luc D'Heere, peintre et schulpteur gantois. Ms. 2466 University Library Ghent, Belgium.

Hemming, E. 1994. Representation of archaeological theories or social myth? Unpublished MA dissertation, Department of Archaeology, University of Southampton.

Henle, J. 1973. *Greek Myths. A vase painter's notebook*. Bloomington: Indiana University Press.

Henry, R.D.D. 1771. *History of Great Britain*. London: T. Cadell.

Herdeg, W. 1973. *The Artist in the Service of Science*. Zurich: Graphis Press.

Hesiod. *Works and Days*. Translated by M.L. West, 1978. Oxford: Clarendon Press.

Hobbes, T. 1651. *Leviathan*. London.

Hodgen, M.T. 1964. *Early Anthropology in the Sixteenth and Seventeenth Centuries*. Philadelphia: University of Pennsylvania Press.

Hollander, A. 1993. *Seeing through Clothes*. Berkeley: University of California Press.

Honour, H. 1976. *New Golden Land. European images of America from the discoveries to the present time*. London: Allen Lane.

—— 1989. *The Image of the Black in Western Art. Vol. IV, pt 2. Black models and white myths*. Cambridge, MA.: Harvard University Press.

Houfe, S. 1992. *Fin de Siecle. The illustrators of the 'nineties*. London: Barrie and Jenkins.

House, J. (ed.). 1995. *Landscapes of France: Impressionism and its rivals*. London: Hayward Galley.

Howell, F.C. 1965. *Early Man*. New York: Time Life Books.

Hulton, P. 1977. *The Work of Jacques Le Moyne de Morgues*. 2 vols. London: British Museum Publications.

—— 1978. Images of the New World: Jacques Le Moyne de Morgues and John White. In K.R. Andrews, N.P. Canny and P.E.H. Hair (eds) *The Westward Enterprise. English activites in Ireland, the Atlantic, and America 1480–1650*, pp. 195–214. Liverpool: Liverpool University Press.

—— 1984. *America 1585: The complete drawings of John White*. Chapel Hill: University of North Carolina Press and British Museum.

—— 1985. Realism and tradition in ethnological and natural history imagery of the 16th century. In A. Ellenius, (ed.) 1985, pp. 18–31.

Hulton, P. and D.B. Quinn. 1964. *The American Drawings of John White*. 2 vols. London: British Museum and University of North Carolina Press.

Hunt, J.D. 1976. *The Figure in the Landscape: Poetry, painting and gardening during the eighteenth century*. Baltimore: John Hopkins University Press.

—— 1992. *Gardens and the Picturesque*. Cambridge, MA.: MIT Press.

Hurcombe, L. 1995. Our engendered species, *Antiquity* 69, 87–100.

Husband, T. (with assistance of G. Gilmore-House). 1980. *The Wild Man: Medieval myth and symbolism*. New York: Metropolitan Museum of Art.

Hutchinson, H.N. 1896. *Prehistoric Man and Beast*. London: Smith, Elder and Company

Huxley, T.H. 1863. *Evidence as to Man's Place in Nature*. London: Williams and Norgate.

Ivins, W.M. 1969. *Prints and Visual Communication*. 2nd edition. New York: De Capo Press.

Jackson, M. 1885. *The Pictorial Press: Its origins and progress*. London: Hurst and Blackett.

Jacobs, M. 1995. *The Painted Voyage – Art, travel and exploration 1564–1875*. London: British Museum.

James, M.R. 1929. *Marvels of the East: A full reproduction of the three known copies*. Oxford: Oxford University Press.

James, S. 1997. Drawing inferences: visual reconstructions in theory and practice. In B. Molyneaux (ed.) 1997, pp. 23–48.

Janowitz, A. 1990. *England's Ruins. Poetic purpose and the national landscape*. Oxford: Basil Blackwell.

Janson, H.W. 1952. *Apes and Ape Lore in the Middle Ages and the Renaissance*. London: Warburg Institute, University of London.

Jefferys, T. 1757–72. *A Collection of the Dresses of Different Nations, Ancient and Modern*. 4 vols. London.

Johanson, D.C. and M.A. Edey. 1981. *Lucy: The beginnings of humankind*. London: Book Club Associates.

Johanson, D.C. and B. Edgar. 1996. *From Lucy to Language*. London: Weidenfeld and Nicolson.

Kemp, M. 1981. *Leonardo da Vinci: The marvellous works of nature and man*. London: Dent.

—— 1992. *The Science of Art: Optical themes in western art from Brunelleschi to Seurat*. 2nd edition. New Haven: Yale University Press.

—— 1993. 'The mark of truth': looking and learning in some anatomical illustrations from the Renaissance and eighteenth century. In N.W.F. Bynum and R. Porter (eds) *Medicine and the Five Senses*, pp. 85–121. Cambridge: Cambridge University Press.

—— 1996. Temples of the body and temples of the cosmos: vision and visualisation in the Vesalian and Copernican revolutions. In B. Baigrie (ed.) 1996, pp. 40–85.

Kendrick, T.D. 1950. *British Antiquity*. Methuen: London.

Kenseth, J. (ed.) 1991. *The Age of the Marvelous*. Hanover, N.H.: Hood Museum of Art, Dartmouth College.

Kircher, A. 1665. *Mundus Subterraneus*. Amsterdam.

Knight, C.R. 1935. *Before the Dawn of History*. New York: Whittlesey House, McGraw Hill.

—— 1942. Parade of Life Through the Ages, *National Geographic* 81(2), 141–84.

—— 1949. *Prehistoric Man: The great adventurer*. New York: Appleton Century Crofts.

Knight, D.M. 1977. *Zoological Illustration: An essay towards a history of printed zoological pictures*. London: Dawson.

—— 1993. Pictures, diagrams and symbols: visual language in nineteenth-century chemistry. In R.G. Mazzolini (ed.) 1993, pp. 321–44.

—— 1996. Illustrating chemistry. In B. Baigrie (ed.). 1996, pp. 135–63.

Knipe, H.R. 1905. *Nebula to Man*. London: J.M. Dent.

Koenigswald, G.H.R. von 1956. *Meeting Prehistoric Man*. London: The Scientific Bookclub.

Lafitau, J.F. 1724. *Moeurs des Sauvages Ameriquains Comparées aux Moeurs des Premiers Temps*. Paris.

Lagardère, G. (ed.) 1990. *Peintres s'un Monde Disparu: La préhistoire vue par les artistes de la fin du XIXe siècle à nos jours*. Solutre: Musée de Préhistoire de Solutré.

Laming-Emperaire, A. 1964. *Origines de l'Archéologie Préhistorique en France*. Paris: A. and J. Picard.

Landau, D. and P. Parshall. 1994. *The Renaissance Print 1470–1550*. New Haven, CT.: Yale University Press.

Larsson, G. 1992. *The PreHistory of the Far Side: A 10th anniversary exhibit*. London: Warner Books.

Latour, B. 1986. Visualisation and cognition; thinking with eyes and hands, *Knowledge and Society* 6, 1–40.

Leakey, R.E. 1981. *The Making of Mankind*. New York: E.P. Dutton.

Leakey, R.E. and R. Lewin. 1977. *Origins*. New York: E.P. Dutton.

Levy, E.K. and D.E. Levy. 1986. Monkey in the middle: pre-Darwinian evolutionary thought and artistic creation, *Perspectives in Biology and Medicine* 30, 95–106.

Lewin, R. 1988. *In the Age of Mankind*. Washington DC: Smithsonian Books.

Lloyd, J.B. 1971. *African Animals in Renaissance Literature and Art*. Oxford: Clarendon Press.

Lovejoy, A.O. and G. Boas. 1935. *Primitivism and Related Ideas in Antiquity*. Baltimore: John Hopkins University Press.

Lucretius. *De Rerum Natura*. Translated by A.M. Esolen, 1995. Baltimore: John Hopkins University Press.

Ludwig, H. 1981–3. *Münchner Maler im 19. Jahrhundert*. 3er Band. München: Bruckmann.

Lynch, M. and S. Woolgar. (eds) 1990. *Representation in Scientific Practice*. Cambridge, MA.: MIT Press

McClintock, H.F. 1950. *Old Irish and Highland Dress and that of the Isle of Man*. Second edition. Dundalk: Dundalgan Press.

McDermott, W.C. 1938. *The Ape in Antiquity*. Baltimore: John Hopkins University Press.

Marvels of the East. Eleventh century. Cotton Ms. Tiberius B.V. British Library

Mathews, T.F. 1993. *The Clash of the Gods. A reinterpretation of early Christian art*. Princeton: Princeton University Press.

Mazák, V. and Z. Burian. 1980. *Prehistoric Man*. London: Hamlyn.

Mazzolini, R.G. (ed.) 1993. *Non-Verbal Communication in Science Prior to 1900*. Florence: Leo S. Olschki.

Mendyk, S.A.E. 1989. *'Speculum Britanniae'. Regional study, antiquarianism, and science in Britain to 1700*. Toronto: University of Toronto Press.

Meyrick, S.R. 1824. *A Critical Inquiry into Ancient Armour, as it existed in Europe, but particularly in England*. 3 vols. London: R. Jennings.

Meyrick, S.R. and C.H. Smith. 1815. *The Costume of the Original Inhabitants of the British Isles*. London: R. Havell.

Michell, J. 1982. *Megalithomania: Artists, antiquarians and archaeologists at the old stone monuments*. London: Thames and Hudson.

Miller, A. 1984. *Imagery in Scientific Thought: Creating twentieth-century physics*. Boston: Birkhauser.

Millon, H.A. and V.M. Lampugnani. 1994. *The Renaissance from Brunelleschi to Michelangelo. The representation of architecture*. London: Thames and Hudson.

Molyneaux, B. (ed.) *The Cultural Life of Images*. London: Routledge.

Montagu, M.F.A. 1943. *Edward Tyson MD. FRS.* Philadelphia: The American Philosophical Society.

Morgan, H. 1997. Festive Irishmen, an 'Irish' procession in Stuttgart 1617, *History Ireland* 5(3), 14–20.

Morris, D. and D. Morris. 1966. *Men and Apes.* London: Hutchinson.

Moser, S. 1992. The visual language of archaeology: a case study of the Neanderthals, *Antiquity* 66, 831–44.

—— 1993a. Gender stereotyping in pictorial reconstructions of human origins. In H. du Cros and L. Smith (eds) *Women in Archaeology: A feminist critique*, pp. 75–92. Canberra: Department of Prehistory, Research School of Pacific Studies.

—— 1993b. Picturing the prehistoric, *Metascience* 4, 58–67.

—— 1996. Visual representation in archaeology: depicting the missing-link in human origins. In B. Baigrie (ed.) 1996, pp. 184–214.

—— 1998. The dilemma of didactic displays. Habitat dioramas, life-groups and reconstructions of the past. In N. Merriman (ed.) *Making Early Histories in Museums.* London: Cassell.

Moser, S. and C. Gamble. 1997. Revolutionary images: the iconic vocabulary for representing human antiquity. In B. Molyneaux (ed.) 1997, pp. 184–212.

Myers, G. 1990. Every picture tells a story: illustrations in E.O. Wilson's *Sociobiology*. In M. Lynch and S. Woolgar (eds) 1990, pp. 231–65.

Newton, S.M. 1975. *Renaissance Theatre Costume and the Sense of the Historic Past.* London: Rapp and Whiting.

O'Malley, C.D. and H.W. Magoun. 1962. Early concepts of the anthropomorpha, *Physis* 4, 39–64.

Osborn, H.F. 1915. *Men of the Old Stone Age.* New York: Scribner.

Ovid. *Metamorphoses.* Translated by F.J. Miller, 1951. London: William Heinemann.

Pagden, A. 1986. *The Fall of Natural Man: The American Indian and the origins of comparative ethnology.* Cambridge: Cambridge University Press.

Panofsky, E. 1955. *The Life and Art of Albrecht Dürer.* 4th edition. Princeton: Princeton University Press.

—— 1962. *Studies in Iconology: Humanistic themes in the art of the Renaissance.* New York: Harper and Row.

Parry, G. 1995. *The Trophies of Time. English antiquarians of the seventeenth century.* Oxford: Oxford University Press.

Partsch, J. 1891. Philipp Clüver der Begründer der historischen Lünderkunde, *Geographische Abhandlungen* 1(2), 1–47. Wien: Eduard Hözel.

Pausanias. *Description of Greece.* Translated by P. Levi, 1979. Harmondsworth: Penguin.

Pfeiffer, J. 1978. *The Emergence of Man.* 3rd edition. New York: Harper and Row.

Picardt, J. 1660. *Korte beschryvinge von eenige vergetene en verborgene antiquiteten der provintien en landen, gelegen tusschen de Noord-Zee, de Yssel, Emse en Lippe.* Amsterdam: Tymon Houthaak.

Piggott, S. 1965 Archaeological draughtsmanship: principles and practice. Part 1: principles and retrospect, *Antiquity* 39, 165–76.

—— 1975. *The Druids.* 2nd edition. London: Thames and Hudson.

—— 1976. *Ruins in a Landscape. Essays in antiquarianism.* Edinburgh: University of Edinburgh Press.

—— 1978. *Antiquity Depicted. Aspects of archaeological illustration.* London: Thames and Hudson.

—— 1985. *William Stukeley. An eighteenth-century antiquary.* Revised and enlarged edition. London: Thames and Hudson.

—— 1989. *Ancient Britons and the Antiquarian Imagination.* London: Thames and Hudson.

Plato. *Protagoras.* Translated by W.K.C. Guthrie, 1973. In E. Hamilton and H. Cairns (eds) *The Collected Dialogues of Plato*, pp. 308–52. Princeton: Princeton University Press.

Pliny the Elder. *Historiae Naturalis.* Translated by H. Rackham, 1942. London: William Heinemann.

Porter, C.M. 1983. The Rise of Parnassus: Henry Fairfield Osborn and the Hall of the Age of Man, *Museum Studies Journal* 1, 26–34.

Pratt, S. 1989. The Imagery of the Native American *c.* 1750–1850. Ph.D. thesis, CNAA.

Pressly, W.L. 1981. *The Life and Art of James Barry.* New Haven, CT.: Yale University Press.

Prest, J. 1981. *The Garden of Eden: The botanic garden and the re-creation of paradise.* New Haven, CT.: Yale University Press.

Rainger, R. 1991. *An Agenda for Antiquity. Henry Fairfield Osborn and vertebrate palaeontology at the American Museum of Natural History, 1890–1935.* Tuscaloosa: University of Alabama Press.

Ray, G.R. 1976. *The Illustrator and the Book in England from 1790–1914.* New York: Pierpont Morgan Library and Oxford University Press.

—— 1982. *The Art of the French Illustrated Book 1700–1914.* 2 vols. Ithaca, NY.: Pierpont Morgan Library and Cornell University Press.

Reader, J. 1981. *Missing Links. The hunt for earliest man.* London: Book Club Associates.

Reynolds, G. 1966. *Victorian Painting.* London: Studio Vista.

Rensberger, B. 1981. Facing the Past, *Science* 81, 2(8), 40–51.

Ring, G. 1949. *A Century of French Painting, 1400–1500*. London: Phaidon Press.

Ritterbush, P.C. 1985. The organism as symbol: an innovation in art. In J.W. Shirley and F.D. Hoeniger (eds) 1985, pp. 149–67.

Ritzenthaler, C. (ed.) 1987. *L'École des Beaux-Arts du XIXe Siecle les Pompiers*. Paris: Mayer.

Roberts, K.B. and J.D.W. Tomlinson. 1992. *The Fabric of the Body: European traditions of anatomical illustration*. Oxford: Clarendon Press.

Robin, H. 1993. *The Scientific Image*. New York: W.H. Freeman.

Romm, J.S. 1992. *The Edges of the Earth in Ancient Thought*. Princeton, NJ.: Princeton University Press.

Rudwick, M.J.S. 1972. *The Meaning of Fossils: Episodes in the history of palaeontology*. London: Macdonald.

—— 1976. The emergence of a visual language for geological science 1760–1840, *The History of Science* xiv, 149–95

—— 1992. *Scenes from Deep Time: Early pictorial representations of the prehistoric world*. Chicago: University of Chicago Press.

Rupke, N.A. 1993. Metonymies of Empire: visual representations of prehistoric times, 1830–90. In R.G. Mazzolini (ed.) 1993, pp. 513–28.

Rykwert, J. 1981. *On Adam's House in Paradise: The idea of the primitive hut in architectural history*. Cambridge, MA.: MIT Press.

Sammes, A. 1676. *Britannia Antiqua Illustrata*. London: for the author.

Sawday, J. 1995. *The Body Emblazoned. Dissection and the human body in Renaissance culture*. London: Routledge.

Schama, S. 1995. *Landscape and Memory*. London: HarperCollins.

Scheuchzer, J.J. 1731–5. *Physica Sacra*. Augustae Vindelicorum and Ulmae.

Schnapp, A. 1996. *The Discovery of the Past*. English translation by Ian Kinnes and Gillian Varndell. London: British Museum Press.

Schultz, B. 1985. *Art and Anatomy in Renaissance Italy*. Ann Arbor, MI.: UMI Research Press.

Shirley, J.W. and F.D. Hoeniger (eds) 1985. *Science and the Arts in the Renaissance*. Washington DC: Folger Shakespeare Library.

Shortland, M. 1994. Darkness visible: underground culture in the golden age of geology, *History of Science* XXXII, 1–61.

Smiles, S. 1994. *The Image of Antiquity*. New Haven, CT.: Yale University Press.

Smith, B. 1985. *European Vision and the South Pacific 1768–1850*. 2nd edition. New Haven, CT.: Yale University Press.

—— 1992. *Imagining the Pacific*. Melbourne: Melbourne University Press.

Smith, W.G. 1894. *Man the Primeval Savage*. London: Edward Stanford.

Sparkes, B. 1989. Classical Greek attitudes to the past. In R. Layton (ed.) *Who Needs the Past?*, pp. 119–30. London: Routledge.

—— 1997. Some Greek images of others. In B. Molyneaux (ed.) 1997, pp. 130–58.

Speed, J. 1623. *The Historie of Great Britaine*. 2nd edition. London: George Humble.

Spencer, F. 1990. *Piltdown. A scientific forgery*. London: Natural History Museum and Oxford University Press.

Stafford, B.M. 1984. *Voyage into Substance: Art, science, nature, and the illustrated travel account, 1760–1840*. Cambridge, MA.: MIT Press.

—— 1994. *Artful Science: Enlightenment entertainment and the eclipse of visual education*. Cambridge, MA.: MIT Press.

Stewart, A. 1997. *Art, Desire and the Body in Ancient Greece*. Cambridge: Cambridge University Press.

Stoczkowski, W. 1992. Origines de l'homme: quand la science répète le mythe, *La Recherche* 244, 746–50.

—— 1994. *Anthropologie Naïve, Anthropologie Savante: De l'origine de l'homme, de l'imagination et des idées reçues*. Paris: CRNS.

—— 1997. The painter and prehistoric people. In B. Molyneaux (ed.) 1997, pp. 249–62.

Strachan, J. 1957. *Early Bible Illustrations. A short study based on some fifteenth and early sixteenth century printed texts*. Cambridge: Cambridge University Press.

Stringer, C. and C. Gamble. 1993. *In Search of the Neanderthals: Solving the puzzle of human origins*. London: Thames and Hudson.

Strong, R. 1984. *Art and Power. Renaissance festivals, 1450–1650*. Woodbridge: Boydell.

Strutt, J. 1777–9. *The Chronicle of England; or a compleat history, civil, military and ecclesiastical, of the ancient Britons and Saxons, from the landing of Julius Caesar in Britain, to the Norman Conquest*. London: T. Evans and R. Faulder.

Strutt, W. 1896. *A Memoir of the Life of Joseph Strutt 1749–1802*. London: Printed for private circulation.

Sturtevant, W.C. 1976. First visual images of native America. In F. Chiapelli (ed.) *First Images of America*, pp. 417–54. Berkeley, CA.: University of California Press.

Tacitus. *Germania*. Translated by H. Mattingly and revised by S.A. Handford, 1970. Harmondsworth: Penguin.

Tattersall, I. 1992. Evolution comes to life, *Scientific American* August, 62–9.

—— 1993. *The Human Odyssey*. New York: Prentice Hall.

Thomas, A.G. 1975. *Great Books and Book Collectors*. London: Chancellor Press.

Topper, D.R. 1990. Natural science and visual art: reflections on the interface. In E. Garber (ed.) *Beyond History of Science: Essays in honor of Robert E. Schofield*, pp. 296–310. Bethlehem: Lehigh University Press.

—— 1996. Towards an epistemology of scientific illustration. In B. Baigrie (ed.) 1996, pp. 215–49.

Trinkhaus, E. and P. Shipman. 1993. *The Neandertals*. London: Jonathan Cape.

Tulp, N. 1641. *Observationum Medicarum*. Amsterdam.

Tyrrell, W.B. 1984. *Amazons. A study in Athenian mythmaking*. Baltimore: John Hopkins University Press.

Tyson, G.P. and S.S. Wagonheim. 1986. *Print and Culture in the Renaissance*. Newark: University of Delaware Press.

Unger, F. 1851. *Die Urwelt in ihren verschiedenen Bildungsperioden*. Vienna: Beck. English translation, 1863. London: Sam Highley.

Unstead, R.J. 1955. *Looking at History: Britain from cavemen to the present day*. London: A. & C. Black.

Van Riper, A.B. 1993. *Men among the Mammoths. Victorian science and the discovery of human prehistory*. Chicago: University of Chicago Press.

Vercoutter, J., J. Leclant, F.M. Snowden and J. Desansges. 1976. *The Image of the Black in Western Art. Volume 1. From the Pharoahs to the fall of the Roman Empire*. Cambridge, MA.: Harvard.

Virgil. *Georgics*. Translated by C. Day Lewis, 1966. London: Oxford University Press.

Vitruvius, P.M. 1511. *M. Vitruvius per iocundum solito castigatior factus, cum figuris et tabula, ut iam legi et intelligi possit*. Venice.

—— 1521. *De architectura libri dece traducti de latino in vulgare affigurati: comentati da Caesare Caesariano*. Como: Gotardo da Pote.

—— 1522. *M.V. De Architectura Libri Decem . . .* Florence: Haeredes Phillippi Iuntae.

—— 1547. *Architecture ou art de bien bastir . . . mis . . . en Francoys, par la Martin secretaire de monseigneur le cardinal de Lenoncourt*. Paris.

—— 1548. *Vitruvius Teutsch. Alles mit schoenen kunstlichen figuren and antiquiteten, und sonderlichen commentarien zu mehrerem bericht*. Nürnberg.

—— 1960. *The Ten Books on Architecture*. Translated by M.H. Morgan. New York: Dover Publications.

Volkommer, R. 1988. *Herakles in the Art of Classical Greece*. Oxford: Oxford Committee for Archaeology, Monograph no. 25.

Vries, L. de 1967. *Panorama: 1842–1865. The world of the early Victorians as seen through the eyes of the* Illustrated London News. London: John Murray.

—— 1974. *History as Hot News: 1865 to 1897*. New York: St Martin's Press.

Wakeman, G. 1973. *Victorian Book Illustration – The technical revolution*. Newton Abbott: David and Charles.

Ward, R. and C. Stringer. 1997. A molecular handle on the Neanderthals, *Nature* 388, 225–6.

Weaver, K.F. 1985. The search for our ancestors, *National Geographic* 168(5), 561–623.

Wees, J.D. 1944. *Darkness Visible. The prints of John Martin*. Williamstown, MA.: Sterling and Francine Clark Art Institute.

West, M.L. 1978. Introduction to Hesiod's *Works and Days*. Oxford: Clarendon Press.

Wiebenson, D. 1978. *The Picturesque Garden in France*. Princeton, NJ.: Princeton University Press.

Winkler, M.G. and A. van Helden. 1992. Representing the Heavens. Galileo and visual astronomy, *Isis* 83, 195–217.

Wittkower, R. 1942. Marvels of the east. A study in the history of monsters, *Journal of the Warburg and Courtauld Institutes* 5, 159–97.

—— 1977. *Allegory and the Migration of Symbols*. London: Thames and Hudson.

Yates, F.A. 1959. *The Valois Tapestries*. London: Studies of the Warburg Institute, Volume 23.

Index

Page numbers in *italics* refer to illustrations.